The
Last
Berliner

A Memoir by
Edie Williams

TRAFFORD

Note for Librarians: A cataloguing record for this book is available from Library and Archives
Canada at www.collectionscanada.ca/amicus/index-e.html
ISBN 1-4120-8566-7

Printed in Victoria, BC, Canada. Printed on paper with minimum 30% recycled fibre.
Trafford's print shop runs on "green energy" from solar, wind and other environmentally-friendly power sources.

Offices in Canada, USA, Ireland and UK

Book sales for North America and international:
Trafford Publishing, 6E–2333 Government St.,
Victoria, BC V8T 4P4 CANADA
phone 250 383 6864 (toll-free 1 888 232 4444)
fax 250 383 6804; email to orders@trafford.com
Book sales in Europe:
Trafford Publishing (UK) Limited, 9 Park End Street, 2nd Floor
Oxford, UK OX1 1HH UNITED KINGDOM
phone 44 (0)1865 722 113 (local rate 0845 230 9601)
facsimile 44 (0)1865 722 868; info.uk@trafford.com
Order online at:
trafford.com/06-0322

10 9 8 7 6 5 4 3

In memory of my Brother Peter –
who knew Berlin better than anyone and loved it
more than most.

∝

Für Wilma!
du other Ihrand.

Pedro Wilhem

Contents

Johann Wolfgang von Goethe visited Berlin in May 1778 and complained: "One does not get very far with politeness in Berlin because such an audacious race of men lives there that one has to have a sharp tongue in order to keep oneself afloat.

He summed up Berlin in a single word: 'Crude!'

The Last Berliner

I AM A BERLINER - born, bred and certified by the incumbent 'Oberbuergermeister' (Mayor) of the City in 1939 to be the *Honorary Godchild of the City of Berlin*. I found the certificate attesting to this honour in my Father's night table, tucked away behind a lifetime's accumulation of other unimportant paraphernalia.

The Meyers Konversations Lexikon of 1874 describes me thus:

> *"The Berliner is always quick at repartee, always able to find a sharp, suggestive, witty formulation for every event and occurrence."*

The image of a Berliner in the rest of Germany is of a cunning, streetwise character, who is witty, self-assured, irreverent and sometimes crass and speaks a sassy dialect, comparable only to the Cockney slang of London.

I am all of the above. **I am also one of a dying breed.**

Chapter 1
The Godchild!

Finding this historic paper carelessly filed away in the nether-regions of his night-table convinced me that Papa had not set much store in the certificate, although he surely appreciated the benefits that came with it. They were substantial and I owe my entire existence solely to the fact that my Papa was an opportunist and a bit of a scrooge.

In Germany's world, under National Socialist rule, having a third child entitled families to all kinds of benefits, one of which being the entitlement to a new apartment to accommodate a larger brood. Before I came on the scene, my parents, their two children and their grandmother, occupied a one-bedroom and kitchen flat with the toilet outside in the staircase, to be shared with two other families, a normal mode of accommodation for working class people in the Berlin of the 1930's.

The production of a third child, however, entitled the family to a modern, one-bedroom apartment in the green-belt zone which included a proper bathroom, a balcony and a small garden. It also committed the authorities to pay a monthly pension to the as yet unborn infant until he/she reached the age of 21. I have been told that I had a nice little nest egg by 1945 but, after devaluation of the German Mark, it was practically worthless and may have kept the family alive for a week. It's nice to know that I contributed somewhat to the family's welfare.

There wasn't anything in the world Papa liked more than saving money and his objections to Mama's wish of adding another mouth to feed vanished with the generous prospects offered. He filled out the necessary forms to be eligible to produce another blue-eyed, blond

Aryan to add to Adolf's dream of a master race. Happily no one ever inquired as to the real reason for his application, nor did they ask for a picture of the family, all of whom were small of stature, olive-skinned, black-haired and did not in the least live up to the expectations of the prototype of German folklore.

Prior to giving the go-ahead to produce this ideal Aryan, relatives on both sides of the family were called to report for health check-ups and the family's trees were searched back through the centuries. Turned out, everyone was very healthy but differed greatly in every other respect.

Papa's ancestors had been sitting around the Berlin area for ever and ever, barring one enterprising young man who emigrated to the United States, took one look at it, and high-tailed it home. No adventurers on that side of the tree.

Mama's family was found to have originated in France and had emigrated to the Hartz Mountains in Germany with a slew of other Huguenots fleeing the wrath of the Queen of France who, probably having a bad PMS problem, let out her anger on the Protestant population and almost succeeded in wiping all of them off the face of the earth.

When we were children, my brother and I saw it thus - *there they were, our ancestors, huddled in the basement of their home, listening to the howling mob of Catholics running through the streets, killing, robbing, raping, pillaging – basically doing what mobs out of control always do. "That does it", said the man of the house, "as soon as it cools down up there, we're getting out of the country. We're going to settle where no one will bother a Protestant. We're going to the cradle of Protestantism, to the town where Martin Luther grew up. We're going to Mansfeld in the Hartz Mountains."* Reality may have looked somewhat different but we always thought our version was so much more romantic.

Over the years these French emigrants forgot that they had ever lived anywhere else. Marrying into the native population, they lost their Gallic looks, their language and their culture, so that in the end they were always slightly puzzled when every generation or so they were blessed with the birth of a baby who had olive skin, black eyes, black hair and a Gallic temperament to boot. My Grandfather was one of them, my Mother another.

Having declared French background to be suitably Aryan and the family considered to be of a healthy longevity, Papa got the go-ahead. The flag went up and my parents went at it in earnest.

The result was born on December 27th, 1938 and declared to be the

Honourary Godchild of the City of Berlin. Heil Hitler and all that Jazz.

On December 25, I interrupted Papa's birthday present from Mama, which was a visit to the STERN movie theatre to watch "Die Feuerzangenbowle" (The Punchbowl). They never let me forget that my efforts at entering the world in the dark of a movie theatre prohibited them from seeing the ending. Twenty years later, we finally saw the whole movie on television and I apologized profusely - it was a very good movie indeed.

Taxis were not as predominant then as they are today. In any event, they couldn't find one readily available and by the time they arrived at the hospital, on foot, I had given up and snuggled back down into the warmth and comfort of my home for nine months. Moving is such a hassle.

This was Mama's first visit to a hospital, her two previous children having been born in the sanctity of her home with doctors attending. Papa was therefore a little worried about leaving his wife alone in a strange place, but as he trudged through the snow on his way home, he heard an unmistakable "ululating" sound which only Mama could make, never having mastered the knack of whistling. Upon turning, he spotted her on a balcony where, barefoot in the snow and grinning from ear to ear, she turned her back and mooned him. That's my Mama.

Patience is a virtue, but after two days of watching twenty other women on the ward produce babies, Mama lost hers. The method to hurry an overdue birth seems to have been of installing an arc with light bulbs over a woman's belly, thereby heating things up and hopefully inducing the Baby to get going. No one was suggesting this method to Mama, so she figured out her own system and leaned against the radiator, alternating between the front and the back. It worked.

In the afternoon of December 27, Christmas holidays being over, Papa called the hospital from work to inquire as to how the birth was coming along. Mama being in the delivery room, they patched him through to that department and, having just emerged from my cocoon, they put the receiver to my head and I had my first conversation with my Father. My screams of outrage at having been thrown out of my nest into a decidedly cold environment nearly blew his eardrums. If I had known what was coming, I would have screamed even louder.

In my teens, I read a book about a fellow in the jungle who had a snake slide into his sleeping bag overnight. His fellow campers tried everything to make that snake move until finally someone came up with the idea of letting the sun shine on the poor fellow. Snakes do not like heat and true to form this one exited promptly, only to meet his doom via a machete. I always associated with that poor snake. I wasn't met by a machete, but they were trying to starve me to death. This is living?

Being endowed with an ample bosom does not mean you are actually a great milk producer. Mama knew her shortcomings but assumed that the nurses were subsidizing my food quota and consequently, for the first five days of my life no one really fed me. I tried to tell them but only ended up with the reputation of the greatest screamer they'd ever had the misfortune to encounter in the nursery.

Three nights after I was born, Mama woke up thinking she had wet the bed. Feeling rather embarrassed, she nevertheless decided to put in a call for help. Minutes later, she found herself packed in ice, feet elevated and a towel blocking a massive haemorrhage. I don't think I was to blame as I only weighed 5 pounds and had the dubious distinction of being the smallest baby born on that ward which wasn't premature but actually overdue, but all my life I was grateful that Mama decided to give birth in a hospital. Had she been at home, we would have lost her and that would have been an awful shame. There was no one like my Mama.

Arriving home after five days, my grandmother's inspection of the newborn resulted in the famous quote: "If that was a rabbit, I wouldn't buy it." I'm sure Mama thought I was beautiful but according to less biased descriptions, I was really just skin and bones. Mama took charge - I was changed, my hands were bandaged (I had sucked on my knuckles until were raw) and bottle-fed. One bottle finished, another started, Papa's eyes started to bulge and he offered his opinion on how much a baby should be fed at any one time but Mama was more down to earth. "When she's had enough, she'll let me know." One and a half bottles later, I fell asleep and didn't wake up for eight hours. And I never screamed again.

Chapter 2

Grandparents and other Relatives!

In 1934, the family addition of a little baby boy coincided somewhat with the departure of my grandmother to a nursing home. To my then 5-year old sister, however, this was not a coincidence but a planned strategy on Mother's part.

Grandmother become very sick with anaemia and one of her medications consisted of eating raw liver. That should have been enough to turn her sour on the world in general but she turned on mother in particular. Familiarity breeds contempt and Mama was a handy subject to vent Grandma's frustrations. Sickness does things to people and Mama understood that and gave her mother-in-law the best care she knew how. Sadly, it wasn't enough to keep the peace. Every night, Papa had to listen patiently to his mother's complaints against his wife, all of which he knew very well were fabrications of a tortured mind and body. There was nothing much either one of them could do except wait for an opening in a nursing home.

Unfortunately, what neither of my parents realized at the time was that Grandma's imagined slights were also relayed to my Sister who, at that tender age, could not possibly figure out why Grandma was turning on Mother or understand the health problem which made her do it. I'm very sure that if the old lady had known what her tirades did to the little girl's mind, she would never have opened her mouth. By all accounts, she was a very nice woman.

Then I came along and Mama's attention span turned to the baby in the crib which did not faze Brother, who instantly turned protector of the weak, but greatly influenced Sister's position in the family. She had not yet forgiven Mother for adding a brother to the family, resulting in the disruption of what had so far been a harmonious existence. By the time I came along, the scene was set and I only added to her unhappiness. Happily, I had no idea what I was getting into. I was fed, loved, cuddled and, once I had put on some weight, proclaimed by all and sundry to be the cutest baby that ever lived. So far, so good.

To get Grandma into the nursing home hadn't taken much time. Getting a new apartment took a bit longer. What happened on the world scene did not affect me too much. War was declared, people disappeared over night, and someone screamed a lot on the radio. Today, no one admits it, but I know that Mama liked Adolf and listened avidly. Papa didn't. Papa had problems. Papa wouldn't join the Nazi Party and neglected to put out a flag on the Fuehrer's Birthday, which was promptly reported to the authorities by politically correct neighbours. That resulted in a visit from some very grim people and a promise from Papa to do better next year. He did. He staked out three small flags on thin wooden sticks amongst the red geraniums on the balcony. No one could see them, but they were there and that was that.

He could not afford to leave his identification papers at home because of continual inquiries by the authorities stalking the population as to whether or not he was Jewish and, if so, why he wasn't wearing the famous armband. Papa was small, dark and sported a rather large, hooked proboscis. Papa became a thorn in the side of the officials and, things getting a little too hot, his employers at Telefunken transferred him to a managerial post at the company's branch in the city of Breslau, very east of Berlin and basically out of reach of the officious party snoop.

The rest of the family spent their time walking to and fro, visiting Grandma in her nursing home. And there I remember her. An old lady with big felt boots on her feet, a shawl around her shoulder, with a little green Easter basket in her hand, filled with sweets which she saved every day to give to us children. Mostly I remember the sweets in the green basket. It would have been nice if she had lived long enough for me to remember more than that. Unfortunately, Grandma did not live happily ever after.

In 1941, the war was going strong and casualties were increasing. Hospitals were needed urgently for the troops and, in Nazi Germany, old people did not have the right to take up breathing space. So one day we arrived at the home and found the whole place empty. It took Papa almost a week, pulling every string and palming hands before he finally managed to find out what had happened. Every living soul in that place had been put on an open truck and transported to a Convent east of Berlin. Grandma spent the next two years in that place, with as many visits from Papa as he could possibly squeeze in. The rest of the family was evacuated by that time and was no longer able to pick up any sweets. In 1944, Grandma went into a coma and died. Papa said it was mostly homesickness and loneliness. It cost him a small fortune to transport her back to Berlin for burial. How he managed to do that is a testimony to his love for his Mother. In 1944, a single ticket on a train was barely available, all of them being used for troop transport. To get a coffin on a train was just short of a miracle. But Papa had promised his mother that she would be buried in Berlin and this was one son who would not renege on that, come hell, high water or the Second World War.

So thanks to Adolf's dream of a United Europe under German ownership, I was denied the companionship of a very nice lady, not to mention the donations of sweets and other assorted goodies. Life is not a bowl of cherries.

What you don't know, you don't miss, they say. So I don't know what it's like to have any grandparents at all. For one reason or another, everyone left the scene prematurely. The only survivor, Mother's mother, lived to a ripe old age but didn't seem to have had any interest in meeting me as she only came to see us once after I was born, and that visit didn't go down very well. Brother was being confirmed in the Church and Grandmother Hedwig and Aunt Elizabeth thought it important enough to visit to witness the occasion.

Grandma seemed old and very stern and, at one point, slapped Brother on the head for a perceived uncivil remark. That did not sit well with me, being loyal to the point of idiocy, and so I kicked her in the shins in retribution, whereupon I got my own slap on the head, which was not to be borne by my equally loyal brother. The two of us jointly requested my Mother to send the witch home. End of relationship.

Hedwig's husband, by the name of Gustav Adolf Otto Zilling, died when the copper mine he was crawling around in collapsed, burying everyone in it. He was apparently putting in some extra hours, probably trying to earn some much-needed cash for his growing family. "Never work overtime," my brother would proclaim fervently once he learned of Gustav's fate, "it's absolutely deadly".

His wife of seven years, eight months pregnant with my Aunt Fanny, was left holding the bag. 1907 was not a good year to be a single mother with three children - no welfare, no social service, no anything. However, they bred them differently in those days. Hedwig rolled up her sleeves, cleaned up her husband's body on the kitchen table, baked some goodies for the guests at the funeral and went to work in the fields.

As soon as my Aunt Elizabeth and Mother were strong enough, they joined her there at about 5 AM, leaving only to attend school at 8 AM where my mother promptly fell sound asleep most of the time. The children were fed, dressed immaculately and used to help keep the family going. Hugging and kissing did not fit into the equation. None of them suffered psychologically, either because there wasn't a psychiatrist handy to tell them they had a problem, or because they were too darn tired to worry about the situation. Either way, family ties did not have a chance in hell to become close and, although Mama visited her old home occasionally in the first years of her marriage, by the time I arrived she had other things to worry about and visits pretty much ceased.

Grandfather on Papa's side, one Arthur Edmund Ernst Krause, did himself in via an exorbitant intake of alcohol. Wasn't entirely his fault. He was a galvanizer by trade and one of the hazards of that profession is a great thirst. Beer is a German staple anyway and the consumption of said beverage is not considered dangerous, however, once you graduate to hard liquor you have a problem and by the time anyone realized that he was an alcoholic, he was fighting ants crawling on the walls and pink elephants attacking his bed. He died in an institution. Of course, being a baby, none of that tragic history was of any interest to me whatsoever.

Chapter 3

Paradise Found and Lost!

Back at 212 Hermannstrasse, life went on. In 1940 we finally moved and Mama thought she'd died and gone to heaven. One bedroom, one living-room, kitchen, hallway, balcony, an attached garden and, last but most certainly not least, a bathroom with a huge bathtub. The days of trotting to the public bathhouse were over.

Paradise was Britz, Franz Koerner Strasse 81E, with a view of a park full of rose bushes, birch trees lining the walk to the apartment building and huge chestnut trees bordering the sidewalks around the park. That it was still a cold-water flat did not hamper Mama's enthusiasm as to her that was merely a way of life. Heating was done with coal briquettes and my earliest memories are of Mama walking every afternoon with a shovel full of glowing coal from the kitchen to the living room, depositing that hot item into the tile oven there and adding some more coal. The bathroom stove had to be heated in the same way, which meant that all of Saturday was taken up with bathing. First Papa (when he was home on leave), then Mama, Sister and then Brother and me. Every one of us needed a stove full of hot water and, as it took about one hour to have enough water for a tubfull, having a bath turned into an all day affair.

So Saturdays were the only days the bathroom was heated. A visit to that facility on any other day of the week during the winter months was not an enjoyable experience and therefore something one got over with as quickly as possible. However, when compared with the facility at Hermannstrasse, this was modern living.

Another modern convenience of the "IDEAL CO-OP", our new

landlord, was the washhouse that sported washing machines, some sort of dryer and a mangle machine, which scared me silly. This contraption consisted of two huge rollers, quite hot, through which sheets, towels, handkerchiefs and pillow slips were pushed, coming out the other end ironed to perfection. Pushing them through meant getting ones hands quite close to these immense rollers and I was petrified that one day my mother's fingers would get caught, she'd be pulled through and come out flat as a pancake at the other end. To be blessed with a vivid imagination is not always a good thing.

Paradise, however, was soon lost. Bombs started falling and nights were nightmares of hearing sirens blaring, getting dressed into jumpsuits and getting carried, half asleep, into the cellar. Brother and I would sit with Mama who told us stories and sang songs. Sister basically missed the whole thing; grabbing her pillow and blanket and dropping onto the nearest pallet, she was out cold within minutes. Neither Brother nor I remember being afraid. Mama was cool and as long as Mama stayed that way, the world was a safe place. Never having experienced the terror of those nights as a grownup, I will never know how much it cost her to appear so calm. The rest of the cellar's occupants were freaking out left, right and centre. One of our neighbours religiously peed her pants, which was a great source of amusement to the children in attendance. We would bet on how long it would take before Mrs. Richter would lose control of her bladder, four minutes being the absolute world record.

People died all around us, whole blocks of flats disappeared and women cried when they saw the Postman because all he ever brought in those days was bad news of their loved ones from the front. But Mama sang songs and laughed with us and showed no fear and, therefore, all was well with the world. Well, not quite.

On one of Father's visits, he surprised us with tickets to a variety show in the "Deutschlandhalle", a coliseum-style building and the pride of Adolf's architects. Being Papa, he bought the cheapest seats; we were way up in the rafters and the arena below was a small circle of light where magic happened. There were people flying through the air and lions and tigers roared and there were horses that shone and glittered in the light and a lady in black who made them walk on their hind feet. It was breathtakingly beautiful.

Then the sirens blared, the lady and her horses disappeared and a voice said: "Ladies and Gentlemen, tonight's performance cannot be continued because of an air raid. There is no need to panic. Please proceed to the staircase." "Scheisse", said Papa. "Couldn't the damn Tommies (Englishman) have waited until the end of the show? Those tickets were expensive," which was definitely not true. However, being cheap sometimes has its advantages. Up in the rafters, it was so cold that we had not bothered to take our coats off, so now all we had to do was collect our shopping nets which, popcorn and concession stands not having been invented, were full of sandwiches and coffee in thermos bottles.

Getting to the staircase was easy - getting down the stairs was impossible. Someone from the top called down, asking why no one was moving and someone from the bottom advised us that the doors were locked from the outside and we had to wait until the animals had been removed from the building before we could descend. People started laughing and made jokes about animals definitely being more important than people and Mama told us that there was nothing to worry about. Then there was a thump and the mysterious voice came back and asked every soldier on leave to please come up to the roof. We had been hit and people were needed to put out the fire. When the voice called for every single male available to proceed to the roof, Mama asked me to entertain the masses with my particular version of the popular "Lily Marlene" song, which kept people amused for a little while. Halfway through my performance, I lost my audience. The doors opened and we were moving and finally emerged into the night.

What a show. Talk about fireworks! Planes flying about, lights flickering, explosions in the sky and on the ground. The Krause clan stopped dead in their tracks, sheltering underneath the roof over the cash register. "You want to stay put or should we try to get to the train station?" asked Mama. "Stay put?" Papa was incredulous. "The building is on fire and you want to shelter here? Everybody grab on to someone. We're off!"

And we went. Mama held Brother's hand, Papa grabbed Big Sister and between them they almost pulled my arms out of my sockets on take-off. My feet hit the ground about every ten meters, in between I just flew until, quite suddenly, the line came to a dead stop. Brother's shopping net had become entangled in some woman's coat button and he was trying to untangle it. Mama grabbed the net and pulled hard. Off came the net, including the offensive button, and we continued our flight, leaving behind a furious woman screaming "You've ruined my coat" or something like that. "Jesus, Maria and Joseph," gasped Mama. "The world is coming to an end and the stupid cow is worried about a button." And then she laughed. As long as I've known my mother, nothing was ever serious enough for her not to find something laughable in it. It's a gift.

Somehow we made it to the train station and slowly the noise of airplanes subsided and the fireworks stopped and the sirens blew the all clear. We sat close together on a bench, huddling for warmth and human companionship and waited for the train.

"Annie, you can't stay here any more. You've got to get out of Berlin."

"I know. I'll get our name on the list tomorrow".

Those few words sealed my fate for the next three years as we joined thousands of other women and their children and became an entity known as "Evacuees".

Chapter 4
THE EVACUATION SCENE

We packed everything. The feather beds, the hi-fi commode, dishes, cutlery, toys - if it wasn't nailed down solid it made its way into our trunks. Mama was moving but she wasn't leaving the comforts of home behind. The town of Milken in East Prussia, our new home, was somewhere near Poland - way up north so to speak - and Mama didn't expect to find many conveniences in a place that far removed from civilization, namely Berlin.

I don't remember much about the train ride or the arrival, but I do remember the enormous horses that pulled the wagon of our host farmer who met us at the station. Brother was put upon the back of one of them but when that man reached for me, I hid behind Mama's skirt. I didn't want to die just yet.

We settled in on a farm a few miles outside the village. Brother took to the farm life as though he had never done anything else and I dogged his heels. Mama went back to hairdressing and soon became the most sought after evacuee in the district. Every girl who got married between 1942 and 1943 had her hair done by my Mama. Payment was usually in the way of aliments, such as geese, chickens, rabbits and vegetables.

I went along to fix up a bride once at the one and only hotel. To this day I remember the room where the wedding party was going to take place. The tables were set up in a horseshoe fashion and absolutely glittered with glasses and cutlery and beautiful dishes on white tablecloth. It was the most beautiful sight I had ever seen. I would have liked to see others but any further trips were curtailed because I embarrassed the family on that occasion. I got drunk.

There were about 15 women in attendance and they were all served glasses of liquor which they drank before disappearing into the next room to watch Mama perform her magic with the curling irons. I thought I'd be helpful and tried to clean all the glasses with my tongue, which was a pleasant task as the liquor was very sweet. When that was done, I tried to navigate my way into what had become the hairdressing salon but the world had become rather unstable and a few furnishings bumped into me and the ruckus made people come running. The sight of a 4-year old tipsy toddler trying to sit on a footstool and missing it made even the bride forget her decorum.

There is a fly in every ointment and my fly was the farmer's wife who thought there was something missing in my diet, being way too small for my age. The recipe was two raw eggs, beaten with sugar, which she poured down my unwilling throat every morning. My height of 4' 11" (and as age approaches probably even less) is proof of the fact that this concoction does nothing at all. All it did was leave me with a life-long aversion to eggs.

So Mama curled hair, Brother learned to ride horses and milk cows, and I tagged along. Mama was busy surviving and keeping the family fed and together. Brother was never officially designated babysitter but he became my protector and guardian angel nevertheless. I was always two steps behind him wherever he went and basically turned into his permanent shadow. Sister was 14 years old, miserable and someone to be ignored at all costs. She probably missed home and her friends and thought to help Mama out by bossing us around. It didn't go over very well.

We could have lived happily ever after except for Hilde Richter, Mama's friend of panty-peeing fame from the cellar. Every afternoon she turned up and cried on Mama's shoulder, she just couldn't cope. They had put her up in the village and she missed us and couldn't we please move closer and wouldn't it be nice if the little ones could play together again, etc., etc., etc.

Inquiries were made and a home found for us in the village - with the Pfarrer, a Protestant Minister by the name of Schwartz. The Pfarr-Haus was beautiful, an old, ivy-covered Mansion set on a hill with lawns sloping in huge steps down to a little brook. To fall in love with Pfarrer Schwartz was inevitable, to hate his wife was unavoidable. There never was a good man who was more blessed with a shrew than our Pfarrer. She was a control freak and compulsive cleaner. Every speck of dust was attacked as if her life depended on eliminating the little mote. Her windows sparkled, her floors sent everyone flying and her mouth kept even the Postman at a distance. Worst of all, she hated children and we reciprocated with everything we had. Every trick we could think of was used and her life became a nightmare of mud in the halls, fingerprints on the banisters and doorbells ringing with no one there. I think we won.

Summer in East Prussia was swimming in the lake, which unfortunately harboured a lot of leeches which had to be burned off with cigarettes. Brother learned how to swim, or at least he told Mother he could swim as otherwise she would have objected to him joining the village boys jumping off a raft far away from the beach. He mainly dog-paddled.

Winter was building snowmen and sledding down those lawn steps over the brook and into the woods. We had to learn to walk in wooden clogs, which was an entirely new experience. Either the snow builds up underneath the sole, making you grow to unusual proportions within seconds or the clog gets stuck in the snow, making the next step a rather soggy one. But they were surprisingly warm once you learned the knack of keeping them on. Life was at its best - but in the spring the Russians came.

It sounded like thunder - Ba Bumm, Ba Bumm - and we started packing again. The Pfarrhaus was being abandoned entirely as Pfarrer Schwartz and most everyone in the village and surrounding farms was packing up to get away. It was in the middle of this mess that Mrs. Schwartz gave a new meaning to the word 'ridiculous' by requesting Mama to clean all the windows before she left. Mama didn't think the Russians would appreciate the effort and threw her out. Everyone was very touchy that day.

The train left in the evening. The noise of thunder was much closer and the sky on the horizon was lit up by anti-aircraft guns, flashing lights that flickered across the sky. Fireworks again - how exciting. Only no one else seemed to appreciate the beauty of it. And beautiful it is when you're four years old and you don't know there is a war on or what it means. I kept wondering what Russians were and why everyone seemed to be so terrified of the word. As usual, everyone was too busy to tell me.

Next stop - the quaint little village of Kirchsteitz, near the town of Zeitz in Saxony. About 50 farms, one church and one schoolhouse surrounded by acres and acres of fields in which potatoes, wheat, sugar

15

beets and hay grew in abundance. Our new home was one room on a prosperous farm belonging to the Herbst family, which consisted of a roly-poly Mrs., a stolid Mr., teen-aged daughter Irene and a son who was away at the front.

Life in Saxony proved agreeable. Mother went to work in the fields for some extra rations and also to keep boredom at bay. "People who don't work, don't need to eat," was Mother Herbst's favourite saying and so we proceeded to earn our keep. Mama didn't just play at field work, she surprised everyone by beating the men in loading the wagons with the yellow hay stacks. The reputation of the Berliner evacuees was greatly enhanced by her accomplishments as she never bothered to tell them that she grew up in a farming community far away from her adopted, and beloved, home town of Berlin.

Brother turned into an all-around farmer's helper and I was part of the delegation to take the lunches out to the field workers. We reported to Mother Herbst who, if one was lucky, could be caught still in the process of cutting up the huge, round, home-baked bread. She would hold the bread in her left arm, pressing it against her ample bosom. With her right hand, and with the biggest knife I ever saw, she sliced the bread, again and again and again, starting on the outside and finishing inches away from her breast. The lunch brigade, consisting of a few 4 to 6 year olds, would watch open-mouthed, waiting for the inevitable plunge of the knife into that ample bosom. It never happened but we were pretty sure that one day it would.

Butcher day came and we were right in the middle of it. Pigs were slaughtered and cauldrons full of hot water were steaming up the yard, their contents a mystery but smelling delicious. Off and on someone would toss me a piece of white meat, still hot from the pot, which, with a little bit of salt sprinkled on it, still remains one of the tastiest delicacy that ever passed my tongue. I don't know what it was and I don't want to know.

Fruits were picked from the trees lining the country roads and Mama produced an apron with a pocket on the inside where cherries and plums, apples and pears could be hidden effectively and brought home to her ravenous family. We were not the only evacuees on that farm and old Mrs. Herbst must have hated the whole thing of accommodating all these strangers and, consequently, was rather tight in the provision of aliments to sustain us. So Mama used the apron to help feed us. I was four years old and I watched my Mama stealing. Stealing was alright as long as you didn't get caught. First lesson in survival - duly noted.

Old lady Herbst was also kind on occasion. She arrived on our doorstep one day and handed Mama a whole pot full of Sauerkraut, ready to eat and smelling wonderful. "The dogs don't like it and the pigs don't eat it. I thought you might like to have it," she said. Mama assured her that her family had far better tastes than the pigs and the dogs and gracefully accepted the donation. Everybody was happy.

Autumn came and the churchyard became a preferred playground, especially when it got dark. We huddled in the shadow of ancient gravestones and told scary stories. The first one to run was a coward. One night a goat lost its way and startled the entire congregation out of imaginary stories into believing they were seeing a real ghost. Not having heard of the "women and children first" commandment, everyone took off at once, resulting in numerous bloody noses, scraped elbows and bruised ribs. Everyone was a coward that night.

Winter arrived and big wooden sleds were found in attics and cellars. The run started at the church and went all the way into the village proper and onto the village pond. The walk back was long and arduous but Brother, being the good brother he was, always towed my sled back to the top. Water was poured onto the snow at night and by morning we had a long 'Schlitterbahn', for those who preferred sliding on their own two feet. For adults, this presented a constant aggravation as they couldn't see the ice under the snow and, not being smart enough to ask the children just where they had fabricated this death trap, many a grown-up ended up on his/her backside. There is nothing funnier to a child as an adult flat on his back. It was constant warfare and fraught with danger because, if one was caught pouring the water, one got a licking. Every adventure has its drawback and you learn to live with it.

Spring meant watching the thermometer. At 10 degrees Celsius, we were allowed to take off the long, scratchy, home-knitted stockings. At 15 degrees, ankle socks replaced the knee highs and 20 degrees meant you could throw the shoes away - except for Sundays when white socks and shoes were a must. I didn't like wearing shoes, so Sundays became unendurable tortures. I resolved to boycott the edict and took off shoes and socks, found a hiding place and got back to wiggling my toes happily in the dust and dirt all day. Lunch was a sandwich that Brother picked up for us and, come supper time, I was all prim and proper again with shoes and socks in place. Then we got ready for bed and Mama went ballistic. For the longest time, I couldn't figure out how she always knew that I had broken the golden Sunday rule.

I thought it was one of those Mother things - they just know! Brother finally came to the rescue. I hadn't washed my feet before putting back the socks and shoes. That was easily fixed and Mama and I were again in perfect harmony - until the next time.

Mama had problems with my logic. I tried to do what I was told but I took what she told me literally. She would ask me to tell my siblings to come into the house as it was getting late. I searched for them outside, gave them the message and they dutifully went home. I didn't. It took them another hour to find me and, when an exasperated Mama pounced on me, I patiently explained that she had asked me to tell my siblings to go inside but had not mentioned me at all and therefore I had not been obliged to return home. Perfectly logical. Mama took care to be exact in her instructions but never quite succeeded. We spent my entire childhood trying to figure out what the other one was saying.

Spring brought dandelions and Brother thought he should give me some identification mark in case I got lost some day. When you break the stem of a dandelion, a white juice drips out and Brother put three dollops of that on my right wrist. He made me sit, holding my wrist up to the sun, for what seemed like a very long time and, when he finally wiped the plant juice away, I was left with three brown spots. I don't know anything about the ability of dandelion juice to brown skin but I still have the three dots on my wrist and they darken in the summer sun. Unfortunately, I never really got lost so Brother missed out on the chance of identifying me.

Spring meant planting and we watched as men strode across newly ploughed fields, throwing seeds in all directions. Mother Nature got active and we were fascinated as the bull was brought to the cow, the stallion to the mare and they all got very busy. Sex is not something mysterious when you grow up in the country; it's just funny to watch. There were kittens all over the place and baby rabbits to play with and I got a job - herding geese. This sounded quite romantic and, according to the fairy tales Mama read to us at night, I was supposed to be discovered by a handsome Prince. Unfortunately, all I was blessed with was a very vicious gander who would peck at my feet and herd me in all directions instead of the other way around. It was painful, degrading and, in the end, rather expensive. One day my persecution by that irate goose was witnessed by Brother, who quickly came to the rescue. He grabbed the offending bird by the neck, swung him around and only threw him down after we heard a distinct click. He'd broken his neck. Poor Mama had to pay for the damage, which didn't even taste good. I quit.

That summer I started school. One room, one teacher, an outhouse, approximately 20 kids, ranging from Grade 1 through Grade 9. First grade occupied the first row of desks, second grade the second row, third grade the third row, and so on. Brother occupied row No. 4. No talking, no laughing, no whispering allowed. There was a solid stick lying across the teacher's desk to remind one of the consequences of such frivolous action. It was used quite frequently on culprits, a situation thoroughly enjoyed by the audience who, listening to the woeful cries of their classmate, took pride in the fact that they hadn't been caught - this time.

One night, Brother took off his shirt for his nightly wash and Mama gasped. His back was criss-crossed in lines of blue and black and red, and he winced when she touched him. "Who?" asked Mama. "Teacher" said Brother. And that was that - or so we thought.

We had barely finished our "Good Morning, Teacher" the next day when the door flew open and there was Mama. Seeing that certain look on her face, I could have told my teacher that she was in deep trouble but I didn't like her, so I didn't. In two strides Mama was at the desk, grabbed that dreaded cane, brought up her knee and snapped the thing in half. Then she turned and snarled: "You touch any of my kids again, you'll regret it." The door slammed shut, leaving behind a totally flabbergasted teacher and an adoring fan club of kids who thought that that was the bravest thing they had ever seen anyone do. It came pretty close to Siegfried or Saint George slaying their dragons.

None of the Berliner Kids were ever touched again but, unfortunately, the village kids were not blessed with a champion and their education continued to be a painful experience, the moral being that it had worked with their parents and if it was good enough for them, it should be good enough for the next generation. I have no idea whether or not it worked.

Life was perfectly wonderful but the situation couldn't last. It was becoming clear to me that, every time I settled in for a harmonious existence, things started to unravel. In late summer, the War caught up with us.

Our living room window overlooked the village street and the schoolhouse, which put Mama into the position of being the Paul Revere of Kirchsteitz. Planes were flying overhead and every time the radio announced a slew of bombers coming our way by imitating the sound of a cuckoo bird, Mama would yell out the window: "the cuckoo called, the cuckoo called," and our one and only teacher would send the children scattering to their various homes or take the ones living too far away to the tunnel which had been dug into a mountain nearby. Those RAF flyers never knew how much the children of Kirchsteitz appreciated their appearance.

If you were lucky, you were somewhere where your mother couldn't find you when the planes came. Then you could sit on a hillside and watch real-life action - a car driving along the 'Landstrasse', the plane zooming down out of the sky, the car stopping, people running and jumping into ditches, the 'bupbupbupbup' of the guns and then the explosion. Greatest show on earth. And here were the innocent children - "Yeah, got him. Told you he would. You owe me 10 Pfennig." We were too young to take sides or understand that people were getting hurt. It was just a game. Today they have video games.

If one was at home, one had to run to the tunnel in the mountain, which was considered the safest place during a bomb attack. We had a ways to go and if it was night, we had a chance to watch the sky explode and appreciate the huge lights that flickered across the heavens, searching for an airplane. When they found one, it was pretty well sunk, as the circle of light that surrounded the plane would not let it go, making him an easy target for the anti-aircraft gunners.

The tunnel in the mountain was dark and dank and we hated it. People cried and screamed when the walls shook and, as I never saw an exit, I always thought we were extremely lucky not to have been buried alive in our attempt to survive the action outside.

In February of 1945, I received my first report card that stated that I was very good at keeping up appearances but my actual performance on the academic level was not considered genius category. Nobody acknowledged the fact that I had only turned 6 in December of 1944 and had therefore started school way before I was ready for it. I threw my little "Schiefertafel" (slateboard) into a corner and decided that school was a waste of my time.

Spring meant we could finally stop listening in secret to a whispering voice on the radio telling us how the war was going, because apparently it wasn't going anymore. Mama turned the BBC to full volume and we were saved from going deaf. The war was over and all it meant to me is that the birds took back the sky.

Spring brought the Americans - and some of them were black. We couldn't believe it. There is a German children's story which has a Moor in it but we didn't actually believe that there was such a thing as black skin on real people. No one was quite sure what to make of it. Having inherited Mama's genes, I elected to volunteer to find out the truth. There is a dark-skinned American somewhere in the United States who tells a tale of a little, pigtailed German girl who grabbed his hand, licked it and started rubbing vigorously with a rather soiled handkerchief. He's still black on that patch and everywhere else and he's also probably still laughing.

The Americans were a great catch. They had stuff, lots of it. They had chewing gum and chocolates and dried fruits. They didn't like to part with it too much, so we didn't bother asking either - we stole them blind. I remember one convoy stopping right in front of our house for lunch and Brother milling about their cars and then hunkering down in the corner of the schoolyard. When Mama called him in for lunch, he shook his head. "Leave him be," Mama said. "He's got something." He sat for almost two hours, an immovable little Buddha, watching the 'Amis' (as we called them, never having heard of a Yank), eating their lunch, dozing on their trucks and finally going on their way. What he finally brought home was a huge can full of preserved cherries. Man the provider had struck again.

Another item of importance he brought home one night was a map. It showed, in the smallest detail, the area we lived in. There was our insignificant little village, including all the streets that ran through it. Mama was totally flabbergasted. "My Goodness, they couldn't have got lost in Germany had they tried." I thought Kirchsteitz must have been pretty important to the Americans to bother making such a detailed sketch of it.

The Amis had a strange habit all of their own. One day they declared our farm to be their headquarters and gave everyone two hours to clear out. People ran to and fro, trying to take with them as much of their belongings as was possible in so short a time. We grabbed the bedding, the pots, the pans, the toys, the clothes and our last trip was for the cherished hi-fi commode which Mama had so diligently transported from Berlin to East Prussia and Saxony and which she hoped to return to my father's care in due course.

It was only 1½ hour into the battle when we were stopped at the farm gate by the Military Police who said that the time was up. Mama lost it. The precious hi-fi commode was still inside and they wouldn't let her have it. The third world war almost started at that point but Mama had no leg to stand on. If you're on the losing side, you've got to learn to live with injustice. Two days later, our farm was declared too small, the Amis picked another farm and we were allowed back into our home. The hi-fi had disappeared, never to be seen again. I hope whoever took it got a lot of enjoyment out of it. It was a very good Telefunken hi-fi commode and Papa missed it.

In the meantime, unbeknownst to me, somewhere in a place called Potsdam, representatives of four victorious armies sat down to decide Germany's fate. They cut the place up like a cheese cake and in the process gave the State of Saxony to the Russians.

Chapter 5

FROM RUSSIA - WITH LOVE

So the Amis left for greener pastures and the dreaded Russians finally caught up with us and turned up in the village streets. Hilde Richter, of peepee cellar fame, went back to being hysterical, being deadly afraid of the Russkies who loved blond women. Hilde was very blond and very pretty, so she probably had cause to panic. Fortunately for us, the troops filing through our part of the country were ordinary, conscripted soldiers and not the ravenous mob of Barbarians who for 24 hours, raped and killed the civilian population of Berlin. It's a historical fact that the Russian troops had been promised full access to the women of Berlin for 24 hours if they took the city. I'm sure glad we missed that.

We were the lucky ones, encountering mostly smiling young men who seemed just as happy as we were that they didn't have to shoot any more. However, that didn't prevent the women all around us to blanch and shiver every time a Russian came near them.

One day, most of Mama's neighbours from Berlin turned up and big discussions were going on about something they needed urgently and it was only to be had in the next town, which was a place called Droyssig, approximately 1 hour walk away. The chances of encountering a Russian in the middle of nowhere were not imaginary worries and no one was brave enough to volunteer. Into the breach strode my Mama. "But Annie", yelped the blond bombshell called Hilde, "what if you get raped?" Mama never suffered fools gladly. "Heavens", she said with a straight face, "then it is someone else for a change. That's all." Gasp, gasp, all around. They didn't mind her risking her life by sending her off on this errand but they did object to her frivolous attitude towards the worst fate that could befall women. That later a number of them had affairs with not only Russians but also other occupying forces, who were a source of providing nourishment which was not available anywhere else, never made them forgive Mama for that remark and gave her a life-long reputation as a loose cannon. Fortunately, Mama didn't give a hoot.

She told us later of her walk through the fields to Droyssig and back. Not having encountered a living soul on the way there, she was hoping for a peaceful return trip. No such luck. Half way home, surrounded by trees, fields and nowhere to hide, two Russian soldiers turned up on the horizon. Her mouth went dry and her knees started to wobble. Sweaty palms could barely hold on to the shopping bags but somehow Mama kept the panic down and commenced walking. As the two soldiers came nearer, they parted company, which meant they would be passing Mama on each side, assuring her that an attack was in the making. She dropped the bags, bent her knee and, pretending to tie her shoelaces, waited for the inevitable.

"Guten Tag," said the two young men and, smiling widely and very proud of themselves for having spoken in German, went on their way. "Guten Tag," croaked Mama and thanked God for sending two decent sons of Russia her way. Nevertheless, it took her quite a while to be able to come out of her crouch because her legs simply were not in any condition to support the rest of her body.

None of the Russians we encountered ever attempted to do harm to anyone, however, being an occupied country meant doors were to be left unlocked at all times which allowed the odd visitor in the form of a young Russian soldier to enter, look around the place, smile a lot and take whatever it was that took his fancy or, not seeing anything interesting lying around, leave us alone.

Brother was caretaker of a watch inherited from Grandfather Krause. It was a watch that was worn on a chain on a waistcoat but now sat in a little wooden box that could be propped open, thereby exhibiting the watch like an alarm clock. The back of the box was decorated with two swallows in flight made out of mother-of-pearl. It was very beautiful. Off and on Brother would take it out of its hiding place and admire it. I could only watch because, as low man on the totem pole, I had no rights whatsoever involving anything important going on. Mama repeatedly warned him about the Russian's love for watches and, one day, disaster struck.

Bang went the door, grab went the Russian and gone was the watch into his uniform pocket.

"Well," said Mama, "I don't know what your father will do to you when he finds out." To me, Father was by now a mystical figure that came and went at infrequent intervals but Brother, remembering that authoritative figure and the wrath Father was capable of, probably thought dying was preferable to admitting he had lost the watch. He promptly went hysterical.

I had no idea what was going on but Brother was crying, which was highly unusual, and that meant he was in deep trouble and needed my help. I started howling myself and the poor Russian now found himself attacked by two children, totally out of control, pulling on his clothes and weeping their little hearts out - in German. Mama took charge.

Pushing the young Russian into a chair, she explained in very loud but slow german that stealing that watch would mean disaster for my brother. She showed him a picture of Papa, pointed to the watch and then to Brother and cut her throat with her finger. He didn't get the message. Firmly clutching his treasure, he walked out the door. He wasn't alone for long. Following in his footsteps were two totally out of control, heartily sobbing children, who clutched at his jacket and could not be shaken off however much he yelled. He took refuge in the local Commandatura and requested a translator who could unravel the mystery and relieve him of his burden. Fortunately for all of us, one was available and, once the circumstances were explained, the young man released the object of his desire. If he hadn't, we probably would have followed him all the way to Russia, which would have been preferable to facing Father's wrath.

Being quite young, I think he perfectly understood what Brother would be facing. He probably had a Dad just like that at home. Handing back the watch was likely the hardest thing he ever did in his life, but hand it back he did and got hugs from two relieved members of the Krause clan in return. I think he liked the hugs better than the watch. He left smiling.

The adult population's problems with Russians were a little more severe. The occupying forces were constantly trying to find something called a 'Nazi', and everyone they encountered swore to high heaven that they were not and had never met anyone who was of that persuasion.

Our Mayor and various other city officials had always been quite upset with our Mama, who had consistently replied to their 'Heil Hitler' with a cheerful 'Good Morning'. She never did take to the new world order of greeting someone with other than 'Guten Morgen, Guten Tag, Guten Abend or Gute Nacht'. So, as soon as peace was declared, Mama thought it was extremely funny to now greet all those who had given her a hard time before with a loud and spontaneous 'Heil Hitler' in the village streets. Our public functionaries went to great lengths explaining to her, in whispers, that times had changed and she could now go back to the original ordinary German 'hello, how do you do thing'. "Well," said Mama, "will you people make up your mind." It was pretty funny to watch the ex-party bigwigs squirm with embarrassment.

With the Russians came not only fear for the adults, there also came one of the greatest discomforts of my life. With the Russians came head lice.

All of a sudden, everyone was scratching their heads and Mama was called into action. She turned up at school with a louse comb and went through the entire class with a vengeance. We all had them and we all had to be shorn of our tresses because that is the easiest and least costly way to get rid of lice.

In no time at all, most of the adults and the entire children population were sporting the skinhead look. We were way ahead of our time. Except for me.

Never having followed a fashion trend before or after, I was a minority of one refusing to part with my long tresses that by this time had grown way past my shoulder blades. I was proud of that hair and, even though Mama explained in detail how much it would hurt to keep it and get rid of the lice, I would not relinquish one inch of it. Vanity had taken hold and I persisted.

It was much worse than I had imagined. Scratching ones scalp raw and then having a concoction of vinegar and other acidy stuff poured all over one's head, covering that up with a towel and enduring was pure hell. It was the longest week of my life but, in the end, it was worth it. I was the only one left with a mane and the envy of my companions.

So - Germany had lost the war and we could now go home. Home? I thought I was home. Or rather, I had no idea where or what home was. Home was where my Brother and Mother happened to be but "Home" they wanted to go and no one bothered to ask my opinion, and that was that.

The problem was finding a truck to take us back to the city of my birth. Not an easy task. Hilde Richter, Mama's incomparable bosom pal, found one, driver and all. She stormed into our little room one day, all flushed and happy, announcing triumphantly that she was ready to leave in two days. *"Great,"* said Mama, *"I'll be ready by then."* Hilde somewhat lost her bounciness. *"Annie,"* she said, *"there isn't enough room for us all. It is only for my family. I'm sorry, but in times like these everyone has to look out for themselves. You must understand that."* Mama didn't.

It isn't easy for people as tanned as my Mother to blanch, but blanch she did. She had the look that usually pre-cursed a spanking and I was looking forward to Hilde being trounced but it didn't happen. Too bad. The woman deserved it. Instead, Mama took her by the shoulders and shoved her out the door. Then she sat down at the table and put her head into her arms. I knew despair when I saw it. Brother and I put our arms around her and held fast. I think it helped.

Years later, I heard Lee Marvin sing (horribly) a song in a movie called 'Paint Your Wagon' which, among other things, mentioned the words "snow can burn your eyes, but only people make you cry" and it brought back the memory of Mama losing faith in people and women in particular. It was a terrible thing to watch.

Hilde and her two children left and Mama put Sister on a train to join Papa at home. My Father, residing in Breslau until almost the end of the war, had heard the noise of the advancing Russian Army and, grabbing a bicycle, pedaled all the way from Breslau to Kirchsteitz. He was very lucky. The Russians closed off Breslau when they got there and almost every male over the age of 16 disappeared into Siberia. War being over shortly after his arrival, he went on to Berlin to see what he could do to find work and provide for his family.

Mama kept trying to get a truck and Brother kept working in the fields, until one day they brought him home injured. Some tool had fallen off the wagon carrying the field crew home and Brother jumped to retrieve it. Unfortunately, he jumped over the side, stumbled and the rear wheel drove over his leg. They didn't tell Mama the whole thing, just that he fell off the wagon, and not until he started crying when she tried to make him wash up did she realize that things were a little bit more difficult than we thought.

A car was organized and Brother disappeared into the hospital with a broken leg. That left Mama and me, which was fine. I got a lot of attention and was taken everywhere Mama went because the permanent baby-sitter was temporarily incapacitated. We were constantly on the roads, trying to track down a truck big enough to take us and the feather beds back to the mythical place called home. The date Mama finally managed to establish for the return trip also happened to be the date they were cutting off the plaster cast on Brother's leg. It was not to be helped. That day or no day. Mama agreed and advised the hospital.

We left very early on a cold October morning. First stop, the hospital, from which they carried Brother to the truck and deposited him on the precious feather beds that Mama had made into a nice little nest. While they were thus occupied, I went to pee into a ditch.

I took off my gloves, put them down next to me, did my business – and then couldn't find the gloves anywhere. Story of my life. I swear there are little people running around in the world who steal things off some people. I'm one of their victims. Everyone, from the truck driver to the hospital staff to Mama, went into that ditch looking for the missing gloves. Nobody found them. Gloves cost money of which there was very little around, so my carelessness was rewarded with a solid swat on my backside. It wasn't fair, of course, but nothing ever is when you're a child dealing with grown ups. So my Brother had a comfortable bed and I sat on the floor with a sore butt. I made his life miserable all the way home. Loving your Brother means you can let your frustrations out on him.

Chapter 6

Home from the Hills!

Home - endless rows of apartment buildings, all of which looked the same. No fields, no animals, no familiar sights at all, just doors, windows with nosy faces staring at us and children of all ages taking our measure with calculating eyes. "Go ring the bell," Mama told me, pointing to a door right next to a tunnel which was cut into the row of buildings. I remembered the tunnel. We used to play there when it rained, invoking the wrath of the people living on either side, including my own family, because of the noise we made - the tunnel made a terrific echo when one screamed.

Inside the building, up a small staircase, were two doors, one on each side. There were name plates but they were written in elaborate German lettering which I could not read, not properly having mastered the alphabet in block letters as yet. I rang the first one, which promptly turned out to be the wrong one. Inquiring after my Papa seemed to be very funny to the woman answering. "*You must be the little girl from Krauses,*" she laughed. "*You live on the other side.*" Thank you and good night.

My second ring was answered by Sister whom I recognized immediately by her attitude. "*Finally,*" she said. "*It's about time.*" Thank you and it's nice to see you too.

Sister disappeared, leaving me standing in a dark hallway. There was a little light coming through the door on my left so I pushed it open - and promptly screamed and bolted. I had encountered that magical being who had visited us off and on for the past three years - my Father who, unfortunately, had been afflicted with something called 'hunger boils', an illness men have a tendency to get when hunger reigns supreme. He was scheduled to go to the hospital next morning to have the boil on the back of his neck lanced and in the meantime sported a tremendous white turban all around his head and neck. The combination of a candle on the table, throwing shadows on his face, and the white bandages on his head produced a picture straight out of an Edgar Allan Poe book. The fact that I can't abide horror movies probably stems from my encounter with the man from outer space in our kitchen.

Papa had to come outside and be properly introduced to the youngest member of his family before I was convinced that it was safe to go back inside. I returned to the chamber of horrors because I thought that, just in case he wasn't the real thing and Mama just couldn't see it, I had better be there to protect her in case something went wrong. I'm a very protective person. Unfortunately, I fell asleep five minutes after I was put to bed, but it's the thought that counts.

In the morning, my parents were gone and I had time to survey this new situation. The rooms were definitely bigger than anything we had lived in lately, mostly because there was no wall between the living room and the bedroom. Brother had to explain. Our building had not been hit by any bombing but the buildings around us sure had and one of the effects of a bombing is air pressure which reduced our living room/bedroom wall to rubble no higher than myself, which wasn't much. He assured me that someone would build the wall up again eventually. I thought it was fine as it was. You could practice gymnastics tumbling back and forth over the remaining bricks.

Papa returned and went straight to bed. Sporting now only a bandage around his neck, he started to look familiar and, as everyone was busy moving things around and pushing me out of the way, I found refuge with Papa. There was a smell about my Father, hard to describe. A smoky, strong male odour which, combined with his embrace, made you feel secure, protected and invincible towards any threat that life had to offer.

The feeling of protection, however, did not translate into survivor. Papa was an honourable man who could neither beg nor trade nor ask for help. If it wasn't for my Mother, we would not have survived the years following the war. Honourable men do not survive in hard times. Mother, on the other hand, was very good at survival.

The winter of 1945 was probably one of the worst ever encountered in Germany and Europe in general. There was no heat, no electricity and no coal to heat the wood stove. Thousands of people froze or starved to death but my Mother had no such fate in mind for her own family.

The city of Berlin is surrounded by forests of immense proportion. Off and on, the foresters went in and cleared dead wood and chopped down injured or diseased trees. Due to the shortness of firewood, the general population was allowed to pick up what was left on the ground and that meant three trips a week to the forests of Berlin for the Krause clan.

Mother, Brother and me - bundled up to the eyebrows, pulling a wagon and carrying rucksacks on our backs, took off in the dark and freezing cold for the half hour walk to the train station where we boarded already packed compartments for the one hour ride into the country. Another hour or so took us to where Mama wanted to go - near birch trees. "Birch trees burn the longest," was what she drummed into us, and birch trees were what we were looking for diligently. The problem was that none of us were actually allowed to cut down a living tree at all, so my job was to stand guard while Brother sawed through the precious wood. Pretending to pick up pinecones, my eyes would scan the road continuously for the arrival of the dreaded foresters.

One day, as Brother was halfway through the trunk of a particularly nice specimen, I spotted four men coming our way. "Mama, I've got to go pee," I yelled. That was our code for 'foresters on the horizon' and the best Mama could come up with, as I couldn't whistle. Coming from a 6-year old with the stature of a 3-year old, it sounded totally innocuous and left nothing much to the imagination. But what was Brother to do?

He did the only thing that would not arouse suspicion in the evil minds of our persecutors. He opened his fly and pretended to urinate, all the while propping up the leaning tree with his shoulder, a feat that put him into the category of superman. He was under-weight, under-height and his leg was still weak from the break. But Brother knew that Mama needed him and he stood and held that tree for at least three minutes. As soon as the coast was clear, he let go, the tree came down and he collapsed beside it. Mama cradled him in her arms until he recovered and I burst into tears because he was lying on the ground and was awfully pale. Then he told me to shut up and that meant he was alive and well and I went back to picking up pinecones. Mama brushed the hair out of his face and said 'thanks'. Brother smiled and proceeded to cut up the precious tree. Those two were two peas out of one pod

31

and didn't need words to communicate.

Rucksacks packed to the hilt, wagon fully loaded, we made our way back to the train station. All the people going through this exercise were usually extremely angry and certainly selfish in the attempt to board the train compartments with all their belongings intact. It never took my Mama more than about five minutes before she had everyone laughing at the situation, which in truth was ludicrous. Here was the glorious master race, in rags, stealing wood out of their own forests and going begging in the country. If you can't laugh at that, you've got a problem.

Brother was best at the begging part. There was no food and the only way to get some was to get into the country and try to trade things to the surrounding farms. Off came Mother's rings, earrings, bracelets and family heirlooms in general. Out went all our toys, stuffed animals, books and pretty towels. Off went Brother to exchange these items for food. He was very cute and very polite and he always came back with more food than anyone else, having himself been fed by the farmer's wife to the hilt before leaving. His story brought tears to their eyes and opened their hearts - and they were all lies. He told them his Father was in Russia and his Mother had pneumonia and lay near dying. His little sister coughed a lot herself and he was the only one left well enough to look after us. Survival instinct brings out the best in us and he was very, very good!

Papa only went once. It was a disaster. Between Papa, Brother and Sister, they managed to trade their goods for a sack of frozen potatoes, which some Russian soldiers promptly confiscated at the train station. Then they missed the last train home and had to sleep in a filthy hotel room where they nearly froze to death. The only thing they came back with was body lice. Papa never went again.

Somehow, we made it through the winter of 1945/46. I wouldn't want to repeat it. There was a soup once out of someone else's potato peels, which was awful and which I threw up after a short stay in the stomach. And then there was the cow udder. It was chewy and had a sweetish taste and, stomach growling, I declined the honour. I couldn't get it down. Brother loved my queasy stomach. He could eat anything.

There were all kinds of strange concoctions Mother invented and to ask about the ingredients of a particular soup was not recommended. Standing in line became the norm for shopping and I was not exempt from that duty. Once I stood in line for three hours for a pail of substitute molasses and fainted dead away in the line-up. People propped me up and I kept my place. Iron deficiency does that to you. I also developed rickets to a slight degree and the curvature of my legs resulted in the loss of a few precious inches in height. This forfeited any future chance of entering the Miss Germany contests and also prevented me from ever getting a job as a flight attendant whose height requirements were out of my reach. I should sue someone.

Ration cards were introduced and food turned up in stores, but not much. Fifteen rabbits took up residence in cages on the balcony and now there was meat sometimes. Chickens pecked away in the garden, sleeping the night away in the basement where Papa had built a coop, and now there were eggs. Something called the Black Market started happening and apparently there you could get absolutely anything - if you had the money, which we didn't.

What we did have was a garden. Actually, we were the proud owners of two garden plots, one small one attached to the apartment and one big lot approximately half an hour away at a brisk walk. Papa had acquired the big lot when Sister was born, originally intending to get the family out of the city and into the country during the summer months. Leased from the church for 99 years, the land had consisted of nothing but sand which Papa had turned into paradise. He built a house, a work shed and an outhouse, planted trees, berry bushes and flowers, never realizing that a few years later his summer residence would help his family to survive the aftermath of a war and to that purpose, the 'Garden of Eden' was now turned into a tobacco field.

People will do anything for a cigarette. They will go without food, without drink, without sex, and they will lose their dignity - but they have to have their cigarette. I watched American soldiers throw down what was left of their 'Camel', step on it, ground it into the soil, walk away and turn to watch the Germans dive for that stump and scrabble in the dirt for it. It leaves an impression when you're young. I didn't like it.

Papa, being a chain-smoker himself, understood the need. The exercise of harvesting the leaves, hanging them up to dry in the summer cottage and spending days rubbing the stuff into small bits and pieces, turned me permanently off smoking. It stank to high heaven and no matter how often you washed your hands, you didn't seem to be able to get rid of the smell. Papa built cigarette machines and we rolled cigarettes to be sold to the general public. Papa had a lot of customers at work and Mama was the salesperson for the neighbourhood. We were lucky to have that kind of opportunity.

But some of our playmates on the street were even luckier. They had relatives in affluent countries like Canada, Australia or, the pot of gold at the end of the rainbow, America. We didn't. So we went outside to play and were shown pieces of chocolate, chewing gum and other assorted goodies but we weren't allowed to touch, never mind bite into these heavenly tidbits. I had encountered the first examples of 'show and tell.' We proclaimed we wouldn't touch that junk anyway but back inside the tears flowed. Papa had forbidden to beg but Mama's children were crying and a way had to be found to make them stop.

She took out the map of the world, closed her eyes and stabbed her finger. Sweden. Out came the map of Sweden, the eyes closed again and the finger stabbed. A Protestant Pastor in a small town in Sweden got a letter from Mama asking if he would be so kind and send her children a few pieces of something sweet. She promised to make it up to him as soon as she could.

A few weeks later, the postman stopped at our door and brought paradise. Chocolates, dried milk, cocoa, cookies, sugar, flour, dried fruits and a letter from a Pastor by the name of Axel Leyonborg who lived in Falun and who had been given our missive by a neighbouring pastor, who was over-burdened already with requests for help. Papa watched us gobble, but he never touched anything himself. Instead, he started work on toys for Mr. Leyonborg's three sons to be sent to them at Christmas. To be beholden was not in my Father's dictionary.

Every two months, regular as clockwork and until we did not need help any longer, Mr. Leyonborg mailed his magical parcels and assured himself of a place in heaven and most certainly in our hearts.

Every two months, regular as clockwork, Brother and I would be quite sick from the dried milk which we mixed with sugar and ate by the spoonful. One evening, after having indulged in our treat, I felt a bit worse than usual and soon got violently ill. While Mama was busy cleaning me up and putting me to bed, Brother joined the party - first to the toilet, then to the bedroom.

Mama was pretty mad, accusing us of being gluttons for punishment and promising stern rationing in the future. Then she promptly fell asleep, joining her husband who was already snoring with his head resting comfortably on the kitchen table. Sister saved our lives.

That particular night she was out and about with her friends but, for some reason or another, got bored early and came home. She smelled the gas as soon as she set foot into the apartment building. As electricity was only available at intervals, we would spend our evenings in the birch-tree warmed kitchen, dimly lit by a round little ball attached to the gas line. That ball had developed a leak, something that is hard to detect. So I owe my own and my family's life to Sister who alerted the neighbours, helped drag her parents out on the balcony and opened the windows, blessing her siblings with fresh oxygen and a chance at more mischief in life.

So now we had the occasional sweet on our plate, but the rest of the food was still rationed and hunger was a daily companion. Mama had to put padlocks on the food cabinets because we had no control and stole from our own. Being small for your age means nobody ever notices you're there, which has its advantages.

Watching Mama put away bread and other assorted goodies, I noticed that she locked the padlock with the same key as the one that opened the broom closet on the balcony. I told Brother. For the next few days, Mama was perplexed by the disappearance of certain food items in her cupboards. Luck has a way of running out on me and it didn't take long for Mama to catch on - and my hero was in for it. Out came the bamboo stick and, crying herself at the injustice of it all, Mama spanked Brother's rear. I watched and wept but did nothing because, when I made an overture to confess my complicity, Brother caught my eye and shook his head. Really, what was the point. I would have got the same. He took his punishment like the gentlemen he was, for me, for him and for the whole rotten world we had got ourselves into.

Stomachs may have been growling but in the evening we listened to the team of irreverent political satirists called "Die Insulaner" (the Islanders) on the RIAS Radio station. They showcased not only political satires, they portrayed life as it was, harsh and ugly, and made us see the humour in the situation. They were Berliner comedians and they did what Berliners had done for generations and what they were famous for - they laughed at adversity. Nothing was sacred on that show. They laughed at hunger, at cold, at ruined buildings and Nazis whom nobody could find. They laughed at the new process of "de-nazification" which was the funniest thing of all. They exhibited the wicked sense of humour that is typical of a true Berliner and they helped us survive. Names such as Guenter Neuss, Edith Hanke, Brigitte Mira, et al, were household names in the dark days after the war and they will remain in my memory forever. They were Berliners at their best - the way we were.

On Sunday mornings, the RIAS station broadcasted 'Onkel Tobias' who entertained us with Kasperl Theatre, the German version of a puppet Punch and Judy show, sang songs and played games. In the evenings, there were "Hoerspiele", basically a movie without a screen. We sat and listened, spellbound, and our own imaginations served up better pictures than any movie ever could. It was magic.

Every afternoon at 5 PM, we turned to the BBC Radio. I learned my first English words - 'Frolic at Five.' No one had any idea what it meant but there it was. *Swing, Swing, Swing, Swing* - the chairs flew into the corners and the family danced. Glen Miller, Artie Shaw, Benny Goodman, Frank Sinatra, Bing Crosby and Louis Armstrong invaded the German airwaves and won entire generations over to their music.

Sister turned 17 and started dating. His name was Heinz Wenk and we called him 'Wenky the Cowboy", because his ambition in life was to ride a horse and he was very proud of the acquisition of a saddle to fit upon it. He never got the horse but the name stuck.

On the whole, in her selection of boyfriends, Sister was a great disappointment. A lot of my friends had sisters, the same age as mine, who had acquired international boyfriends - French, English, Scottish, Canadian and, the preferred variety, American. They brought food into the households, the desired chewing gum and Hershey Bars. My own sibling refused to find herself one of these exotic gentlemen and I thought that maybe she was to shy. I have a habit of fighting for the underdog, especially when the outcome could be profitable, and so I leaped to the rescue.

I waylaid one of the 'Amis' on his way to the girl of his choice, grabbed him by the arm, told him I had a nice sister and dragged him home. He thought it was pretty funny. Sister did not. I came pretty close to being killed but was rescued by the rest of the family who thought that that was the most hilarious thing they had ever seen. A 7-year old procuring for her 17-year old sister. A sign of the times and, for my part, entirely innocent in nature. The Ami was another matter; he quite liked the girl I introduced him to and we had a problem getting rid of him.

As if Sister wasn't a big enough disappointment, Brother became an even bigger one. He started lording it over me with his 4-year advantage in age and newfound intelligence. In the process, he took away my trust in the 'Weihnachtsmann' (Santa Claus) and that was a belief that I was not quite ready to relinquish.

Christmas starts early in Germany. On the evening of the 5th, every child in the country polishes their shoes to perfection and then places them outside the bedroom door. Overnight, Saint Nikolas appears and fills them with sweets. This, of course, necessitates that the child has been a good child for most of the year because, if it hasn't, it will find no sweets but a bundle of twigs, tied together with string, denoting a warning of dire things to come if no improvement is evident in the last few weeks before Christmas. I'm a slow learner. Finding the bundle one year did not turn me into the model child I should have become and, when Christmas Eve arrived, I was ill prepared for the consequences.

Waiting for that white-bearded, sack-carrying old man was nerve wracking. Germany's 'Weihnachtsmann' is both loved and feared and his arrival with a very loud "Bang, Bang" on the door made us shake in our boots. He would ask whether or not we had been good children, to which we always replied in the affirmative. Unfortunately, that answer was not always to his liking as he usually shook his head and proceeded to relate to us stories of our wrong doings all through the year. It was mind-boggling. The memory of that man was incredible. We were asked if we knew any Christmas songs or poems, which we recited eagerly and, only then, did he finally fish our presents out of his sack.

This was normal procedure except for the particular year when there weren't any gifts for me. Instead, that bearded maniac took out a big bundle of twigs, tied together with strings, and proceeded to give me a spanking. I have the dubious distinction of having been beaten up by Santa Claus. I've never met anyone else who has. I should be in the Guinness Book of Records.

The year I turned eight, Brother spotted an earring beneath the old man's bushy beard. The earring strongly resembled our neighbour's dangling ornament and the mystery of the "Weihnachtsmann" was solved. Brother was 11, he could deal with this loss. I was devastated.

In the years that followed, I helped Papa trim the tree in the afternoon of the 24th. and hand over my presents for the family which he then put under the tree. After supper, Papa lit the candles on the tree, turned on the music and rang a bell, which prompted the remaining four family members to charge through the hallway and into that hallowed room. It was magical and holy and fun. But it was never quite the same without the 'Weihnachtsmann'.

In 1947, Christmas taught me the biggest lesson of my life. I don't know what gave me the idea or where I ever heard of a coconut but that was what I wanted for a present that year and nothing else. In 1947 it was pretty hard to find any food at all, never mind something as exotic as a tropical fruit, and I never knew how far my Father traveled and how many days he spent looking for that darned coconut, but travel he did and the miracle happened - he found one. It was gorgeously ugly and hard to break. We spent a long time on a freezing cold balcony, trying to smash it with a hammer on the concrete floor and Papa was pretty well cursing the darn thing and ready to throw it somewhere when it finally came apart.

I was generous. Everyone got a piece to chew on - and everyone spit it out seconds later. It tasted awful. We didn't know anything about this kind of fruit. We couldn't know that sometimes a coconut goes bad. We thought they all tasted that way and that nut became one of my biggest disappointments in my life so far. Lesson duly noted - not everything you badly want in life actually turns out to be what you expect. Life goes on and you learn to deal with its harsh realities but it sure takes the fun out of things.

But life after war was also paradise. Our parents were simply too busy trying to survive to pay much attention to their offspring. The emphasis was on providing food, a place to sleep and watching for the children's health. Apart from that - we were on our own. Which suited us just fine.

Life after war was also very dangerous. There were unexploded bombs, hand-grenades, all sorts of ammunition and a landscape of ruins that could be explored at random. A lot of our friends got hurt but that didn't stop any of us. It always happens to the other guy.

Brother found a little container one day which, when opened, revealed a lot of grey sticks looking like spaghetti and a little silk bag with powder. If you laid the sticks on the ground and concentrated sunlight on them through a magnifying glass, they exploded. A little firework never killed anybody, right? Wrong! He almost bought it. As it was, he got away with his eyelashes and eyebrows singed off, burns like freckles all over his face and the shock of his life. He was more worried about what Mother would do to him when she saw him then he was about his rather bald looks. Many others weren't so lucky.

We built caves in the ruins and sometimes they collapsed and knocked you out cold. We found some long, iron beams in a heap somewhere and our imagination turned them into the most magnificent ship ever to roam the seas - the Titanic. I've been on a lot of ships since, but nothing ever compared with the thrill of that first ship of my imagination. It went down, came back up, went down again, and we drowned and came back to life and were rescued or left to rot in the ocean and it was glorious.

We climbed on ruined walls to swing in bathtubs, which were precariously attached to the pipes still imbedded in the bricks. And we swam in the dirty shipping lane called the 'Teltow Canal', until polio came along and put a stop to that.

Towards the end of the war, people were throwing all kinds of things into the canal, guns, uniforms, Nazi paraphernalia, etc. It was a veritable treasure trove but you had to dive for it. As Brother was still dog paddling and I couldn't swim, we missed out.

One summer day, swimming in the dirty Teltow canal, the boys got a competition going to determine who could stay under water the longest. We all watched as they disappeared beneath the surface and then, one by one, re-surfaced. All - except one. We waited. Nothing happened. Boy, that kid was good. Finally some of the older boys started worrying but, while they were still debating as to what to do next, out of the water shot the missing competitor, screamed, and disappeared. We were stunned. Then the boys dove in.

What they brought up was a sobbing, swearing youngster whose lower leg was bleeding all over the grass and everyone who came near him. Someone came up with the bright idea of taking him to the hospital which, lucky for him, wasn't far. His leg bandaged with reluctantly donated towels, they dragged him on a little wagon to get help in the adult world. This was too big for us to handle.

His story came out much later. He had dived all the way to the bottom, crouched down and got his leg entangled in a coiled bedspring. The more he tugged, the worse it got. In desperation, he tucked himself into a ball and then pushed as hard as he could towards the surface, leaving half his calf embedded in the coil. He remembered screaming and nothing else until he came to in the hospital. He probably fainted and so missed all the excitement. When the wound had healed, he was a hero and to be permitted to touch his scar was an honour few of us were granted.

Paradise was having adventures every afternoon of your life. In the morning - you had to go to school.

Chapter 7

The Good, The Bad and the Ugly !

After Papa died, I found a little slip of paper in his wallet. In Brother's handwriting, it said the following: *Dear Mrs. Fiedler! Edith has forgotten to get the signature of her father and she is crying because she is afraid. Please don't be mad at her. Peter Krause*

That note is a testament to the courage and love of a boy who, by trying to avoid disaster for his little sister, dared the establishment to have mercy. A bad mark necessitated the signature of one's father or mother to verify to the teacher that the parents had had the pleasure of witnessing the feeble efforts of their offspring. Brother's intentions were honourable and the mere fact that Papa carried the note around with him for almost 30 years showed that he appreciated the gesture. But mercy was not a word that was in my teacher's dictionary. Her name was Mrs. Fiedler and she became the bane of my existence for three long years.

Being in charge of children ranging from the first to the ninth grade is not easy and I doubt my teacher in Kirchsteitz ever even took notice of me. I know that I didn't take much notice of her. I scratched the alphabet onto a black slate board with chalk and got myself covered in white powder. That is all I remember.

By the time we got back to Berlin, I had basically forgotten everything I had learned, which wasn't much to begin with. That didn't stop Papa from registering me in Grade 2, which had already been underway since the start of September. The fact that my classmates were older and towered over my head like giants didn't faze Father, whose vocabulary did not include the word 'back.'

Teachers were a commodity in 1945, most of the male variety having died for the Fatherland, and therefore anyone with a modicum of intelligence could apply for the position. After a short course, they were let loose on the unsuspecting post-war children. Most of them were terrific, dedicated to teaching and bringing new and innovative methods to the classroom. Some of them deserve a place in hell that is especially reserved for bad teachers.

To be a Berlin child was to have a reputation that stank to high heaven. They called us 'Berliner Spatzen," (Berlin Sparrows). We were sassy, loud-mouthed, fight-picking braggarts who did not take kindly to authority. Someone made up a song about us and we sang it heartily at every opportunity. It went like this:

Berliner Jungens die sind richtig	*Berlin Boys, they are alright*
Berliner Jungs sind auf dem Kien	*Berlin Boys are on the ball*
Mit keinem Sechser in der Tasche	*Without a Penny in their pocket*
Da fragen se frech, wat kost Berlin	*They boldly ask, how much for Berlin*
Und wenn auch manche Leute schimpfen	*Even if some folks complain*
Oh diese Bengel sind mit recht so sehr verschrien	*Oh these boys have earned their bad name*
Berliner Jungens die sind richtig	*Berlin Boys are alright*
Ja solche hellen Jungs die gibts nur in Berlin	*Yes, such bright boys exist only in Berlin*

Although it addressed the male version of Spatzen, none of us girls ever thought we weren't meant by it too.

To deal effectively with this bunch, one needed patience, strength and a very good sense of humour, all of which were sadly lacking in this particular educator. Mrs. Fiedler was in charge of 44, very unruly, little Berliners. In retrospect, I suppose the poor woman was very likely already taxed to her limits and the arrival of No. 45 was the straw that broke the camel's back. We didn't hit it off at all. I couldn't count very well. I couldn't write except in block letters and I stuttered when I read. I tested her patience and we both found out she didn't have any. Her methods of teaching left a lot to be desired and not only in my case. If you didn't have an answer, she cut you to pieces and scared you witless. I hated that woman with a passion and she reciprocated heartily.

Being told you're stupid at least once a day does not encourage confidence in your abilities. Teachers being the ultimate authority on the subject, I firmly believed her - but only as far as school was concerned. On the street, I held my own among the giants. On the street we ignored the classifications of teachers and set our own standards. On the street, I was equal to any challenge and the giants knew it.

Having been upgraded from Grade 2 to 3 on 'probation', Papa thought I needed help and came up with this terrific idea of after-school instructions. He hired, of all people, Mrs. Fiedler, to give me extra lessons in the evening. She made a lot of money and it didn't do any good at all. All it did was to not only turn my days into nightmares but my evenings as well. Somehow, I made it from Grade 3 to 4 and from Grade 4 to 5, albeit always with that lovely sentence on the bottom "On Probation", whatever that meant.

A few months into Grade 5, salvation came in the form of our principal with a rotund, motherly looking female in tow, announcing that the two Grade 5 classes were way too big and we had finally acquired another teacher and anyone who wanted to join the new class should put up their hands.

My hand was in the air before she had finished speaking and an annoyed Mrs. Fiedler told me she would take my decision up with my Father. "You leave my Father to me!" It was a statement made out of desperation and it took a lot of courage. It was also the first and last time I ever dared to talk back to her.

Telling Sister of my plan for emancipation was a mistake. I was advised to quickly change my mind as Papa would not only never allow me to switch, he would also in all likelihood kill me for having made this decision all on my own. Very dependable girl, my sister. The words 'positive thinking' never entered her vocabulary.

When Papa came home, I promised him heaven on earth. I would turn myself into a model child, such as had never existed before or ever would again. I would never lie, never cheat, wash the dishes, clean the shoes - anything at all. But please, please let me switch to the other class.

"If you don't improve, you're going back." End of discussion. Thank you, thank you, thank you.

Mrs. Dahler was sweet, had infinite patience and loved children. Most of all, she loved teaching. It helps when you're taking up the profession. Within a few months, my math was up to scratch, spelling was a cinch and any time there was a story to be read out loud, I was the one requested to do it. I could do it better than anyone. What do you know?

But Mrs. Dahler was also quite sick. Something to do with a gall bladder and eventually she had to give it up. Next one up - Mr. Schaar - and if Mrs. Dahler had been sweet, Mr. Schaar was the absolute best. He was young, tall and handsome - and within weeks we were willing to die for him. All of us, without question.

In 1948, a teacher was someone heading up a class of about 30 children and teaching everything from Math to Geometry, German to English, Geology to Drawing, Physics to Biology and even Gym. Mr. Schaar drew the line at needlework. Every class was an adventure where mysterious things came to life.

Once, a classmate slammed a door on someone who happened to have his hand on the door frame. Into the fight that ensued strode our hero Teacher. Fists do not solve problems, he exclaimed, and next morning we found ourselves on a streetcar, heading for the Law Court to watch minor court proceedings for a few hours. Upon return, we created our own court. He was the Judge who appointed Prosecutors, Defence Counsels and the Jury. I was intimately involved. I was the hapless 'Witness for the Prosecution'. It all went really well. The door slammer was found guilty, mainly due to my evidence, and was sentenced to three days staying after school for an hour, writing, I don't remember how many times, that one should not slam doors on fingers. He did his time and forgave me my testimony, but only after he had cuffed my head - off the schoolyard and out of sight of Mr. Schaar, of course.

He was the first teacher I encountered who was willing to spend time away from school with us. He scrounged around, found some old army tents, and proceeded to organize a camping trip into the wilds of the forests surrounding Berlin proper. A few parents volunteered to accompany the class, not exactly appreciated by their offspring or the rest of us, but necessary for the safety of the group. It was a long haul on the train and, to save time finding our place, Mr. Schaar parked the entire tired and sweaty mass of children, plus 2 of the volunteers, at the train station and took off with one other adult and myself in tow to scout out the shortest route. I do not remember why I was taken along but I do remember that they walked very fast and that I was running most of the time. We found what we were looking for on a hill overlooking the lake at Glienicke. There was a beach at the bottom of an overgrown pathway where a lot of people already frolicked in the water.

Sensing that I would hold them back on their return trip, the two adults made the wise decision to leave me alone on the hill, promising a quick return. Mr. Schaar gave me his watch and told me to time their progress. Then they left.

I had never been entirely alone in all my life. I lived, ate and slept surrounded by my family. I played surrounded by my friends and I studied surrounded by fellow students. Solitude had never been experienced and at first, being a novelty, I enjoyed it. There were no sounds but those of insects humming, creatures swishing about in the grass and the wind moving the tops of the great fir trees. Before long, however, imagination took over. Insects started to grow in size and seemed to be in attack mode, things crawled over my bare feet and the soft wind in the trees changed its tone and became menacing. I freaked out. I needed people and my watch told me that no people were coming for at least another half hour. There were, however, lots of people on the beach and a pathway leading to that area was close at hand. I bolted.

When Mr. Schaar and the rest of my class arrived on the hill, they were at a loss as to what happened to the watchdog they had left behind. The pathway being the only way out, they followed it down and found their guard sitting on a log, clasping a watch as though life depended on it. When the irate parents were finished yelling at me, I told them that some boys had arrived on top and threatened to steal the watch and that is why I had run. Before they could contradict my story, Mr. Schaar, who was the only one not yelling, picked me up, shook my hand and congratulated me on a job well done and saving his precious watch. We looked at each other and I knew that he knew that I was lying. It didn't matter. He also understood that there was something else that had made me run and that that was something I could not admit to because I didn't think anyone would understand. So, instead of being ridiculed, I was hailed as a sensible person doing the right thing. Now that's a teacher!

Camping proceeded in an orderly, and very German, fashion. As the tents had no bottom sheet, the first thing we had to do was dig ditches around the outsides for the eventual rain to run off. This was home for a while and needed a personal touch. The ground was brushed clean around the tent, stones were collected and the name of our abode was spelled out in front. What other people go to such extremes but the Germans? After all the excitement and toil, sleep was not long in coming. Morning brought the first chores.

While everyone else took a morning dip, my roommate and I got the task of cooking breakfast. Mr. Schaar started the little stove, we filled a pot with water, waited for it to boil and added Cream of Wheat powder. It didn't thicken. It was supposed to. So we added a little more. It didn't thicken. Neither one of us ever having even boiled water before, we were quite at a loss as to what to do. By the time the concoction in the pot did what it was supposed to do, we had almost emptied the bag of Cream of Wheat. Needless to say, when everyone assembled for breakfast, they didn't need a spoon to feed themselves. We cut the thicker than molasses glue into slices and ate it with our fingers. Demotion was quick in coming and was gratefully accepted.

The only other memorable thing sticking in my mind was the glass of honey that my roommate's mother had packed in between her clothing. The seal came undone and all her clothing were covered in a sweet, smelly mess of runny honey. We soaked everything in the lake and the fish got a real treat, but the stickiness never left and we finally gave up, stuck it all back into her bag and forgot about clean clothes. Washing and changing clothes is an adult obsession anyway. Who needs it.

We came back to our families tanned to perfection, sporting dirty fingernails and a ravenous hunger. Mother's cooking was never more appreciated. We had survived rain storms, black nights and bad cooking. We had had a ball.

Mr. Schaar was the best and no one ever figured out why he left. It was all very sudden and had something to do with politics among teachers. We cried and swore we would not attend school in September if he was not there but, when the time came, we made our way back to find out what kind of an individual we had been assigned to. In 1950, children didn't have any clout at all.

Mr. Kauffman was very tall, skinny and dedicated. You couldn't love him, he didn't ask for it. We respected him and were loyal to him because he was better at teaching than anyone else. He made us want to learn and insisted that we were better than we thought we were. He didn't spend his free time with us as other teachers did. He was sarcastic, argumentive and stubborn. He didn't believe there was such a thing as a stupid child and set out to prove it. And we tried our best not to let him down.

His only fault was that he believed in snitching. He asked us outright to report any shenanigans going on, i.e. people copying homework, cheating with cheat sheets, etc. We did not understand that. Snitching on your pals was the worst thing any one of us could do. It was punishable by ostracism of the culprit on the playground and in the school environment and was to be avoided at all costs. One of us did not think so.

Benita was Class President and teacher's pet. Benita was a 'Streberleiche', a word that cannot possibly be translated into any language but the meaning of which could be describing someone who strives so hard to please, it kills them.

Benita was the first one in the classroom in the morning, cleaning the blackboard, organizing teacher's pencils or other paraphernalia on his desk and watching whether or not anyone disobeyed the rule of 'no cheating allowed.' She had it coming.

At a time when class elections came close, some of us started scheming as to how to get rid of her and, in the process, teach her a lesson in classroom unity. The perfect plan accepted became the tool for her ruin. It was my plan. It was a good plan. It was also pretty horrible to watch an egomaniac lose it.

What we concocted went like this. My best friend went to class early, encountering Benita, making herself useful as usual. Five conspirators were also in early attendance, albeit outside the classroom, hidden by the barely open door. We watched in amazement the Oscar-winning performance of my pal, crying and whining for help with a particularly difficult mathematical problem in her homework which she had not been able to figure out and asking to copy Benita's results for just this one time. Whether it was the power of tears produced at random or a soft spot in an otherwise snitching soul, Benita gave in and handed over her book. It was probably the last time she ever helped another student in need.

Five minutes into the class, Mr. Kaufmann demanded the results of our homework. I stood up and asked permission to make a report on a snitching witnessed by four classmates. Mr. Kaufmann was so pleased that his admonitions had finally taken root, he never bothered to figure out why the change of mind happened and why his favourite pupil was involved.

I reported the incident in detail, backed up by four respectable classmates and my best friend's tears, which by now came in earnest as she realized that some punishment would also come her way. Benita was immediately demoted from class president to ordinary student and not permitted to run in the next election. Her tears were prodigious but the looks she threw me through the veil of tears could have killed an elephant. I don't know whether or not she ever understood the lesson we were trying to teach her. I don't remember her ever snitching again but she held a grudge far beyond our childhood and never spoke to me again. Poor Mr. Kaufmann expected more but in the end had to be happy with the one and only instance of the class letting down its guard. Childhood has its rules and unwritten codes. It is 'Us' against 'Them' and one had better comply with the rules.

Life under a new president went on. New ideas came and went and the school system changed intermittently and children survived. In 1950, a whole generation of Grade 7 was asked what they wanted to do with their lives. Both the students and their parents had to make a decision on whether to attend school until Grade 9, 10 or 13. Upon completion of Grades 9 and 10, one was expected to enter the work force as an apprentice to the industry. Grade 13 incumbents would move on to University.

Mr. Kauffman was convinced that no one needed to go to school for 13 years to acquire all the knowledge required to proceed to the higher echelons of society. Consequently he talked most of our parents out of the 13 years and then proceeded to teach us a curriculum far beyond Grade 9 or 10. He proved what he said. By the end of Grade 9, we had learned way more than we were entitled to and had run out of things to do.

Another American invention hit the schools in the way of IQ tests. Papers were handed out and Mr. Kauffmann explained - if the best student and the worst student got 98 questions right - but the worst student was younger than the best - then the worst student was smarter because of the age difference. This induced hilarity and, as I was the youngest by a year, everyone pounced on the idea that I just might turn out to be the smartest after all. I laughed heartily along with the rest of them. I was a mediocre student and I knew it. We sat down and doodled. 45 minutes later I had finished answering a lot of very strange questions while everyone else was still doodling. I thought I had made a mistake. I went over the puzzles, the figures, the questions but nothing new occurred to me and so, watching three others handing in their paper, I made my way to the front.

When Mr. Kauffmann turned up four days later and asked us whether he should start from the bottom or the top, we all yelled 'the bottom'. I yelled the loudest. Having been the butt of every joke about intelligence for days, I wanted the ordeal to be over soon.

Half way through the pile, I was convinced he was keeping my paper to give everyone a good laugh by making them think I was brilliant, when I really wasn't. When he finally called my name, there were only two papers left in his hand. I had scored 97. I was the third most intelligent kid in the class. *I knew that*! Thank you America!

Next on Herr Kauffman's agenda – "social etiquette". He brought in glasses and bottles, dishes and cutlery and we learned what spirit to pour into what glass and out of what bottle, what to cut with a knife and what not and how to set a table when you have five courses to serve - which none of us thought was real, having only ever been served with soups and the odd roasts, potatoes and vegetables, all of which our mothers ladled onto the plate before putting it in front of us. Thanks to Mr. Kauffman's efforts, we left school with an outstanding education, social graces and high hopes for the future. We had encountered the best and the worst of the teaching profession and we had survived.

Chapter 8

War and Peace!

I don't remember a day when there wasn't a fight happening outside the schoolyard. Inside was neutral territory. Outside, school bags would go flying and fists would hammer away, creating bloody noses and bruises. It was great entertainment if you weren't the one getting hammered.

In the fall of 1945, Brother and I were the new kids on the block and that meant earning your rank in society. Mostly it meant finding out how much punishment you could take before you buckled. Brother, through a badly administered cast, was encumbered with a leg whose foot was pointing sideways instead of forward. At first he was the recipient of verbal abuse, which he ignored, and then physical action, which he endured. However, the giants soon found out that there were two of us on the team and to trifle with one meant earning the wrath of the other.

Zooming through the tunnel one day on my homemade, wooden pushbike, I encountered one of Brother's classmates on top of my hero, slapping his face, over and over. I didn't even stop to think. Leg pumping furiously, the pushbike hit the offender's rear with a crunch that broke my steering pole, damaged his tailbone, and catapulted me over the two combatants head first into the bushes. Before the enemy could say 'ouch', I was on my feet and my nails were in his face. When you're very small and slight, you use whatever is handy and fair fight doesn't come into it.

Having established our reputation, we were accepted by the general population and allowed to join in their plays. We played bandits and princesses, hide and seek, re-enacted whole movies and tried to ignore the boys who were bothering us.

Those were the good plays our parents liked us participating in. Putting buckets full of water against doors and ringing the bell, putting wallets attached to strings on the streets and hiding in the bushes to pull them back when someone bent down to pick it up, or throwing balloons filled with water out of windows were not acceptable, but much more fun.

There was a permanent war situation with the kids living on Rungius Strasse that was declared enemy territory. I have no idea why. It started way before I came on the scene and peace was not declared until we had basically outgrown throwing stones at each other.

It was an unfortunate fact that the nearest grocery store that sold milk was situated on that street and, therefore, to be handed the milk can and ordered to attend to its being filled without finding a friend to accompany you, was synonymous to walking down death row with your last appeal denied. If you were lucky, the warriors of Rungius Strasse were otherwise engaged. If you were not, you could lose your milk, your money and your health. Likewise, if one of the Rungius mob was caught in our territory, which unfortunately did not have a store but luckily was the street that had to be crossed to get to the major shopping area of the Britzer Damm, the outcome was no different. West Side Story in Britz. No guns though. Just stones thrown from a distance and fists used in close ups. School was neutral territory. Everybody played with everybody else.

Car owners being far and in-between, the streets belonged to us. Anyone daring to drive through 30 to 40 ball players on a bicycle or in a car took his life into his own hands. The adult population was not amused. They also did not understand what Mother's Day meant to us.

Every evening before that important event, as the sun slowly sank below the horizon and dusk fell over a peaceful neighbourhood, fathers emerged from their lairs to stand guard over their precious little garden plots. Mothers screamed names at the tops of their lungs but no one answered the call. An eerie quiet had descended on the streets and there wasn't a child to be seen anywhere. It was as though the Piper of Hamelin had come and whisked all the children away.

There was a tradition. We stole flowers. Never out of our own garden and never from the public flower beds in the park. Everyone stole from everyone else and never once did anyone get caught doing so. Half of that was due to the fact that we practiced crawling among bushes while re-enacting Indian battles of the Wild West and half of it probably because our fathers played along and managed never to see anyone. Once a bunch of flowers was thought to be deserving, it was hidden in boxes and under steps, only to be brought forth in the morning, drooping and sad looking, for presentation to astonished, surprised and eternally grateful Mothers. It was a lovely tradition but not overly appreciated by some of the more mean-spirited adults in the neighbourhood. They clamoured for action and demanded the Kids be got off the street.

The first club we joined was run by the Communist Party which, until approx. 1947, still functioned in Germany. I couldn't have cared less about the party affiliation. Twice a week we went to a basement underneath a butcher store to play, sing songs, have costume parties and do crafts. In summer they took us camping. We learned about nature in the forest of the Mueggel Berge and sat singing around campfires in the dark.

On one trip, they gave us books on mushrooms. There were pictures about good ones and bad ones and, with this intricate knowledge in tow, we headed for the woods to bring home the bacon, or better the mushrooms. I collected an enormous amount of the tasty morsels and then gave it all to my friend who lived across the street. Two days after we returned, Mama found out that every family in the vicinity was having feasts of mushrooms added to their diet and she was understandably upset that I hadn't collected any. But I did, I assured her. I just wasn't quite sure whether every one of the mushrooms was entirely safe to eat and had therefore decided not to put my own family at risk and handed them over for consumption by our neighbours. Mama took off like a house on fire. Luckily, the Staehler family had survived my generosity. It is sometimes hard for adults to understand the logic of children. Mama had a real hard time with this one.

Our new club put on shows that we presented in schools and community centres. I was singled out one year to be the last person on a pyramid consisting of eight young men. Five of them were standing in a row, balancing three more on top of their shoulders and I was supposed to be the crowning achievement by standing on the shoulders of one of the three, waiving a communist flag. This was my moment, my claim to fame, on top of the world - well, a pyramid anyway.

With the proud parents in attendance, Brother and I started practicing. Feet firmly planted on the floor, he pulled on my arms while my feet tried to find a foothold on his legs. I got to the shoulders, accompanied by oohs and aahs of my adoring fan club - and that's when we found out that I am afraid of heights. Losing my balance, I grabbed the kitchen cabinet for support which promptly came away from the wall and utter disaster was only avoided by Papa propping it back into position while it took all of Mama's strength to pry my hands loose from their support. On the day of the show, I was delegated to sitting at the side of the stage, in a split, waiving that ridiculous flag in the air. End of stardom.

My real claim to fame was reciting poetry. I loved poems with a lot of action, like Nils Randers who was a Frieslander and who watched a ship being wrecked on the rocks and decided to rescue the one man clinging to the mast. His mother didn't want him to go. She had already lost her husband and son and Uwe, another son, was missing and she didn't want to lose Nils too. But Nils was heroic and brave and asked her to think of the mother of the man clinging to the wreck. Then he talked some other men into jumping into a boat and rowing, in a terrible gale, out to the sinking ship. Well, the boat went up and down, got swamped and survived and they rowed with mighty strokes and it was a breathtaking description to listen to. Then, as they neared the shore, they heard him calling, "Tell Mother, it's Uwe." Wouldn't you know it; he had rescued his own brother. I could make people weep with that one.

One evening, shortly before bed-time, some members from the youth club turned up, asking if they could borrow me for a performance at the Volkshouse. One of their performers had been taken ill and they had a gap and I was to fill that gap with a poem that I didn't much like but which was very much in line with the Communist Party doctrine of working people. It had something to do with a father's hands, which were rough and hurt when they stroked the child's cheeks but that the child didn't mind because her father worked so hard. I couldn't quite comprehend that as my Papa's hands were not like that and I couldn't understand why that particular father couldn't look after himself a little better.

Mama was delighted that they requested me and off we went. They sat me on a stool in the back of the stage to wait for my entrance. By now I knew I had a problem. I couldn't remember the entire poem. While frantically trying to refresh my memory, I promptly fell asleep. It was way past my bedtime. On stage, the show took its inevitable course and, in the general excitement, my recruitment team forgot about me.

Making a last sweep through a dark auditorium, they found their poem recitor fast asleep, slumped on the chair they had put her on hours earlier. Everyone was very apologetic and nice. I didn't deem it necessary to tell anyone what a disaster I would have been on stage. I have a Guardian Angel.

So the Youth Club was a total success until the day I tried to tell Papa about Marx and Lenin and the glorious cause of communism. That was something our adored arts and crafts instructors threw in on the side and we didn't think there was anything wrong with it. We were on our way to become young Pioneers, which entitled you to wear a red bandanna around your neck. Adults have an incredible talent for spoiling the fun. Papa went ballistic. We were immediately removed from our evening entertainment, which was tragic but, within a few months, the whole Communist party was outlawed anyway.

Then, in 1947, those darn Russians were at it again, this time cutting off my entire city from the rest of the world. The Blockade had started and I thought that, if that was what Lenin and Marx had in mind, I didn't want to have anything to do with them. Papa was forgiven. Food got even scarcer and only came in by airplane, now piloted by the very ones who had formerly thrown bombs down on us. People are full of surprises.

Lunch was a handful of dried, square pieces of carrots, which needed a lot of saliva to be digested. Dinner was Spam (which resembled mashed potatoes in looks but left a lot to be desired in taste) or dried potatoes that needed to be soaked forever. No one will ever understand hunger unless they have been hungry as we were. There was no soup kitchen to run to, no food bank to help out and no one to beg from. Every night Mama made sure we included the welfare of every pilot who flew the "Raisin Bombers" into the city in our prayers and we did so heartily. Wars are fought by men but the real victims of every war that has ever been fought are the women and children they leave behind.

Now school started being something one looked forward to. They gave you lunch, courtesy of our Allied friends. Hanging on our school bags were aluminium canisters for the collection of the noon meal of the day. Heaven is a white bun with raisins and a hot, thick chocolate brew in your canister. I can still taste it but have forgotten everything else they fed us. I'm sure it was nourishing because we made it through the blockade in a relatively healthy state.

In the end, the Russians gave up their starvation game, Mama was able to go shopping again and we joined a new club, this time run by another party, who fortunately, concentrated more on games than on their political agenda. At any rate, Papa approved and we were now called 'Falken' (Falcons) instead of Pioneers. The songs we sang had to do with wandering and exploring and being 'Kameraden' who stand together in adversity. Camping was back and the basement underneath the butcher shop re-opened. We didn't care about the names, the policies or the colour of the bandannas. We just wanted to play.

Ruined houses were re-built and new playgrounds had to be found. The CO-OP Housing Corporation vacated the former Kindergarten premises and we were blessed with a Club House that stood in a huge, fenced-in park which sported a swimming pool. Movies came from Hollywood and every Sunday afternoon the neighbourhood emptied of children who headed to the FilmEck, our local movie theatre. It was a very noisy affair until the lights dimmed, the curtains opened and the entire audience let fly with a very drawn out "AAAHHHH!". Then magic happened.

Johnny Weissmueller battled Amazon women, and the child population of the female gender went to work on fabricating bows and arrows. Until someone came up with the fact that Amazon women cut off one breast to shoot better. None of us sported any growth in that particular part of our bodies as yet but we weren't going to fool around with it in the future. The bows went the way of the dodo bird.

Joel McCrae battled the Ogallala Sioux and we tied one girl to a torture post and set some leaves on fire around her feet. By the time she announced that her toes were getting hot and the leaves had been removed, the front of her shoes did not even vaguely resemble brown leather but looked rather like a piece of charcoal. It cost six of us three months of pocket money to pay for the damage and that was the end of the Ogallala Sioux.

Gene Kelly danced. Oh, how he danced. Both Mama and I swore that if we could have just one dance with Gene, we would gladly die right after. I wore out the soles of my shoes imitating Ann Miller's tap dancing routines and drove poor Papa crazy. How can one read a newspaper in peace when there is a constant tapping sound all through the house. If I could have afforded proper tap shoes, I would very likely not have reached my next birthday. I was forbidden to tap in the house and as it didn't work on the sidewalk, I gave up my career. I could have been a somebody.

I wanted to swim like Esther Williams. The pool in the park being only waist deep, I could keep one foot on the ground and make the top part look as though I was doing a crawl just like Esther. But you couldn't call it swimming with the best of intentions. Brother had taught himself to swim but I was no natural talent.

Money was squeezed out of Papa's tight wallet and swimming lessons started. I spent a year hanging on a fishing pole in the waters of the beautiful swimming pool at Ganghofer Strasse, advanced to a cork ring surrounding my skinny breast and, acquiring a dependency, promptly went under every time they took the cork thing off. I learned to swim the hard way.

Once a year, Papa insisted on getting the whole family together for a picnic at the Wannsee, one of the beautiful lakes surrounding the city of Berlin. The rest of the family prayed all year that he would forget this trip. Unfortunately, he wasn't a very forgetful man.

The evening before every one of these memorable outings we spent hours making innumerable sandwiches, boiling eggs, filling thermos with hot coffee and sorting bathing suits, towels and blankets. We took off very early in the morning. Four people loaded down with all the paraphernalia of a successful picnic. The originator of this exercise walked in front, delegating the packhorses in the right direction. Half an hour walk to the train station, one hour on the train, half an hour walk to the beach of his choice - and a happy tyrant surveyed his exhausted crew slumped on the ground.

Papa was a good swimmer and, after having spent a lot of money during 1 ½ years of lessons, figured that I should be just as good. So, one year, watching me paddling around in the shallows, he thought of all the money spent and the results not living up to expectations. I was taken to the end of the pier and thrown in.

It took all Papa's strength to keep Brother, who by now had the ability to rescue a drowning sister, and Mother, who had never bothered to learn to swim, from throwing themselves in after me. The object of this exercise went down, came up, went down, came up, went down and finally came to the realization that no one was coming to the rescue. I started swimming. Mama didn't speak to Papa for a week.

Brother was not only a natural swimmer, he was also a natural clown, always eager to entertain the masses. On one picnic, he told us he would show us how a drowned man looks upon reaching the beach after a shipwreck. Into the lake he went, coming back on all fours, throwing himself theatrically into the waves and attracting a lot of attention. One intrigued customer was a gigantic German Shepherd dog who trotted into the lake to investigate this erratic individual. Brother didn't notice that dog until he came out of the water, to find himself nose-to-nose with a very hairy face. Neither one of them was prepared for the shock. Brother jumped backwards a foot in the air and the dog jumped just as high in the other direction. The audience was thrilled, what an entertainer. It was the best performance he ever gave.

Our picnics continued until the day we arrived at the beach and found that every sandwich had absolutely nothing on it. No butter, no sausage, no egg salad. Nothing at all. All we had were dry bread slices. Mama had packed them up before the crew had filled them with the necessary ingredients to deserve being labelled a sandwich. Papa had to fork out money for food and somehow, in the years that followed, picnics went out of fashion. Hallelujah!

Back in Britz, the youth club was striving under the leadership of the mother/daughter team of Herta and Baerbel Albin. Until they went camping one summer and someone came back with the juicy tidbit of young people swimming naked at night in the lake. Wow! Brother was there and vigorously defended what happened, which was mainly nothing. They went swimming in the dark. They took off their bathing suits, girls on one side, boys on the other. They never so much as looked. An innocent escapade was turned into a lurid nightmare and it cost Herta and Baerbel their job. We missed them.

Their replacements were two hunch-backed sisters named Hahn. A Hahn being a cockerel in German, they were immediately dubbed "the chickens". They did all right but they never got the loyalty and admiration they probably deserved. It's kind of hard to be authoritative when you're no taller than your charges and hunch-backed to boot.

We kind of outgrew them eventually anyway and the club disbanded, to be replaced by the Youth Home with the Park and the swimming hole. Whenever you think that you have reached Paradise, something or someone comes to spoil it. There was a caretaker.

He was an invalid with only one arm and, in retrospect, was probably in pain a lot of time. Whatever the circumstances, he was not especially fond of children. If one wanted to play table tennis, he was too lazy to set up the table. If one wanted to play netball, he was too busy to hang up the net. If one wanted to play cards, he couldn't find them. What do you do with a person like that.

I took the problem to Papa. "Strike," said my authority. Strike? What's a strike? "Nobody goes in to play," said Papa. "You make up a sign that says we're not playing here until changes are made and then everybody stays outside and people notice." Thank you, Papa.

Brother, the natural talented swimmer and entertainer, was also a naturally talented artist. He made me a beautiful sign saying "Wir Streiken" and three of my friends joined me in front of the Youth Home, marching up and down and attracting a lot of attention. Within minutes, we had not only taught scores of kids what 'streiken' meant, we had also acquired a following that spilled over the sidewalk onto the street. Then someone had the idea of walking to the office of the CO-OP to tell them about our problems because how else would they find out otherwise. The old man inside who peered through the blinds was surely not going to tell them that there were no kids inside but lots of them outside the building.

Off we went to snitch. My first strike was very successful and it almost cost that man his job. Luckily, a truce was declared, our caretaker got very active and life went back to normal.

The most surprised person was poor Father who had thought he was cracking a joke. He promised Mama to be more careful when giving advice to his daughter in the future. I was still taking things at face value.

Chapter 9

Bullies and Other Tormentors!

No.1 Bully on the block was named Irene and resided above my head. The story was that Irene was not really her mother's daughter but the result of an affair her father had had with another woman and therefore was not very popular with the Mrs. The other story was that Irene had been 'verschuettet', meaning a bomb dropped on the building she lived in and she was buried in the rubble for quite a while and therefore not quite right in the head. Whether or not any of that was true, I have no idea. The fact was that Irene definitely marched to a different drummer than the rest of us. She told us that every time her father beat her up, it was with a seven-thronged whip. Today's social workers would have a field day with that one.

We didn't really believe her but that didn't stop us from stopping dead in our tracks and listening open-mouthed to Irene's blood-curdling screams penetrating through closed windows and curtains. Imagining those seven-leather strips descending on her bare bottom was enough to give you goose bumps.

Whatever violence was encountered upstairs, Irene found necessary to spread around downstairs. I was a very handy target. The fact that Brother would beat up on her every time she beat up on me did not seem to be much of a deterrent. Once, as Sister came up the stairs from the cellar, she found herself face-to-face with that impudent girl who, leaning over the railing, belted her one right across the face. Sister was stunned. She was 18 years old and that sort of thing just wasn't happening. Brother wasn't long in retaliation. Family is family but his loyalty cost him a few strands of hair. Irene was not a fair fighter and beating her was not an easy task.

At one point, the entire gang of girls on the block decided that enough was enough. We sat in judgment on Irene who was advised that she would not be allowed to participate in our games for a whole month. Every one of us would have been pleading to be forgiven immediately and altered our behaviour. Not our Irene. She laughed in our faces and waltzed through the Tunnel to the next street, namely Rungius Strasse, and started playing with our archenemies. So much for that.

Playing meant using your imagination, of which we had plenty. Toys were lacy kitchen curtains that decorated Princesses' heads. Old, deflated cushions crowned a Knight, worn-out blankets thrown over some bushes turned them into caves, tepees or castles, whichever was needed at the moment.

Then the marbles arrived. It started small and became an epidemic. Suddenly there were holes everywhere in the ground, kids congregating around them and adults screaming because of the danger of walking anywhere in the neighbourhood without breaking off a heel or, worst scenario, break a leg in one of those depressions.

Brother gave me two marbles, which I promptly lost. He gave me two more, which went the same way and then he refused to support my gambling habit by further donations to a lost cause. I cried. It worked. Two more marbles started me on a career that had no equal.

First I watched and learned the rules. Then I practiced on my own little hole in the backyard. When I thought I had it down pat, I ventured into the fray - and slew the competition. By the end of the first day, I was the proud possessor of two, very full, bags of marbles with a few coloured glass balls thrown in. By the end of the week, I had a bowl full and started piling them, 50 at a time, in little bags Mama made for me. Then I undersold the shop on Britzer Damm by 5 Pfennig per bag. It was a very lucrative business. I sold, I played, I won them all back, I sold them again. By the end of the week, the bathtub was full and Mama had a price list hanging on the door. When I wasn't home, she sold them for me. The only one who could beat me was Georg Schultz who was declared Marble King for two years in a row to my Marble Queen.

Years later, I wrote a letter to Papa, telling him not to worry about me. I still have his answering letter in which he said: "I haven't worried about you since the affair of the marbles." I never knew he even noticed.

The marble business allowed me to buy a pair of used roller skates off a friend and a decent bike off another. The bike Papa had built for me from scratch parts was a disgrace to the neighbourhood. I never had to ring the bell, the darn thing made so much noise, it drove everyone out of my path on its own. Papa either did not believe in buying toys or really didn't have the money to afford them, we never really knew.

Our favourite game, however, still remained playing tricks on adults. In our world, anybody over 20 had absolute power over your life. They could smack you if your curtsey was not reverent enough, they could scold you and report you to your parents if you forgot to greet them altogether and they frequently did. In consequence, very few of the adult population were considered 'Friendlies.'

Playing tricks on adults is fun, playing tricks on your playmates is just as good. One cold winter day, we found some old newspaper which stank to high heaven of rotten fish. We picked up a piece of ice, wrapped it into that odorous paper, put a clean newspaper on top of that and tied it neatly with a string. Then I was sent to Christel Spika's aunt to deliver it.

I rang the bell while the rest of the gang watched from the safe haven of the lower staircase. The Aunt opened up and I handed her the parcel with the compliments of her sister, Christel's mother. She thanked me and asked me to wait while she got me a sweet. I bolted.

I don't know what the reaction was when she unpacked that stupid gift. The whole episode was probably a conversation piece for the next few coffee parties and the neighbourhood likely had a good laugh. In any case, we never heard anything about it, but over the next week, good old Christel made me do whatever she wanted me to because if I didn't, she was going to report me to the police and I would end up in jail. I'm not good at obeying orders but with jail hanging over my head, what was a girl to do. One week later, I'd had enough and went to Mama, confessing my crime in detail. Mama forgave me my sins, called in my tormentor and gave a good lecture on using people and shunning responsibility. Christel belted me one at the next golden opportunity and harmony was restored. Life was complex but simple.

As we grew older, new words entered our vocabulary. One of them was 'Ficken" (Fuck). Great word that. But what the heck did it mean? One of us volunteered to ask her mother. Her Mother opened the door, the child said 'Mama, what's fuck?" and a resounding slap echoed through the building, accompanied by the advice never to use such language again. End of lecture. Except the mystery was still out there and by now it seemed, considering the reaction, that we had hit a gold mine. No one was brave enough to face another mother and fathers were definitely out. I like to be admired, who doesn't. I volunteered for the task.

Mama opened the door and I said the dreaded word. The woman never even flinched. She just asked me to please step inside, which meant I was not only going to get slapped, but the dreaded bamboo cane would come off its hook and descend on my backside. No way! "I'm not the only one wants to know," I yelled. "Everybody else wants to know and they're right behind me." Mama looked down the staircase and asked everyone inside. Great - now it was mass slaughter.

Instead of the bamboo cane, Mama produced a book as thick as the Bible and bigger in size. What she showed us were pictures of a pregnant woman, with the baby prominently displayed in its various stages of development. It was fascinating. Then she explained what happened when two people of the opposite sex really loved each other and how nature had ingeniously devised to equip a man with a body part which fitted to a tee into a woman. We were spellbound. And then she showed us the multitudes of little fishies who started out as semen and who, at a certain point of loving, were let loose to start racing towards their future and a safe haven for the next nine months. We, the winners of the race. We, the Olympic champions of love making. We were first, then, now and forever. And where did that dreaded word fit in - well, that was a nasty word for a very loving act and why would anyone want to degrade that. Not us. We had to live up to being champions. I never heard the word again among my pals.

Some of us were a little older than the rest. Some of us were all of a sudden not capable of joining us in the swimming pool because of a condition called 'period'. Not a problem. They stayed behind and we swam. Until one of us couldn't stand it any longer and asked another what the heck a 'period' was. Nobody knew. We didn't bother with any other mother. Mama was the ultimate authority on the mysteries of the birds and the bees and periods in particular. Most mothers in the neighbourhood thanked her, others ignored it. It was easier that way.

The only trouble we ever had with our sex education was when, in Grade 6, a young woman turned up to explain the reproductive process to an out of control classroom. With pamphlets and a chart draped over the blackboard, she depicted the course of the semen into the ovaries. The girls giggled and the boys laughed out loud and the result made her so nervous that she got very muddled and her semen ended up in the vicinity of the gall bladder. I thought I'd better set her straight and pointed her in the right direction, which resulted in Mama being called to school to explain my precocious behaviour. They didn't get very far. She had them rolling in the aisles with her fishies in no time at all.

Chapter 10

One is a Lonely Number!

Ten years age difference between sisters is a gap that neither Sister nor I ever managed to breach. We had absolutely nothing in common. She wore a lot of make-up and powdered her nose and I thought that was terribly silly. She spent hours mending nylon stockings and reading silly books that dealt with highly improbable people falling in love and out of it and getting married in the end. Sister hardly ever spent time with me and, when she did, it usually turned into a fiasco and an embarrassment for both of us.

She took me to my first adult movie. It was very thrilling to go to the movie theatre in the evening. The atmosphere was totally changed, no one talked out loud, they all sort of whispered. I thought that was strange but hey, when in Rome do as the Romans do. I whispered. Then the lights went dim, the curtain opened, and I let fly with a very drawn-out "AAAAAHHHH," until a hand clamped down hard on my mouth and a voice hissed, "If you don't shut up, I'll kill you." I was quiet for the remainder of the movie and didn't enjoy it one bit. To my recollections, she never took me along again. So when she disappeared one day, it didn't make much difference in my life. At home, there had been angry shouts, arguments and counter arguments and an ugly atmosphere poisoning our evenings.

I was told that she had gone to a country called England, like so many other young German girls who had had their fill of empty stomachs and grey, ruined landscapes. She was working in a hospital kitchen, peeling potatoes. I couldn't imagine her liking that. She didn't peel much at home. I didn't miss her in the daytime but she left a gap at bedtime. No one could tell stories like my sister could.

There was a lamp hanging in the middle of the square outside our bedroom and, when the wind blew, the shadows of the trees around the lamp would make pictures on the ceiling of the bedroom. What big sister saw up there was awesome. Castles came to life with knights in shining armour, witches flew on broomsticks, dragons attacked innocent maidens and mythical beasts climbed down the window curtains, ready to jump and devour us in our beds. She was a dynamite storyteller and we missed that. But life went on and soon there were other things to worry about.

There came a letter from our old Swedish friend, Axel Leyonborg. One of us three children was invited to travel to Sweden to stay with his family over the summer holidays.

Sister was gone and would have been too old in any case. I was willing and eager but way too young. The unanimous choice, "the best horse in the stable," was Brother. And then there were none. Suddenly I was an only child. I didn't like it.

Brother stayed with the Leyonborg family for the prescribed three weeks. Then he went down on his knees and begged to be allowed to stay longer. So much for missing your loving family and your adoring little sister in particular.

Mrs. Leyonborg was pregnant with her third child, so our Pastor found a place for Brother on a farm in Lindholmen, where Brother reverted back to farm-boy, making friends wherever he went. Two weeks after that, still begging to stay, the adorable child was sent to an island near Stockholm. There was a mission school on that island which was run by a school friend of Mr. Leyonborg and Brother enjoyed whatever they do in mission schools, while practicing and perfecting his Swedish accent. When he finally came home, after two long months, I had lost my sidekick.

What came back from Sweden was a young man towering over me, sporting a strange little knitted cap with a tassel who threw Swedish words into every conversation. He locked the bathroom door during bath time and I was not allowed to enter the bedroom until he was properly undressed and hidden away under the sheets. I hammered the bathroom door with my fists and cried my eyes out. But I couldn't stop him from growing up and leaving me behind. It broke my heart. Something had to fill the gap and that something was called Monika.

The Berg's moved in with their two daughters in early summer and, being new on the block, Monika and her sister spent their days

64

sitting on the doorstep, watching the rest of us ignoring them. It was not the custom in my neighbourhood to associate quickly with people with whom one was not acquainted. It was a custom which did not agree with my personality. New faces fascinated me. I couldn't take it for long and two weeks into their forced isolation, I broke. "You want to play with me," I asked, and got booed by my fellow citizens for my effort at neighbourly hospitality.

My new friend was a year younger than I, had beautiful red hair and was as stubborn as an ox. Our relationship consisted of competing against each other and trying to make each other give in. Neither one of us ever did.

Another new face was a boy who was sent from East Germany to spend his vacation with an Aunt in Berlin. His name was Gerhard Lenz and he came from Nordhausen Salza in the Hartz Mountains.

I met him one sunny afternoon while he was manhandling a boy much smaller than himself. You don't do that in my book. I took immediate action by walking over and smacking him one right across the nose. Once he explained that the little fellow had beaten up on one who was even smaller than himself and that, what had appeared to me to be an attack, had only been the effort at teaching manners to the next generation, I apologized and he forgave me. Thus started a loving relationship that lasted the summer.

We went to movies, swam at the Columbia Bath, a newly opened swimming pool complex, walked in the parks and sat on the benches holding hands. Monika didn't like it. For lack of anyone else, she started holding hands with Bodo, Gerhard's bosom buddy, but he wasn't what she wanted. So she proposed a race. We would run between the posts that separated one street from the other and the winner would get Gerhard for the rest of the summer. I don't know why I agreed. I already had him. I have a weakness for gambling though and that almost did me in.

The boys had no idea what was happening. Boys never do. They thought it was a race to see who could run faster, nothing else. On your mark, get ready, go! I broke the Olympic record. Monika was taller, had longer legs and gave it everything she had. I had love on my side and love gives you wings. I flew. I won. I kept my Gerhard. It was too bad I couldn't tell him that I had nearly killed myself for him. He would have thought I was crazy about him and that just wouldn't do.

We played a game called love ball. The boys sat on one bench in the park, the girls on the other. One girl would throw a ball at another and call out a boy's name. If the ball receiver did not like that particular boy, she'd bounce the ball back with a hard thud on the floor. If she just liked him, she'd throw it back at waist level. If she wanted to kiss him, she'd roll it back on the floor and if she really, really loved him, she'd throw the ball high up in the air. It was a great game; everybody knew where they stood without having to say anything.

The day they threw the ball to the love of my life and called my name, my heart stopped. He toyed with the ball, pretended to thump it, and then let that ball fly - way up in the air, higher than anyone else had ever thrown a ball, way over the tops of the poplar trees. Love is a many splendoured thing. It also doesn't last long when you're 10 years old. He left at the end of summer vacation, promising to be back next year. I never saw him again which was probably just as well. For me, that boy is always 11 years old, handsome and daring and kisses my cheek in a darkened movie house.

Chapter 11

Growing Up Is Hard To Do!

At age 10, Mother took me to school for an examination. We knocked, the nurse opened the door, took one look at me and snarled "We don't take school beginners today". Slam went the door. Story of my life.

I didn't ever seem to grow. My shoes would wear out before I ever had a chance to remove the absorbent cotton in the toe part, which was put there in anticipation of my toes reaching the end. My pants wore out before the hem needed to be undone and my shirts and sweaters, which were hand-me-downs from Brother, fit me forever. Papa liked that because it meant he hardly ever had to buy new clothes for me. Mama worried and so did the rest of the neighbourhood. Any greeting was usually followed by the words "Aren't you ever going to grow?" How should I know. I got pretty tired of these people.

I also got pretty tired of playing dwarfs on stage at Christmas school plays. I had beautiful, long, dark hair. I wanted to play Snow White. They told me it was impossible to find dwarfs who were smaller than I was unless they recruited in Kindergarten. Once I was a snow-flake, they are small. And once I was a flame, trying to wake up the Sun who had fallen asleep and winter kept going on and on and on. That play was a big problem. Brother, who was tanned even in winter and had the pitch-black hair of his French ancestors, was assigned the role of Northwind. Lothar Staehler, who had survived my mushrooms and who was blond and pale and thin, was appointed Southwind. Now Northwind liked the cold and wanted the sun to stay hidden, but South wind wanted to help fan the little flame so that the sun would see it and wake up. Result - stage fight. North against South. It was a terrible sight. It took a lot out of my Brother. He could have laid Lothar flat with one hand tied behind his back. Instead, he had to endure defeat, night after night, in front of friends, relatives and other assorted audience members. So I wasn't the only one suffering.

The school examination result at age 10 indicated that I was under-nourished, under-sized and under-developed. In other words, I was basically like every one else in the neighbourhood, except for the growth problem. I just couldn't keep up with the giants who kept on growing. Therefore, the powers that be thought it would help if I were sent to a holiday camp where good food and lots of sleep would turn the situation right around. In next to no time, I found myself on a bus with a load of screaming children, waving goodbye to a lot of rather happy looking mothers.

My seat partner turned out to be an 11-year old from Neukoelln by the name of Doris Unrath. We clicked. Half way to our destination, she talked me into pretending to be 11 years old. Doris had been there before; she knew the ropes. If you were 10, you were sent to bed earlier than the older girls and they always had a lot of fun at night. I didn't want to miss any of that.

Upon arrival in a spacious mansion in the Dahlem district of Berlin, we were called up by name, asked our ages and told our room numbers. I said 11. They gave me my room number and my assignment. I had been put in charge of 5 little girls, ranging in age from 6 to 8. I was den mother. I had to make sure they brushed their teeth, washed their hands before meals and didn't get lost on outings. And I wasn't allowed to leave them alone when they went to sleep. The 10-year olds had fun at night - I baby-sat my charges and fretted. I thought they had immediately known that I was lying and had therefore given me this assignment as a punishment. While waiting for retribution to descend upon my head, I proceeded to turn myself into the best den mother they had ever had. It was a hard job and it cured me of lying. There is just too much hassle involved in not telling the truth.

We ate good food, took long walks in the forests and played lots of games. There was a swimming pool but, instead of water, it was full of leaves and dirt. Someone in the mansion came up with the wonderful idea of cleaning up that pool as a new game and, like so many idiots, we jumped in and started throwing the leaves out of the pool and at each other. Halfway through that new "game", I suddenly realized that we weren't playing but actually working for something that would never be of any benefit to us. We were leaving in three days. The pool would be clean and available for the next load of Kids who wouldn't even think of thanking us. I went on strike.

Everybody loves a strike. The pool stayed dirty, management scowled every time they saw my face, and we went back to playing for real.

At the end of three weeks we were asked to step on a scale. I hadn't gained any weight, hadn't grown an inch and was declared incurable. I played a dwarf for the rest of my acting life.

The other side of the coin was that, not growing any closer to my contemporaries, I gradually lost the playmates of my own age. They went on to bigger and better things, like boyfriends. Not only wasn't I ready for that adventure, I couldn't find any boy to take any interest in me anyway. When you're 12 years old, you don't want to be seen loading a girl on the front of your bike who looks as though she just turned 8.

My new friends were mostly two years younger but more fun to be with than the old crowd. Our city had become civilized again and so had its children. Ruins were a thing of the past and our playing fields were parks built on top of 'Truemmer Berge", which were mountains of grass hiding the rubble of destroyed buildings. Thanks to those artificial mountains we now had hills you could slide sleds down in the winter months. Summer brought the highlight of the year - the Ideal CO-OP 'Kinderfest'.

At three in the afternoon hundreds of kids of all shapes and sizes, dressed in our very best, assembled in front of the Youth Club House. Then, with a band of musicians in front, we paraded through the neighbourhood, waving at neighbours and singing our hearts out.

Back at the Park, there was a dance floor, booths that sold pickles, ice cream and wiener sausages with potato salad, and booths to play games. In the afternoon, the children danced or hopped about and gorged themselves on sweets. In the evening, the parade started again but this time every child carried a paper lantern with a candle inside. It was beautiful and magical. Every balcony was lit up with lanterns or strings of light bulbs, the music played and we made our way through this wonderland with oohs and aahs and I always looked forward to what my Papa had to offer. He never let me down. Being an inventor, he came up with new ways every year to make our balcony into something very special. His masterpiece was a big board, covered in little bulbs which spelled the name "IDEAL" in glowing colours. I was the envy of my peers.

New Years Eve was another highlight of the year. Germany erupts with fireworks at midnight and Berlin is no exception. Out of every window, and from every balcony, an assortment of fireworks explodes into the air and for at least 5 minutes it feels as though the third world war had started. Papa loved the fireworks and usually managed to have the most exciting show around until Brother got clumsy and ruined our display for years to come.

Mama and I had positioned ourselves as far away as we could from the tray containing Papa's ammunition while our two males sorted and arranged their booty for the last time. Then Brother lit a match, started a frog on its way, burned his finger and dropped the smouldering thing onto the tray. It exploded and everyone froze. Realizing what would happen next, Papa grabbed Brother, shoved him into the kitchen and closed the door, totally oblivious to the fact that his wife and daughter were now stranded in the middle of hell. Finding ourselves literally locked out, Mama pushed me into the corner of the balcony, pulled some old sacks lying on top of the rabbit cages over our bodies and then all hell broke loose.

For the next three minutes, fireworks the likes of which no one in the neighbourhood had ever seen exploded all around us. They had no place to go but from side to side, up and down and around in circles. Off and on something hit us and Mama pushed it away. It was an experience. When it was over, Mama got up, made sure the rabbits had survived and then marched into the kitchen and announced that everyone had better get out of her way as she was ready to kill someone. Papa and Brother tried to apologize but, realizing the futility of their words, disappeared into their respective beds. Mama and I had a cup of cocoa and watched the rest of the neighbourhood celebrating New Years at the appropriate time.

Next morning, while trying to remove black marks from the walls on the balcony, Mama was accosted by various neighbours who congratulated her on, once again, having had the best fireworks display in the area, albeit advising her to please check her watch as our display had appeared a little ahead of the prescribed time. That was too funny to resist and both Papa and Brother were forgiven for not opening the bedroom door and rescuing their valued family members. "Men", Mama exclaimed, "they just don't think straight in emergencies." I agreed.

Having lost Monika to the City of Cologne, I found a new playmate who introduced me to 'Folk Dancing'. Twice a week in the evening,

Annelies and I trotted off to a school gymnasium and learned the steps for hundreds of folk dances that originated in the various states of the German union. There was a man with an accordion who provided the musical accompaniment and a teacher who taught us the intricacies of each dance. There were also new boys. We had a ball. For three long years, we danced together and Annelies paid a terrible price for that pleasure. She was the taller of the two and therefore my leading man. She never learned how not to lead. It isn't always advantageous to be tall.

It was a fun time until they served us with a reality check. There once was a girl called Anne Frank and she wrote a diary.

Chapter 12
The Guilt Trip!

Shortly after the war, stories appeared in the papers about people having been killed in something called Konzentration Camps. Then one day, in school, we were handed a book called "The Diary of Anne Frank" and the world turned upside down. Pictures of horribly starved people turned up in the papers. Names like 'Auschwitz' and "Buchenwald" became household topics and my world collapsed. What was a Konzentration Camp and why and who killed some people called Jews? And what, pray tell, was my own father's role in this calamity?

Guilt is a heavy load. Guilt for something you didn't do is even heavier. I decided to work it off - on a Kibbutz in Israel. Permission was sought from Papa, which resulted in a very strange dialogue.

"Why do you want to go to Israel?"

"Because I feel guilty."

"What have you done?"

"Nothing. You did."

"What did I do?"

"You killed Jews."

"I don't know any Jews."

Stalemate.

It wasn't easy for Papa to explain what happened in a nation known for its thinkers and poets and scientists. It hasn't been properly explained by anyone to this day. All he could do is to try to make me understand that to judge a situation from a safe haven is not the same as to judge it from the point of having been there. It was the longest speech Papa ever made but one which I never forgot and which stood me in good stead in many a situation.

"If anyone should go to a Kibbutz in Israel, it should be me," Papa said. "I was there and I let it happen."

No one had asked him whether he wanted to join the army at 18 years of age in 1916 but he had to. No one had asked him two years later whether he should declare for the Bolsheviks or the National Socialists who were battling it out in the streets. No one could replace 26 of his classmates whose bodies were rotting away in the trenches of Verdun. No one offered to give him back his health, his youth or his life.

When he finally managed to get a job, inflation made the money he earned into a joke. He packed billions of marks, earnings for a day, into a knapsack every evening to buy a loaf of bread. It was an unbearable situation and ripe for the likes of Adolf to step in and exploit it. World leaders didn't catch on, so how did the world expect Papa to figure out what exactly Adolf had in mind? Papa started earning good money; Germany started being respected in the world and Papa's priorities changed. He got married, had children and wanted to further his career. He went to evening school and studied to become an engineer. He didn't have time to read a paper or sit around in cafes discussing the political situation.

Until the day he was accosted on the street for not wearing the Star of David, he hadn't noticed the changes taking place around him. He saw the signs in the windows declaring Jewish shops off limits and he thought it would go away in time. He knew he should do something and couldn't figure out what. He looked at his growing family and shut his eyes.

"That is my guilt," said Papa, "and I will live with it for the rest of my life. But not you. You will learn from this and keep your eyes and ears open and you will not put your head in the sand. And last but not least, never follow anyone who has to scream to make his opinion known and don't get caught up in a mob frenzy. Be an individual. Make sure that at the end of your days, you don't have to hang your head in shame because you could have made a difference and you didn't."

Then he reminded me of my dislike of manual labour and my queasiness regarding anything that crawled around in garden refuse heaps. He had watched me once performing my weekly job of loading the garden refuse into a bucket. I used a shovel and a rake and wore gloves, which so irritated Papa that he stormed down the balcony steps, tore off my gloves and thrust my hands into the heap of weeds. Not a very good idea. I lost my breakfast and lunch and deposited the half-digested mess all over his shoes and trousers. Mama thought it was hilarious. I had to pay for the cleaner, which took all my pocket money for three months. So maybe he was right. I don't think they would have got much work out of me on a Kibbutz

Anne Frank's book was an eye opener. It also got me into trouble. I had a problem with the girl. Try as I might, I did not like her. Everything she wrote was full of malice towards her mother, her sister and everyone else in those close quarters. Quite apart from the horrible situation they were in, she seemed to think almost entirely of herself and her beloved father. So when discussions ensued in class and I dared to mention my impression of the girl, I was soundly trashed. Apparently, when someone is declared a heroine, no critique is allowed.

I have read Anne's Diary more than once over the years and I always despair at the thought of what the human race is capable of doing to one another. But I've never managed to like the girl.

Chapter 13

Revolutions and Other New Ventures!

Having been declared too small to even apply for a job after Grade 9, Papa entered me into a business school for Secretaries. My opinion of what I wanted to do with my life was of no importance to anyone. I wanted to be a reporter at a newspaper but Papa had decided that I was to be the third generation working for Telefunken. If it was good enough for Grandfather Krause and good enough for Papa, it was good enough for me. I pointed out that Grandfather could not have been very happy with his choice as he had been drinking himself to death but Papa didn't think that I would run that risk. He was around and he would keep an eye on me. However, before I could start my illustrious career, I had to waste some time waiting to grow.

The girl who collaborated in spoiling the 'Cream of Wheat' breakfast at camp and whose clothes got soaked in honey joined me at this school for secretaries and for two years Ursel and I took the bus or biked to the Donau Strasse in Neukoelln to learn bookkeeping, shorthand and other assorted nonsense needed to get on in the world of business.

Ursel and I were bound not only by the tie of producing the most miserable breakfast anyone ever ate but also of having been exposed to ridicule in front of an entire class. Back in Grade 9, Mr.Kauffman had asked everyone to make a presentation of their intended profession and the two of us were chosen to represent the Secretaries of the future. We did real well and accepted our deserved applause with grace and humility. Until he asked us what in the world the word "Kopje" meant. All through our performance, we had talked of taking copies of various documents, a task that seemed very important to us, but unfortunately we had misread the word 'Kopie' and pronounced it 'Kopje' which, even though the rest of our peers had not even noticed the mistake, made us the butt of their jokes for the rest of the year.

So the two little Kopjes went off to learn about the real thing and found themselves innocent sheep surrounded by wolves. Most of our new classmates had failed their first year. Jobs were not plentiful in the early 50's and sending the girls to school at least kept them off the street.

Interested in school our new classmates most certainly were not. We listened in on conversations about missed periods and abortions and boyfriends who hit girls. We nodded sagely, agreed with everything they said and pretended to understand what the heck they were talking about. I didn't learn too much bookkeeping but a lot about life.

I also entered a new phase originating in France which was called "Existentialism". A few of my newfound school friends explained the theory (which on later retrospection had totally escaped them) and we found ourselves admiring new heroes. There was the writer Jean Paul Sartre, the singer Juliette Greco and the actress Marina Vlady, none of whom looked anything like my Hollywood idols nor did they profess to believe in the same philosophy.

So a new trend started. I painted my lips with white lipstick, put black eye shadow and eyeliner around the eyes and dyed my hair very black. Had I waited six months before cutting my long tresses, I could have been totally in. As it was, I was the only Beatnik with a crew cut. We assembled after school in the bakery on Karl Marx Strasse and discussed life. It was a little hard to be depressed, as a proper Beatnik was supposed to be, while sitting in a comfortable, sunny bakery surrounded by delicious cakes and cookies. It was easier for the people in Paris who sat in dingy, dark cellars and who were older and had at least some experience in living.

It was also very hard to be a Beatnik when surrounded by a family who did not seem to take my newfound outlook on life entirely serious. Every time I entered a room, Papa would recoil as if in fear, scream - and then apologize for not having recognized his beloved daughter, having thought the apparition to be a ghost. Mama smiled. How can one explain the seriousness of life to a person who simply grins from ear to ear. She did make the concession of reading my, for the moment, favourite author, expressed her honest opinion to the effect that she found him to be a very good writer but entirely too depressing for her liking. Brother looked me up and down and requested that I not acknowledge knowing him should we meet in public. This was so depressing that I almost believed in what I couldn't even understand. It couldn't last. I got tired of black, tired of Sartre, tired of Juliette's songs and went back to being the optimistic fool I had been. Life has its ups and it's downs. You've got to roll with it. Sometimes it's hard.

In the summer of 1953, rumours started to spread. The people of East Germany weren't too happy with their Russian occupation, their German "Volkspolizei", who were worse than the Russians, and the continuous upgrading of quotas in their working life, without the wage increases to go along with them. More and more of them decided that life in the East was infinitely worse than life had ever been and, grabbing a few belongings, took the train or subway to the West. The ones who decided to stay thought that showing their unrest and unhappiness in public would get the desired results. They went on strike and I learned that striking does not always work.

On June 17, 1953, the pot boiled over and it wasn't just a strike any more. Brother was at work near the Potsdamer Platz and heard the shooting. He and his colleagues dropped whatever they were doing and took off to participate in the excitement. At the Brandenburg Gate they watched East German Youth take down the Communist flag and watched them being shot at for their effort. Tanks rolled into the streets. The same T-34 tanks that had taken the city 8 years previously. History repeats itself.

We heard about it on the way home. The border for the Russian/American Sector was only 15 minutes away from my house. We changed direction and joined a lot of other people heading for the checkpoint. There was a tank and out of it's turret leaned a Russian soldier holding a gun. He didn't look as if he would love to use it but then someone threw a stone.

There is nothing more frightening than a few hundred people getting mad. It is like a storm exploding all around you, catcalls, whistles, screams and the missives flying through the air, hitting the tank, if not the soldier squatting on top. He wasn't waiting around either. He dropped like a stone, the lid closed - and the tank started moving.

I always thought they sort of lumbered along, being so big, but they don't. They come very fast and all of a sudden this particular one lowered the gun, pointing it straight at the rapidly disappearing young revolutionaries. I froze. I have a problem reacting fast in emergencies. Unfortunately, the soldiers inside that infernal machine couldn't possibly know that. All they may have seen through their slits was a minute figure looking defiant but was, in reality, a shell-shocked idiot.

My guardian angel sent along a man who picked me off the street and threw me sideways into the bushes. I finally found my reaction button and ran away like everyone else. That particular gun never fired, nor did any of the Russian tanks distributed through the rest of the City of Berlin and East Germany. They didn't have to. Their work was done by the East German Volkspolizei to the utmost satisfaction of their superiors. It was a shameful display of people obeying orders they should not have.

267 dead, over 1000 injured and many more to be executed later. Thousands of East Germans disappeared. It was a disaster. And all these people wanted were decent wages for a job well done. So much for Communism.

Capitalism looked a lot better. Germany was changing. There was a Marshall Plan which had put us on the right path to renewal and rebuilding of our economy. There was food on the table, cars in the streets, money in the bank, American movies and Television.

Musicals made Broadway look like heaven. Westerns made the American male into a heroic figure and comedies made me think that life always turned out right. We fell in love with Gregory Peck, Tony Curtis, Burt Lancaster, Richard Widmark and Cary Grant. We adored Rita Hayworth, Ava Gardener, Jean Simmons and Susan Hayworth. We spent more time in the movie theatres than anywhere else and our perception of life was formed by what we saw on the silver screen. Good people looked nice, bad people were ugly and wore black and with a song in your heart you could win the one your heart desired. Reality is somewhat different.

The Russians had a way of intruding on my blissful ignorance of World Affairs. Three years after the German mini-revolution, the Hungarians tried it in earnest. They didn't have a chance.

In November of 1956, the entire family traveled to the Rudolph-Wilde Platz to protest the invasion. There were a lot of speeches, a lot of protestations and a lot of tears. The Red Army was murdering Hungary with planes, tanks and artillery and, in the process, turned Budapest into a sea of flames. At night, we sat around the kitchen table, listening to cries for help from Hungarians who were asking the World to come to their aid. The Americans protested and asked the UN to intervene. Every elected official in the World professed outrage and then went to bed for a good night's sleep. I still have the EXTRA edition of the Telegraph newspaper from Monday, November 5, 1956. It was a story of betrayal by one of their own and of mass murder by one nation of another for the simple reason of holding together an Empire.

They really should teach history to politicians. All these years later, the Russian Empire has gone the way of the Dodo bird, the Eastern Europeans have attained freedom and the people who thought to protect their own by appeasing a great Bully have, hopefully, gone to their just desserts.

"Listen," said Papa, as we huddled around the Radio. "This is reality. This is what it is all about. Heroes, villains and ordinary people who pay the price." I was 17 years old. I did not want my world to be so hideous. I wanted out.

I went back to the movies and dreams. Watching 'The Children of Mara Mara', I professed an interest in Australia. Watching 'Niagara', I told everyone I was going to spend my honeymoon there even though I didn't really know where it was. I intended to die in New Zealand, which looked like Eden, and I wanted to ride elephants in India like Sabu from the Jungle Book. Everyone told me I was crazy.

Papa found an old school buddy who had fled the East and lived in a camp. Heiner Eberle had once been quite rich but had come to a sad end. But he had traveled, had seen the world and was eager to talk about his more affluent and happy days. Except for me, no one seemed interested. So to his audience of one, he related stories of far-flung places, of strange people who spoke languages no German understood and of customs and rites utterly foreign to the German mind. It was fascinating and some of it was probably invented but it opened up my mind to possibilities of travel and having adventures other than marrying the bloke next door and rearing children in the same old neighbourhood.

My interest cost Mr. Eberle his invitations to dinner. Mama got worried about his putting ideas into my head and requested his removal from the dinner table. I missed him a lot and, anyway, it was too late to stop what he had started. I had decided what my life was going to be like only I didn't bother telling anyone anymore. No one can talk you out of something they don't know anything about.

Having attended Business School for 2 years, life turned a complete 180 degrees. I started my illustrious career as the third generation worker at Telefunken. There were three of us. Tall, wide and tiny.

Helga was very tall and skinny, Waltraud was middle-sized and pudgy and I was a skinny midget. We never made friends but we suffered each other's idiosyncrasies and, as we didn't see too much of each other by always working in different departments, we got along tolerably well.

My first assignment was the Bookkeeping Department, my least favourite subject that, even after two years of schooling, was still a mystery to me. Luckily, what was done at Telefunken did not in the least resemble the little T frames we had to draw in school. Debit on one side, Credit on the other, etc., etc. Mostly what every department made us do is file away mountains of material into Leitz folders, a task which is abhorred by every office worker I have ever encountered and therefore gleefully assigned to new apprentices.

For two years, I filed away piles of documents in every department of this big firm. I had my ABC down pat by the end of it and had received a rudimentary education in the workings of office procedures.

The real education was provided by a business school which we attended, twice a week, in the afternoon and which was decidedly more exciting. School was on the Hardenberg Strasse near the Kurfuersten Damm where everything was happening. School meant making new friends from all over the City who were fun to be with. School was a teacher yelling, without ever turning her head to see who the culprits were, 'Schmidt, Stuermer, Krause, Wittke, shut up!" It wasn't always us four who were disrupting class but most of the time we were.

Having to get up at 5:00 am every day was hell but getting paid for it was heaven. My first pay cheque was a measly DM45.00, half of which I handed to Mother for my monthly upkeep.

Surprisingly, it felt good. I was now a member of the adult society, carrying on me at all times my own ID card that every German receives at the age of 15. People addressed me as "Miss" and it made me feel grown up. It also made me feel that I knew everything better than everyone else, which led to some friction in the household. I didn't get very far. Mama and Papa had never heard of the problems that young adults encounter psychologically, being too busy surviving during their own time of disillusionment with the world, and therefore considered my lamentations of boredom a lack of exercise. I was told to weed the garden. End of discussion.

With all that money to spend, my best friend from business school and I decided to embark on our first vacation away from home. We decided on a trip for two weeks to Denmark. I caught a bad cold the week before we were due to leave and our apothecary, ever helpful, provided me with a very potent liquid to battle my nagging cough. I was in a hurry and took a healthy swig which promptly knocked me out cold for a day and a night. Mama and Papa were away but lucky for me, Sister, having returned from England, took it upon herself to check up on my packing abilities only to find me sound asleep and no sign of a suitcase anywhere. She managed to pack whatever item I pointed to and then deposited a very sleepy sister on my pal Helga's doorstep. Helga held on to our luggage and me for the trip to the train station where we met up with our travel group. As soon as we had boarded, I went back to sleep.

Any time one left Berlin in those days, one had to travel through East Germany and the Border Guards would enter the compartments, check passports and generally make a nuisance of themselves. It was at that precise point of their operation that my cough medicine wore off and I found a renewed interest in life, mostly in the fact that there were uniformed people standing on the platform pointing guns. I wasn't sleepy any more. I was now hyperactive. Unfortunately, it was in the middle of the night and my yelling out the window did not endear me to my fellow passengers who were in the middle of their normal sleeping pattern. I was offered two choices, shut up or risk being thrown off the train in the middle of East Germany. I took the hint, sat back down and sulked.

Farum in Denmark was a sleepy little town with a youth hostel resembling barracks. It was clean and comfortable and we settled in for a week of sightseeing around the countryside. Inevitably, groups formed, mine being the most ridiculous assortment of people anyone could imagine. Bodo was tall and skinny and liked me. I liked Klaus, Klaus liked Vera, Vera liked Bernd, Bernd liked Elke and Elke liked Bodo. But Bodo liked me. We were the most star-crossed lovers on the planet and no one got anywhere but neither could we break out of the circle. We just kept on trying and, in the process, provided entertainment for our fellow travelers.

The second week was spent at the seacoast resort of Gilleleje and I fell in love again - this time with the ocean. I dumped my suitcase and ran to the water's edge. The biggest amount of water I had ever seen was the Wannsee and the biggest wave that lake ever produced wouldn't cover your ankles. But the sound of the waves on the beach of Gilleleje was something I couldn't get enough of. I sat and listened while lunch was being served and dinner eaten. Didn't matter. It got even better when the moon came out and the tops of the breakers turned silver. Helga finally dragged me away. With the windows open, you could still hear the ocean. It was magic.

It could also be deadly. Swimming in high waves is not advisable if you are not a strong swimmer, which I wasn't. Some meters away from the beach, there was a sandbank which was the point of no return and which everyone used as a beacon for the return trip. I figured I could make it to the sandbank alright and I did, but I hadn't counted on the pull of the waves on the way back to the beach. I couldn't get anywhere. I swam and swam and when I got tired, drifted back to the sandbank. If that piece of elevated beach hadn't been there, I would have ended up in Sweden. I got very scared when I finally realized that I was the only one left out in the middle of nowhere without the strength to get back on my own. A good set of lungs is a godsend in dire circumstances. They got my message and it wasn't any hardship for the boys to piggy- back me to the safety of the wonderful, safe, solid beach on Denmark's soil. I learned to respect the forces of nature that day but my love for the ocean was undiminished.

A lesson of a different kind was learned at the dining room table. We shared the youth hostel with groups of teenagers from France and Belgium. The French had all the lovely girls and our boys went after them like wildfire. The Belgians had Jean-Claude who broke every heart in the female German contingent.

Helga and I shared a table with six of our German compatriots and six of the French variety. We got along very well. We couldn't communicate except in English which no one was any good at and we smiled a lot. Considering that 12 years earlier preceding generations had shot bullets at each other, I thought we were doing terrific.

Until the day the serving girl brought in a huge bowl of a delicious looking dessert that was handed around the table. The first German took a great big spoonful, which his neighbour perceived as an incentive to do likewise. Number three gouged an even bigger hole and so on and so on. By the time the bowl arrived at Helga's place, there wasn't enough left to feed one, never mind the last two Germans, namely Helga and me, and the six French friends who didn't look very amused right about then. Helga abstained and passed the bowl to me. I couldn't have taken that last spoonful if my life depended on it and, blushing to the eyebrows and wanting to sink into the floor with shame, I passed it on. None of our French pals touched the spoon and the bowl ended up back in the hands of the first German boy, who cheerfully spooned out the remnant and crammed it into his mouth.

It wasn't funny, although I am sure it was meant to be. We didn't contribute to French/German relations in any great way that day and the Teutonic sense of humour went totally unappreciated. But somehow the fact that neither Helga nor I had participated in the humiliation contributed to the fact that we made friends and the rest of the holiday was spent sitting on the beach trying to teach each other our respective languages. They were great fun to be with and my first real encounter with a different nationality than my own. Turned out, they were just like us. Interesting fact that.

We exchanged addresses and promised to write and actually did for quite a while - in English. It was the only language all of us had learned to some degree in school and therefore the only way to communicate. With Helga's help, I managed some letters and they got me an invitation to go to Paris to visit Andre Rey and Denise Autechand the following year. The fights that followed were historic landmarks in my relationship with Papa. I lost the battle but I won the war.

Instead of Paris, I got a certificate from my Doctor advising my employer to give me an extra two weeks off because of a completely run-down physical condition. My health insurance company recommended a recuperation place in the country, namely the little village of Schwelm. I really was run-down but it wasn't because of a heavy workload or any other business related activity. I didn't get enough sleep because I had joined a rock-n-roll club and was out dancing almost every day of the week. Papa's rule was, you can stay out as long as you want but you have to go to work in the morning. 5:00 o'clock is very early. Coming home at 1:00 am does not give one much time to relax and store up energy. The day my head fell into the typewriter basket, bloodying my forehead, was the day my supervisor decided to cave in to my doctor's advice for recuperation. I was freed of my duties and set out on the second vacation of my life.

A two-storied building in the middle of the forest, about ½ hour walk from the town of Schwelm, was my home for four weeks in 1958. Everyone there was between the ages of 16 through 25. The girls occupied the upper floor and the boys the lower, both floors being connected by poles that were a cinch to shinny up on to the upper balcony. The architect of that place had not counted on the interplay of the sexes at that tender age or he wouldn't have put in those connectors.

It was a heavenly place of walks in the country, hitchhiking to places like Duesseldorf and Koelln and making new friends. And I became the mother of a 14 year old.

On my third day, and in the middle of lunch, a young man approached me with the incredible question of "would you mind being the mother of my child." Being a Berliner means you usually have an answer for everything but this one stumped me. I took him literally. Turned out that he was 22 years old and had been paired with a 14-year old who was recuperating from an appendicitis operation. For a joke, they called each other father and son. Problems arose when the father chose a girl to be his paramour for the duration of his stay and the son did not like the object of his affection. His interference resulted in a rapid break-up of a relationship that hadn't even started. Kids do that sort of thing. The person the son finally chose, from a distance, to be the perfect mate to complete the family, was me. It was too good an offer to refuse and the instant family gave me an opportunity to experience what it was like to be on the other side of the fence. It wasn't always pretty.

The two new members of my family being ardent Catholics, I was obliged to attend my first Catholic Mass and, true to form, embarrassed the entire congregation. Holy water may be a blessing but it is still cold and when sprayed over a heated body surface, such as my shoulders and the (indecently) exposed part of my developing bosom, it shocks the senses and provokes a shout of protest which does not comply with the decorous manners usually present during Mass. A great portion of the sermon was spent kneeling to which I wasn't accustomed and my knees started to hurt. I sat back down, which resulted in a very stern finger being poked into my back.

Enough was enough. I turned around, snarled "don't do that" at the old, black-shawled lady behind me, folded my hands and sent a very ardent thank you prayer to my ancestors in general and to Martin Luther in particular for having made religion a little easier on the body for the Protestants.

My new family forgave me my sins and things proceeded as things should. Junior's bedtime was 9 pm, which gave his parents a chance to get to know each other better. It was fun and entirely innocent. This was 1957. We kissed and hugged and talked and discovered that we were both still virgins and, at least on my part, intended to stay that way a little longer. It was wonderful and romantic and a young man from Minden and a boy from Duesseldorf gave me an indication of what a family should be.

When the head of our family left, I turned into a single parent without any chance of getting into another relationship. My son saw to that. It put me in mind of all the single mothers after the war and the problems they encountered when faced with the choice of either continuing solo or dealing with the wrath of their offspring by adding a stranger to the family circle.

It was a hard choice to make and who's to judge when the urge to share one's life with another man turns out detrimental to the children as a whole. It was a sad thing to watch in the years following the war when so many men did not return to take up their place in the family. I had always admired the women who sacrificed their own happiness and simply took care of their children, which wasn't always repaid in kind. I, on the other hand, only had one week to endure. Junior repaid me by keeping in touch through correspondence for years to come. I never forgot father and son but I never saw either of them again. So it wasn't Paris, but it was wonderful and touching and a definite learning experience.

Back home, new faces turned up on the silver screen. Marlon Brando, the "Wild One." Nobody in the neighbourhood even faintly resembled Marlon nor did anyone I knew in Britz or the surrounding area own a motorcycle or sport a leather jacket. Somewhere near the Kurfuersten Damm there was a Hell's Angels Club of some sort but I couldn't get there. Luck was with me. On the way to work every morning, coming the other way, was a young man who first smiled, then greeted and finally asked me for a date. What swayed my opinion of this particular individual, who otherwise was not my type and did not remotely resemble Marlon, was his mention of picking me up on a motorcycle. He had himself a date.

One Saturday afternoon, while the rest of the family went down on their knees and prayed for my safe delivery, I plunked my posterior on the backseat of a huge machine and bathed in the admiration and envy of my friends and enemies.

It was the coconut affair all over again. It didn't turn out the way I thought it should. It was a disaster. Halfway around the block, I found out I hated motorbikes. I couldn't see anything past his broad back. I couldn't feel which way he was turning until he was already in the turn and the bike slanted at an angle, which made me feel as though I was going to end up scraping the pavement. It was noisy, uncomfortable and wrecked havoc with my meticulously teased hair. I was made for better things. Marlon could go fly a kite; this was not my cup of tea.

Five minutes later I was back where I started and lost my one and only chance of joining the rebel generation. My date took off in a huff, never to be seen again. C'est la vie!

Next up on the 'love of my life' list - James Dean. What a sulker. What a perfect model of disenchantment, disillusionment and other teenage maladies. "Rebel without a Cause" was the movie that started an entire generation to think along the lines of how important a teenager really was and how much maligned and misunderstood we were. It was also a movie that I personally did not quite understand.

The title said it all. What the heck were these kids rebelling against? They had cars, they had great clothes, they seemed to have unlimited free time to hang around. They drank milk straight out of the bottle, something my Mother would have clobbered me for even at this tender age. One girl was upset because her father didn't hug her anymore. Big deal. At this stage of the game, I was more interested in hugging young men anyway. One father was a henpecked idiot. Sooo? We had a few of those around. Mr. Berg used to go for the milk on Sunday mornings and cook on the weekends, actions no real man in the 50's would think of performing. So he got laughed at behind his back, a fact that wasn't lost on his daughter, my old friend Monika, who just shrugged her shoulders and enjoyed her father's cooking. He was better at it than her Mom any old day. So what possessed the Americans to hurl themselves off cliffs, destroying a car in the process, for which we would have given anything to own? It was a mystery and a definite culture gap.

In the 1950s, we still did our own stuff while partaking in the cultural revolution that came out of America. America danced in running shoes and white socks. All the girls had ponytails and wore blouses and wide skirts. We danced in high-heeled shoes and either very tight skirts or plumped up wide dresses which stood by themselves, being supported by starched and boned petticoats of immense proportions, while our dates dressed in suits and ties and asked if they could have the next dance.

The Americans played a game they called 'football' but they only touched the ball once on takeoff with a foot and the rest of the time it was handled by hands. Figure that out. Grown up men huddled together, sticking their bums into the air, bumping into each other with great force and trying to catch the one man holding the ball. The whole thing ended up by everyone piling up in a big heap. I thought it was a joke they were playing on us when I first saw it in a newscast at the movies. I didn't find out until years later that it was an actual sport. Different strokes for different folks. But why call it 'foot ball'. It was all very mysterious and needed checking out but at the time I was too busy studying and surviving my apprenticeship.

Chapter 14

Adventures in Corporate Living!

Surviving apprenticeship was a cinch. Surviving the final exam was not. Three months before our bell tolled, three of my classmates and I decided we needed help. Once a week we met, alternating locations between each other's family residences, and studied. Helga was an ace in math and bookkeeping, Ellen was best at the business correspondence, I walked away with shorthand and typing speed and I don't remember what Christa was famous for but it must have been something useful. I don't know if we would have made it without those sessions but I wouldn't have missed them for the world. At almost 18, we laughed at just about everything.

Exam day arrived and we were about as prepared as it was possible to be. All four of us ended up in different classrooms. It was an all-day affair where you weren't even allowed to go to the bathroom without a teacher in attendance, making sure you didn't snitch some information from a class mate. All that for the dubious distinction of calling oneself a Secretary in the years to come. After eight hours of torture, we met in the school yard. Did you? I think I did! I hope I did! Actually, I'm pretty sure I did! We did it! We all did it! Hurrah for the Four Musketeers.

People on the Kurfuerstendamm didn't quite know what to make of four young girls, arm in arm, singing at the top of their lungs, "We always knew we would, get through the exam we would, we always knew we would come out ahead." The actual song was about love and how someone knew that he would love that other person but our words were much more significant. It was a glorious day and only marred by the knowledge that, having survived the written exam, we still had to face the oral one.

My torture day was scheduled to take place at the 'Karstadt' shopping emporium on the Hermannplatz. Mama accompanied me there and disappeared into the restaurant, drinking coffee and praying for her daughter's safe deliverance.

Her little girl faced up to three very stern judges of the male variety who didn't quite know what to make of my answer to their mathematical chain questions. Sorry, I can't count without paper.

They tried again, slowly, '21 plus 34, divided by 4, multiplied by 6, take away 35, etc, etc, etc.' I lost them after the '21 plus 34' problem. I cannot do chain math. Sorry. It's beyond my capabilities. Girl, they said, you got a 4 (D) in math now. We will have to give you a 5 (F) if you don't try. Sorry, can't do. It doesn't matter anyway. I want to become a Secretary, not a Bookkeeper. And I've got two As, they will wipe out the bad marks. So sorry.

They were sorry too. So sorry that they ignored the treacherous chain problem and left my mark at 4. Thank you. I will never forget you. Mama and I celebrated with a great lunch.

Every year, as a reward for having passed the exam, Telefunken put on a party for the graduates. Buses were hired and a day trip taken to the countryside. In the evening, we were provided with a sumptuous meal and then proceeded to a bowling alley. I had never bowled in my life and neither had most of the other participants in this venture. Our organizers announced that each one of us could throw six balls down the lane. Girls were separated from the boys and each team would have a winner and a loser category and the best of each would receive a prize.

My first and second ball went predictably into the gutter. Waltraud scored the highest number of pins toppled. That, I figured, was that. There was no point in trying to win this as she seemed to know what she was doing. First prize was out of my reach. I decided to go for the booby prize and threw every other ball deliberately aside. Six out of six into the gutter, congratulations, you've lost.

Prizes were awarded and Waltraud proudly took possession of a beautiful cup and saucer. I was presented with a pink ribbon from which an animal stamped out of metal and resembling a rat was dangling. As Mr. S. draped the ribbon over my shoulders, he told me not to take it too hard as the inability to bowl must run in the family. Apparently my father had received the rat medal at his graduation party. I wondered about that. Papa wasn't the sort to take losing kindly and

I did not think I should mention his failure to perform unless I was prepared to live with the consequences. As it was, I was happy. I had something to remember the night. The cup and saucer are likely history by now but my rat medal still resides in my box of memorabilia and is dearly cherished as it also sports the signatures of everyone present on the pink ribbon.

Papa was already asleep when I returned from my sojourn into the gaming world but Mama had a good laugh at my first attempt to con the authorities. In the morning, I proudly presented the medal to Papa who, without blushing, confirmed his own medal in the same category. "But I did it on purpose", he said. "I figured I wasn't going to win the first prize, so I deliberately went for the loser medal".

If I had not told Mama beforehand what I did, he never would have believed that I pulled the same stunt more than 40 years later. Like father, like daughter. We had a lot in common after all.

I returned to Telefunken, a full-fledged Secretary, and was promptly put to typing meaningless orders for eight hours a day and DM450.00 a month. It was a totally brainless job and I couldn't quite see why I had spent two years studying for that. Of my two fellow apprentices, one joined me in the typing pool in another department and the other was appointed Secretary even though her exam paper was worse than mine. Excuse me, is there something wrong here?

First lesson in the business world. It doesn't matter what you know, it's who you know. Pudgy Waltraud had an uncle who was running the Bookkeeping Department at AEG, sister company to Telefunken. Pulling a few strings was child's play for that man. Tall and skinny Helga's mother worked in the factory and had absolutely no strings to pull and my own Papa's strings were totally tangled. To my horror, I found out that my Papa was very much disliked by his superiors. Nobody likes a smart guy and Papa was very smart. Trouble was, he let everyone know that.

Running a huge conglomerate like Telefunken requires an excellent management team. What we had was Mr. S. and Mr. K., two guys Papa had known all his life and who had outmanoeuvred him on the ladder to success. Papa couldn't kiss butt. Papa believed that respect was something you had to earn. Papa did not suffer fools gladly and, consequently, Papa managed to alienate his superiors to a level never again achieved by any other member of his family.

Papa's top level was Manager of the Estimation Department, while Mr. K. and Mr. S. soared to the dizzying heights of managing the company - right into the ground. By the time Telefunken went bankrupt, Papa was dead. He would have said - I told you so.

No one likes to be thought a fool. It must have been galling to these two not to be able to get back at Papa at times, which they couldn't. He was very good at what he did. But the day he put my life into their hot little hands, they found their means for revenge. I applied for all sorts of other positions, only to find myself thwarted at every opportunity. Somehow there was always something I didn't quite know which prevented me from fulfilling the requirements of a new position. My one and only promotion was into the very department my Papa was heading. Another typing pool and no responsibility but with the added obstacle of now having to read my Father's handwriting, which was in elaborate old-German writing and a nightmare to decipher. Meanwhile, Pudgy went on to bigger and better things and there was nothing I could do.

In between typing, we had a lot of fun. The room we worked in was immense, with rows upon rows of desks, four of them always facing each other, with one telephone installed on an extended arm which could be swung around to each participant. Very frugal and very efficient.

The typing pool consisted of five Ladies on manual typewriters, hammering away at the keys which could never keep up with speed. Pressing down a key resulted in a little hammer-like contraption to swing up and hit the paper roller. Typing faster than the speed with which the hammer could return to its nest in the basket resulted in four or five of them getting tangled up with horrendous results. My speed was the talk of the Pool but my fingernails were the talk of the entire Department. Through all the punishment, they kept their length, protected by several layers of nail polish, the colours of which changed by the week and caused an uproar. Not one of my fellow workers had ever experimented with green, white or yellow nail polish and it was a lot of fun hearing their lamentations regarding the radical new generation. Within two weeks, however, most of them copied my style and we all enjoyed ourselves tremendously.

Being in close quarters with a mostly-male contingent of staff was too much of a temptation to play tricks on the female occupants and tricks were played all around all the time. They put things into the hole in the typewriters where the levers were situated, prohibiting them to jump up in their normal fashion. Sometimes things went missing from our desks, or signs were put up directing people not to the Steno Unit but to the Snake Pit. It was a way to enliven an otherwise boring existence and we were never lax in reciprocating.

Our masterpiece involved the worst practical joker in the office and he never stopped talking about it. In Germany, people are allowed to drink beer at their desks, although between sips, they store the bottle in the drawer. We watched until that certain beer-guzzling individual left his desk for parts unknown. Being the youngest and therefore most agile, I scooted on all fours between the rows and replaced his bottle with another, albeit filled with pure water. He returned, picked up his bottle, took a swig - and choked. "That's water," he proclaimed to all and sundry but everyone told him not to be silly, it was a beer bottle after all. He glared at us but all he could see were five heads bent diligently over their typewriters. Before any action could be taken, our ally, the Boss's secretary, called him over to her desk, posing some innocuous question. As soon as he turned his back, I was back on all fours, replacing the water bottle with the original one. He returned, picked up his bottle and, smirking, proceeded to pretend water was just fine with him. "It's beer!" he yelled and everyone looked at him as though he was slightly demented. "Of course it's beer, you idiot. It's a beer bottle, isn't it?"

Mama managed to enliven our dreary existence with ideas all of her own. She sometimes inserted a candy or a piece of chocolate in my own and Papa's breakfast bag. We appreciated that immensely, but usually forgot about the treat by the time we returned home. One morning, I unwrapped my package and found a small piece of coal. Coal? What's with the coal? I looked up and saw Papa staring uncomprehendingly at a very small baby hair brush. I showed him my coal and Papa tapped the side of his head, which in any language means 'crazy'. "She's flipped," he said, and grabbed hold of the swinging telephone. His formal inquiry as to the reasoning behind our unusual gifts was answered with a hoot of laughter which everyone within a mile could hear. "Well" said Mama when she finally finished amusing herself, "you two never acknowledge the nice things I give you so I thought I'd try something different and see if I can get a reaction. I was right, wasn't I?" She sure was and it worked. Neither one of us ever neglected to thank her for whatever we found in our packages.

At Telefunken, we started work at 7:00 am in the morning, had a 10-minute break at 9:00, a half-hour lunch break at Noon and a 10-minute break at 2:00 pm. Lunch could be bought with weekly tickets for a very reasonable price and was served at the 'Kantine' army fashion, ladled onto your plate by the kitchen staff. It was good food and sometimes so good that the male population saw fit to describe various items on the plate in a very despicable, if not gross, manner, comparing harmless food to stuff produced by cannibals butchering missionaries. It worked very well on the sensitive stomachs of many of my female compatriots who turned green and left their food for the consummation of their ravenous male co-workers. It was gross and very mean but everyone accepted it as what it was, a joke. We had not heard of harassment and, in any event, we always got back at them somehow. Personally, I drove them crazy. I was immune to anything they threw at me and merrily consumed my own portion. I grew up with a Brother. I had heard it all before.

Every summer, the entire staff at Telefunken partook in the annual summer party which generally took place at some restaurant on one of the lakes surrounding Berlin. We boarded boats and cruised the canals, leading to whatever lake was the destination of the year. It took at least two hours to get there and there was not much else to do but knock back a drink or two (or three) and, naturally, by the time we docked on the pier, half the population on board was tipsy and a quarter of them were too drunk to manipulate the long walk to the restaurant and had to be helped by their less inebriated friends. We were served a meal, more drinks and then the music started and, whatever portion of the population was still standing, took to the dance floor. When it got dark, people were seen disappearing into the bushes. Being young, inquisitive and bored with the old-fashioned music presented, the younger generation thought it fun to poke around outside and dig up some information as to who did what with whom. It wasn't pretty. We found out what it took to get a promotion. We met back at the pier, exchanged information and professed moral outrage at what we had witnessed, swearing never to sink to the same level. I don't know about the rest of them but I kept my promise. Needless to say, at Telefunken, I never got out of the steno pool.

I worked hard and earned my keep but sometimes it was hard to live up to Papa's expectations, especially when the weather was great and the sun beckoned. One year, what beckoned was Mama's strawberry cake. Her birthday, September 7, was always celebrated with a cake made with the last strawberries Papa harvested from the garden. I saw the cake in the morning. I could not get it out of my mind and my brain worked furiously to find an excuse to get out of the office, into the world and at the strawberries. I ate my breakfast, accompanied by a cup of beef bouillon, then proceeded downstairs to the washroom to wash out my cup. By the time I returned, I had it figured out. Holding on to my wrist, I told my co-workers that I had fallen in the staircase and slammed my arm onto the cement step. It hurt something fierce. They cooed and soothed and sent me to the boss who professed sympathy and accompanied me to the company medical officer. They probed, I winced and, within minutes, I found myself in a chauffeur-driven Mercedes company car, on my way to the emergency station nearest to Sickingenstrasse. The situation had run away from me. I wanted an afternoon off and found myself trapped in a vicious spiral of deception. I had no idea how to handle this.

Emergency Stations are for very sick people. Some of them were bleeding all over the floor with cut-off fingers and sliced arms resulting from gory accidents. There were broken limbs, bruised heads - and one little girl with a phoney wrist injury who started to sweat with fear. They called me in for X-rays and I had to keep up appearances of wincing whenever they turned my hand to take another picture. By the time the very gentle giant of an X-ray Technician was finished, my pale complexion produced by fear was interpreted as extreme pain and shock and I was treated with solicitude and extreme kindness.

Waiting for the results of what I was sure was the discovery of my deception, I imagined the outcome. I would be fired, that was a given. My Papa would disown me and I would be thrown out of the house. I would have to join Sister in the exodus to England and spend the rest of my life dishonoured. Only Mama would love me because 'that is what Mothers do'. With all that promising future ahead of me, tears came naturally, which prompted another outpouring of sympathy to which I knew I was not entitled, which made it hard to endure. Then the judge and jury appeared with my X-ray clutched like a sword in his hand. "Oh, you poor little girl" he said, kneeling in front of me. "You severely cracked your wrist. It isn't broken and you won't need a cast, but we have to put your arm into a sling," which he promptly proceeded to do. Talk about a weight lifted off my shoulders.

Returning to my company car, my feet never touched the ground and the drive back was now a thoroughly enjoyable experience. Back at work, everyone hugged me, taking care not to touch the poor injured limb, and, within minutes, I was on the train heading home. Happy Birthday, Mama!

I did tell Mama about my deception because firstly, lying to Mama was useless as she always had a sympathetic ear for whatever trouble I got myself into and, secondly, I couldn't see myself wearing that darn sling for two weeks. Mama was not quite as forgiving as normally and I got a good tongue-lashing about lying, deceiving and bad behaviour in general, which I acknowledged, and then I got the cake, which I craved. In the end, she figured, the way they were treating me at work with their stupid typing jobs and no promotion, they had it coming. We never told Papa but I did tell one of my friends who, the summer following, tried the same stunt and, after X-rays, was diagnosed with a broken arm and put into a cast covering her arm from wrist to past the elbow. She was a perfectionist. To make it look good, she had hit her arm a few times, producing a nice bruise and that was over the top. Sometimes it works, sometimes it doesn't, but I haven't had much confidence in X-rays since.

So life was pretty boring on the whole until one injected some spice into it. Having turned 18, what excitement I missed in my daily chores was now available in the evenings - I was allowed to frequent any nightclub my little heart desired and stay until closing time.

Chapter 15

THE DANCE-HAPPIEST YOUTH ON EARTH

Mama always maintained that I danced before I could walk. The entire family loved to dance and Mama taught us all. She served breakfast in a waltzing step, lunch came in with a foxtrot and dinner was a definite polka. Any time a good tune turned up on the radio, the chairs went flying into the corners and the family danced. All except Papa. Papa was a very good dancer but could have spent his life without doing so. The rest of us could not.

Sister attended the Kather Dancing School at 18 without having to pay as they were short of females and she knew how to dance anyway. Brother went in on the same ticket a few years later and I completed the trio of freeloaders. Dancing was not something that needed to be taught to my family, it came naturally.

At 16, getting ready for my first Sunday afternoon dancing class, I asked my again home-based Sister what I should wear. "Nothing special," said Sister. "Just your usual sweater and skirt." I took off in a very wide sweater, a tight little skirt, high heeled shoes to elevate my frame to acceptable levels and an Anorak in case it rained.

I entered the premises to find the boys uncomfortably lodged in smart looking suits and the girls spread out over two chairs, each in beautiful, stiff, petticoat dresses. I wasn't quite sure whether I wanted to die right there or wait until I killed my Sister first. I didn't need to worry. As always when Sister tried to put one over on me, it backfired. All of the boys were much more comfortable with me in my day-to-day wear than they were with the perfumed, frilly, starched to perfection beauties who they were supposed to swing around the dance floor.

At break time we played cards and got properly acquainted and two hours later we cemented our relationship with a Coke in the nearest 'Kneipe'.

Being escorted home by five good-looking young men was explanation enough for Sister who disappeared out of my vision for the rest of the day. The following Sunday, however, I was suitably attired in the prescribed manner befitting a dance class. Peter Kather and his wife Edith then proceeded to turn an unruly little mob of rock-n-rollers into proper little Gentlemen and Ladies and, on the surface at least, they succeeded.

Two years later, as we promenaded around the room at our final Grand Ball, ready to impress our parents with a perfect waltz, my escort and I, leading the procession, made a terrifying discovery. The head of my family, sitting on a chair in his usual stance of widespread legs, had forgotten to close his fly. A piece of his immaculately starched white shirt was peeking through the opening as though it wanted to be in on the action. My throat went dry, my knees buckled and I hung on to my escort for dear life. He, having been schooled by the Kather pair, never so much as faltered in his step. Passing Papa, he merely bowed his head as though to greet my offending parent, whispered "Your fly is open," and smiling broadly, continued to lead me around the floor. Parents are a continual embarrassment to their children and there should be a law against that. I survived the evening but I didn't speak to Papa for weeks.

Kather's dancing school also provided me with the opportunity of experiencing love for the first time. On my 17th Birthday, it was an embarrassing thought to admit that I had never been kissed. I met the suitable object for lessons on the subject at Kather's New Years Bash. He was tall, blond, had a little moustache and resembled Erroll Flynn - well, somewhat. He was also 22 years of age and I was pretty sure he would know how to go about this venture. At the end of the night, he volunteered to accompany me to the streetcar. I left Sister behind and ventured into the night. We walked and talked and he finally managed to pull me into a doorway, proceeding to show me what I expected to be the No. 1 high point of my life.

I expected bells to ring and sweet music to play in my head - what I got were explosions, glass shattering on the side walk and people screaming obscenities at the top of their lungs. Some idiots had decided to explode some more fire works and had pointed them in the wrong directions. Windows were smashed, doors blackened and people in night shirts were chasing the culprits around lamp posts. We high-tailed it out of there and didn't stop running until we got to Hermann Platz and the safety of my streetcar.

When I got home, I brushed my teeth - for about half an hour. This vigorous action woke up Mama and Papa who were informed that I thought kissing was definitely overrated and I would never do it again. It tasted awful (the guy smoked), it felt weird and it affected an entire neighbourhood. My first kissing venture made the headlines in next morning's paper but I wasn't mentioned.

Having passed dancing school with exceedingly better marks than business school, I was more than ready for the rest of Berlin's dancing establishments and, in 1957, Berlin sported dancehalls of every size and for every persuasion. My stomping ground was the Hasenheide, a ½ hour's ride on the streetcar from home. There was the Roswitha Bar, reserved for those intimate little outings with a date by your side. There was the Klosterkeller which, connected to the world-famous Resi, made up the best-known dancing establishment in the city.

The Resi had a water organ which, accompanied by classical music, presented a colourful picture of flowing, cascading, moving water across the stage every hour on the hour. It also had table telephones and table telegram facilities. Every table had a post with a number on it so one could call any other table and talk to people there without them knowing exactly what table one was calling from. One could send messages in a tube to another table, asking for a dance, a date or simply flirt with whoever took one's fancy. The Resi was expensive and reserved for the older generation, which included anyone over 26.

The Klosterkeller sported the same amenities except the water organ but served up more up-to-date music than the swing and tango stuff upstairs. In the Klosterkeller, we rocked and rolled and danced from 8 pm sharp to 2 or 3 in the morning. No obese people around in those days and no one needed aerobics. We had Elvis and Pat Boone, Chuck Berry and Jerry Lee Lewis and we were known as the dance-happiest youth in Germany. And all that on a glass of apple juice that had to last all night. It was all we could afford and it was all we needed.

Down the road was the Casaleon. It boasted two floors, the lower one sporting a dance floor consisting of colourful glass that I considered to be very chic. It was also quite small and how on earth we managed to pack every one into that wee space, jiving, turning, feet flying, without killing each other is a miracle.

The Casaleon gave me a chance at stardom - which, true to form, I blew. Someone on the political spectrum had the bright idea to intersect election results one year with short scenes from nightclubs all around the city. They came to the Casaleon and everyone piled onto the dance floor. Selection was limited and only the best were asked to stay. Eight pairs survived and I experienced for the first (and last) time the power of those god-awful lights they shine on the members of the performing arts. Dancing rock'n'roll is a sweaty affair in any case and those lights were torture but, hey, its showbiz and the show must go on.

On election night, the family sat around the TV and waited for my moment of glory. That blasted show went all over the place but never got anywhere close to my own district of Neukoelln and at about 11 pm Papa called it quits. I couldn't keep my eyes open either. There is nothing more boring than watching election results, even if they show people dancing around town in the intermissions. And so to bed.

Boarding the train in the morning, we were accosted by many of the regular passengers, remarking upon my excellent dancing skills, which they had watched on TV. I had danced myself into the heart of my fellow Berliners at 10 minutes past 11 pm. Story of my life. When my ship comes in, I'm in the train station.

The Casaleon engaged live rock bands and some came from other countries. I remember the Swedes. They were very young and played a mean tune and the red-headed little drummer thought I was the love of his life. Brother, still speaking Swedish to some degree, had a ball with them and abetted the freckle-faced boy in his pursuit of a reluctant Sister. That did the Swede no favour at all. I was at the point of never doing anything Brother wanted. He cramped my style. His habit of ignoring my presence set my teeth on edge but the attention he paid to the people I danced with was even worse. I'd be dancing with what Brother would call a 'Punk' and who I would think a gorgeous specimen of the male variety and there would be a finger poked into the back of my hero and a voice would growl, "that's my Sister," and that would be the end of that relationship. It wasn't fair. It wasn't appreciated. It was brotherly love and I hated him for it. It also killed any chance the Swedish carrot top ever had of getting a date.

Close to the Hermannplatz was "Die Neue Welt". Two huge dance halls connected to one another by a long hallway. The front one, consisting of two floors, usually played contemporary music with waltzes, tangos and foxtrots and in which old German songs were sung which made you link your arms and 'schunkel', weave from side to side in unison. It was 'Gemuetlichkeit' as only the Germans understand it. It was the place for the Oktoberfest where there was enough space to put an entire oxen on a spit, have a slide from the upstairs floor to the lower floor and provide a Gretna Green chapel where the object of the game was to get married as many times as possible during the night - for one mark each. It wasn't the marriage certificate that made the boys pay up; it was the kissing that went with it. It was the place to stand on tables and sing at the top of your lungs "Ein Prosit der Gemuetlichkeit". It was the place where young and old mixed and got along.

The second facility in the back was reserved for the Boogie Woogie generation. Another big orchestra, but this time it was swing with Glenn Miller and Rock N' Roll ruled and no one over 30 showed his face here.

It was a world of dancing and falling in love and out of it and having fun. And sometimes it broke your heart.

Chapter 16

LOVE IS A MANY SPLENDORED THING - maybe

His name was Wolfgang but everyone called him Windy. I should have paid attention to the nickname. He was absolutely gorgeous and debonair and everyone wanted him. And I thought I got him.

He had a car, which added to his appeal and gave him added advantage in his pursuit of easy conquests. There weren't too many real cars around as yet and, the ones that were, were small little contraptions of two-seaters with doors that either opened to the sky or to the front. Windy could afford drinks at the bar and tickets to movies. Windy sold refrigerators to unsuspecting parents by dating their daughters. Windy took me for drives at night and tried to make love in the backseat. I balked. Something wasn't quite right.

We never went dancing together, we met there. He never sat at my table or escort me out of the hall to his car. I had to meet him in the parking lot. When questioned, Windy explained patiently that he had other fish to fry in the refrigeration sales business and, if anyone found out we were going steady, it would blow his chances of selling his fridges. Made sense at the time.

My competition included a drop-dead gorgeous girl by the name of Doris whom everyone called 'Snow White'. Black hair, blue eyes, white skin and a figure to die for. Not that Windy was serious about her. It was the fridges he was sacrificing himself for. What a salesman. I believed because I wanted to believe. Until the night Doris thought I should get out of the picture and sat down at my table to have it out.

What finally dawned on the two of us was that we were being had. Everything Windy had ever told either of us was a lie and I found out that my existence in his orbit was only due to the fact that my father was supposed to be a future client. There wasn't any future in that proposal, we already had a fridge.

It was unfortunate that our windy friend arrived in time to see the two of us having our little chat and, realizing that his chances of renewing either acquaintance were growing dimmer by the minute, he lost his charming cool and showed us what he was really made of. It was awful.

Obscenities the likes of which I had never heard spouted from a man who was no longer the handsome devil I had adored, but rather an ugly, vulgar and despicable punk who embarrassed the living daylights out of both of us in front of hundreds of people. Everybody loves a show and in no time at all we had acquired an audience who participated in the soap opera with hoots and catcalls and advice on how to proceed. I would have enjoyed it too, if I hadn't been in the middle of it. Question was, how to get out of the dance hall with a modicum of respectability on extremely wobbly legs which didn't feel as though they were capable of carrying me anywhere at all at the moment. It was the worst moment of my entire life so far and I wanted to die.

My 'Knight in Shining Armour' was a blond, quiet young man who was known to me simply by his nickname 'Mille.' He suddenly broke away from the jeering mob and as though nothing out of the ordinary was happening, stopped at my table and asked me to dance. I grasped the lifeline offered, clamped down hard on his arm, and made it down the steps and onto the dance floor in a reasonably decorous manner. My audience didn't like this interruption and now poor old Mille was booed for his efforts at being a Gentleman. He didn't seem to mind.

"Could you please help me get out of here?" I asked politely. "Only to the door," said my Knight. "After that you're on your own. You're an idiot to fall for that pig, he's a cheater, don't you know that?" I didn't. Love is blind. Didn't he know that?

He was as good as his word. Song over, he marched me back to my table, I grabbed my handbag and we left my sordid life behind me. Outside, he merely bid me good night, turned around and disappeared. I fought tears and tore up the street in the direction of the streetcar terminal as though furies were behind me.

I was doing pretty good holding on to my emotions and demolished ego until, two stops past the terminal, my parents, coming home from watching a movie at the Stern Theatre, entered the compartment where their daughter huddled in abject misery. One look at my unsuspecting Mama and the dam broke. A sobbing, wailing and pitiful to behold daughter threw herself at Mama's breast for consolation. Mama obliged. Papa took one look at me and disappeared to the rear of the car. The rest of the passengers, listening to my sniffling report clucked their tongues and commiserated. It helps a great deal having other people's sympathy.

Back home I continued to cry. It was all too much to bear. Suicide looked good but I didn't know how. Life was never, ever going to be good again. Love was the pits and men were mean creatures with whom I never wanted to have anything to do with - ever. Mama sat by my bed, listened patiently, and held my hand until I fell asleep. Papa cursed me for a fool.

In the morning, Mama told me to wash my face and smarten up. No more tears allowed. "One night is enough," she said. "There isn't a man alive worth crying over. Learn from it and pay closer attention to the object of your desire. No one dies from a broken heart." I didn't quite believe her but in the end she was right. I didn't die, not then, not later. I also never cried for another man again - but sometimes I cried for myself.

For the next few months, I stayed home and sulked. I couldn't face the audience who had witnessed my fall from grace and staying away for a while seemed a logical conclusion. I didn't think that anyone would miss me but someone did.

Two months after my sordid love affair ended, my 'Knight in Shining Armour' turned up on my doorstep, inquiring as to the state of my health. Having had no trouble recovering from my broken heart, my mental health appeared good but my physical one left a lot to be desired at that precise moment. I had a frightful cold and when Mother came and told the bundle of sniffling, coughing misery on the couch that a man by the name of Horst Mueller was at the door, asking to see me, I declined. Mother led him in anyway. It was cold and the boy needed a good cup of coffee. Turned out, the one everyone knew simply as 'Mille' had been baptized Horst and had spent the last two months trying to find out where I lived. My knight's efforts brought tears to Mama's eyes and got him a date for the following Saturday, providing my cold had subsided by then. It was the start of a beautiful friendship.

Entering the Klosterkeller premises after an absence of two months and on the arm of a date was thrilling. Expecting the mob to pounce and continue where they had left off, I was pleasantly surprised to find that everyone was simply happy that I was back in action. People are full of surprises.

For the first time in my life, I seriously dated a member of the opposite sex and it was great fun. We did all the silly things young people do when they are in love and it earned us smiles from the older generation who remembered their own days in the sun. The fly in the ointment here was my young man's plan to vacate his mother's flat. Of course, being able to do that meant leaving the country altogether as the chances of the natives getting apartments were getting slimmer by the minute, what with more and more East Germans piling into West Germany and the City of Berlin in particular. It made capitalism look so good to have people streaming into the West but it lost the West many a promising youngster who sought greener pastures in other countries. In the old days, they called it Voelkerwanderung (people migration).

Chapter 17

THE GRASS IS ALWAYS GREENER - on the other Side of the Hill!

On December 27, 1958, I turned 20 years old. It was time to leave home but in the Berlin of housing shortages, his or her own accommodation was something a young Berliner could forget about. So-called 'guest workers' from other countries and East Germans were turning up in droves and prohibited an unmarried Berliner from entitlement to a decent abode. There seemed to be an imbalance somewhere. I paid taxes but accommodation was reserved for newcomers and foreigners and people with large families.

I had no intention of producing children just to be eligible for a "Wohnung" but living at home with aging parents was also no longer an option. There comes a time when the generation gap gets too big to handle and the subsequent friction can only be avoided by parting company. It was time to start on my journey of discovery. I told Papa I wanted to immigrate to Australia.

"NO." End of discussion? Not this time. "If you don't let me go, I will wait until I am 21 and go forever and never come home." We are very cruel when we're young but it's also a defence mechanism. It worked to some degree.

Sister, having encountered numerous obstacles in her job searches since returning for the second time unexpectedly from England, had disappeared to Canada the year before and Papa proposed I start my adventures a little closer to home while, at the same time, having a little assistance from someone already on foreign soil who could give me a helping hand. It was a thought which was made palatable to me by the fact that my boyfriend was on his way to join up with an Uncle in Calgary, a town in the Province of Alberta in the far away land of Canada. He had already gone through the paperwork and two months into our relationship his Visa was approved. It didn't faze us too much. My own Visa was in the works and we didn't figure the distance between Montreal, where Sister resided, and Calgary would constitute a problem.

On the Atlas, it did not look very far. Europeans have a hard time grasping the size and distances involved in countries such as Canada, USA and Australia. It boggles the mind. On trains, a European is never more than 8 hours away from the Capital of the farthest country. The train from Montreal to Calgary takes 3 days. We were blissfully ignorant of this fact and dreamed of reuniting as soon as possible. To cement the relationship, we, very secretly, got engaged. Rings were out of the question as being too noticeable, but a little golden Buddha, hanging around our necks, was unobtrusive and thought of as simply charming by our respective parents. Little did they know.

Spring came to an end and the time of my paramour's departure loomed closer and closer. I wanted to do something special, wanted to make sure he never forgot me or replaced me. Wanted to leave him with something more permanent in his memory than a kiss in the dark doorway of our apartment building. I went to Mama for help and Mama came through.

He left with the memory of an entire day spent at our leisure at his home. It was magical, clumsy and exciting and opened up a whole new universe. We promised to love each other forever and we meant every word. We expected to be apart for only a few months and we believed that fact. We said good-bye a few weeks later without a worry in our minds, never realizing that time has a way of changing people and circumstances alter mindsets. I didn't keep my promise but neither did he.

My own visa arrived at the end of June. Sister had sent me a ticket for the ocean liner "Arcadia" to arrive in Canada on July 17. I packed two suitcases, changed DM100.00 into $25.00 Canadian and said good-bye to friends and family, all of whom thought I had lost my mind.

Mama and Papa waved from the window as Brother's car pulled away from the curb. At this first, and at all future departures, they never came to see me off but waved from the window as though I was just going off to work as usual. It was easier on all of us.

Brother cracked jokes about how long it would take before I would wet my pants and hightail it back home, but he held my hand all the way to the bus station. We might have grown apart somewhat over the years but we were still joined at the hip emotionally.

A surprise met us at the bus stop. My lost lover's mother, the formidable Mrs. Mueller, had decided to accompany me on the trip from Berlin to Bremerhaven, where my ship was waiting. I think she wanted to make darn sure I went after her boy. I was supposed to bring him back within a year.

As the bus pulled away, Brother put his hand to the window and I covered it with mine. It had all been so exciting until now but I hadn't realized that actually saying good-bye was like dying inside. I kept my eyes glued on his diminishing form until he disappeared from sight. Then I started appreciating the companionship of someone familiar, like Mrs. Mueller.

It wasn't a very long trip but long enough to make the acquaintance of my fellow passengers, all of whom had no idea where they were going, what they would do once they got there and only a few had any idea why they were going in the first place. Adventure was what most of us were after. Some of us got a little more than we expected.

In Bremerhaven we went through a passport and visa control, our luggage disappeared into the bowels of an enormous ship and we balanced over a wobbly gangplank into our new home for the next seven days.

Mrs. Mueller and I wobbled into our first misadventure. We tried following the signs for Cabin 138 on D Deck and ended up in the wrong part of the ship. I had an excuse. I was terribly short-sighted and known to stumble into men's washrooms frequently. Mrs. Mueller had no excuse and I blame her entirely.

The way to my designated cabin turned extremely ugly. There were pipes all over the ceiling, the walls were dirty and the door to cabin # 138 was smeared with fingerprints. Pushing it open, we found ourselves staring at two huge men with tattoos all over their arms and a scantily clad woman perched on what I presumed to be my bed. I was aghast. What kind of a ship was this? Straightening myself up to my full 4 feet 11 inches, and backed up vociferously by my future mother-in-law, I told them in no uncertain terms to please get the hell out of my cabin. It broke them up. When they had sufficiently recovered their mental equilibrium, they escorted two highly embarrassed women out of the crew quarters and into the more amenable passenger section of the Arcadia Liner.

Cabin 138 was in the bowels of the ship, had a permanently shut porthole and two bunks. No other passengers had booked themselves into this low-class section and, for the first time in my life, I was the proud possessor of not only my own room but basically my own corridor. Sister had spared no expense. It was the cheapest cabin that money could buy.

Mrs. Mueller finally took her leave, the band played 'Muss I' denn, muss I' denn zum Staedtele hinaus,' the ship's horn blew and we pulled away from the pier. Any thought about having made a mistake disappeared with the rupture of my streamer which fluttered away in the wind and then limply settled on the ocean waves. We were off. We were free. We were full of beans - and one day later most of us were seasick.

The Atlantic is full of surprises. Storms should not happen in July but they do and we encountered a nasty one. Water was sprinkled on tablecloths to hold the dishes, ropes were strung in hallways for people to hang on to and doors were locked to the outside where the waves crashed over the railings and washed anything loose overboard. Within hours, less and less people were able to hold on to their stomach contents and the little containers gracing the hallways were full to overflowing. About 50 of us managed to eat the little food our waiter suggested. Dry buns, only little portions of meat and potatoes, forget the soup and coffee. Just watching the soup move back and forth was enough to make another patient out of an otherwise hale passenger. Going down to my cabin was out of the question as the stench of the overflowing cardboard containers was enough to make even the sturdiest of stomachs lose its hold on still undigested contents. So the survivors sat in the rotunda and sang songs, told stories and got acquainted.

Mrs. D. was traveling with her 15-year old son to catch up with her husband in Toronto. One young man had been persuaded by the occupying Yankees to join a new religion called 'Mormons' and was headed to Vancouver to meet up with his newfound friends. I had never heard of Mormons but learned a lot about them. Never ask a religiously inclined person for something to read when you're bored. I was provided with three books, which permanently turned me off prophets or any other kind of person who presumes to have intimate conversations with God.

One girl called herself an Actress and everyone wondered how she would perform in a language none of us knew much of. The point of that was driven home when we decided to watch a movie in the ship's theatre. It was a Western and I still don't have any idea what it was all about. Discussing the action in the Bar later on, we found that every one of us had a different impression as to what went on in the story. We couldn't even agree on who was the bad guy and who was the good guy. Now that's bad news.

All in all, we had a lot of fun, especially after the storm subsided, the sun came out and the deckchairs filled up with sun worshippers. We even saw an iceberg floating by which sent some of the more timid personages looking for their assigned lifeboats. The Titanic disaster sure left its mark.

On July 17, 1959, some official stamped my passport at the port of Halifax and declared me to be officially an immigrant. At least I think that was what he said. My English lessons in school had taught me a lot about some guys called 'Peter Pym and Billy Ball' who ran around in ghost castles in England but hadn't taught me any practical sentences and therefore, apart from saying 'Good Day' and 'How are you', I was almost entirely devoid of any practical knowledge of the English language.

We spent the last night at the Bar swapping addresses and bolstering sagging spirits. Our friendly bartender declared us one and all to be insane for leaving the beloved Fatherland for something entirely unknown and we declared him a weakling with no sense of adventure at all. We were free of all restrictions imposed upon us by loving parents and determined to make the most of it. Some of us did. Some ran back home. And some went under. That's life.

Chapter 18

TRUE COLOURS!

I was sound asleep when the ship docked in the harbour of Montreal in the middle of the night. At breakfast, someone told me that, upon reaching the Pier, a woman was heard yelling my name. Sister had expected me to eagerly wave to her upon arrival and had brought some friends along to watch the family reunion. Nothing ever turns out right between the two of us. We are on two different wavelengths. When she's up and about, I'm asleep at the wheel.

When I finally disembarked, a not-so-friendly Sister accosted me sternly about my absence on the railing at 2 am in the morning. What was I to say? I usually sleep at 2 am after a strenuous night of drinking and saying good-bye to friends. It was an auspicious beginning, which was followed by a shopping trip to the nearest Deli where she borrowed $15.00 to cook me a nice 'welcome to the country' meal. Then we proceeded to her home-away-from-home in the suburbs of Montreal near Town of Mount Royal.

Looking out the car window, I asked why everyone lived in 'Lauben', which is what we called the kind of wooden summer house Papa had built and which are usually only used as summer residences but seemed to flourish all over the place in Montreal. Sister was horrified. Apparently, houses were built out of wood everywhere, even apartment buildings, and the only bricks visible on the outside were put there more for decoration than insulation. Strange place, this Montreal. I wasn't looking forward to winter. How could they keep these things warm?

Sister lived in the cellar, which she called a Basement, of a house owned by a Greek family. She shared her rather small apartment with a girl from Switzerland and, after having been introduced, we sat down to a meal of 'fried potatoes and scrambled eggs.' Seemed like either sister was broke or potatoes were extremely expensive in Canada - or maybe it was the eggs. This did not bode too well for the image of streets paved in gold. $15.00 didn't seem to get you much in the way of food.

When I proceeded to unpack, I was advised of the fact that, with sisterly love, she had already procured a job for me. I was to start next day, cleaning house upstairs for the Greeks. Suitcases at the ready, I was marched upstairs, introduced to a lady and shown my own room. It was a little overwhelming to say the least. However, it was a nice little room and it was the first room I had ever had to myself, not counting the little cabin aboard ship. I unpacked, lost a couple of items that appealed to Sister's tastes, and settled in with what was left. I was tired, I was scared and I wanted my Mother.

In the middle of the night, I was shaken awake by my irate relative and informed that there was a phone call for me and to please get out of bed fast. It was my lost love from Berlin who, not realizing that Calgary is on a different time zone, woke everyone up and into a bad mood. He had bought a train ticket for me to join him in Calgary. Not a bad idea, I thought. Sister was of a different opinion. Taking the phone out of my hand, she informed my hapless suitor that she had been given responsibility for my wellbeing in this country and, until I turned 21, she had every intention of keeping me out of trouble and out of Calgary and his hands in particular. I promised the love of my life to join him right after I turned 21 but also suggested he might want to leave Calgary and join me in Montreal instead. He declined, being very comfortably ensconced in the bosom of his uncle's family and not willing to face insecurity in Montreal and my Sister in particular. My Knight was showing some rusty spots on his armour.

We all went back to bed, never realizing that the temporary decisions made that night were permanent in nature. When you're old, absence might make the heart grow fonder. When you're young, it's more like "out of sight, out of mind". In the days that followed, I had other things to think about than my love life.

While my fellow immigrants were welcomed to their chosen country by Immigration Officials who put them into a camp and then let them loose on the unsuspecting population of Montreal to acclimatize and familiarize themselves with their new surroundings for an entire week, I scrubbed floors, washed windows and cleaned silver plates. While my friends were assigned jobs as housemaids to families who were fully aware of the fact that they were receiving a person into their homes who did not speak or understand English, my Greek family was blissfully unaware of my shortcomings. Sister had quietly understated my ability to comprehend what was expected of me in my new job.

My employers left the house very early in the morning and religiously left a note on the kitchen table, telling me what to do. Problem was, I couldn't read it. Calling Sister became a morning ritual. I read the note, she translated and I started work. Clean the floors, make the bed, wash the windows, polish the silver. How I hated that silver. They owned tons of the stuff, all put away and covered with plastic, it nevertheless got black and my beautiful long nails were soon sacrificed to the grooves and crannies of endless plates and bowls, spoons and knives. Silver stinks. I decided that, if I ever got rich, silver would not be in my inventory.

My employers also left me provisions for the day's food ration in the fridge. That was very nice of them, except for the fact that I had no idea what to do with a chunk of meat as I had never acquired the facility to cook. Mama had tried but I just wasn't interested and the only thing Mrs. Mueller had taught me was how to do scrambled eggs. There were no eggs, just this unappetizing slab of raw meat that I didn't know what to do with. Down it went to Sister who knew a lot about cooking and appreciated the donation and the saved money that went with it.

One evening I decided to brave my new world and walked to the bus stop to pick up my loving relative and walk her back home. People stared and I kept checking my body and face in shop windows trying to figure out what it was they were staring at but I couldn't find anything wrong with my attire. Then came the policeman and things got hairy. Five minutes into our discussion in which neither one of us knew what the other was talking about, Sister arrived on the scene. It was my shorts. People in Canada were not allowed to wear shorts. They wore something called Bermuda pants which covered your legs to just above the knees and my shorts were simply what their name implied - short.

Sister explained my recent arrival and ignorance of local custom and I was released into her custody. I was beginning to think that Canadians were slightly out of kilt with the rest of the world and morality in particular.

Two days later, on my day off, Sister and her boyfriend took me to the St. Lawrence River public swim park to relax and enjoy the Canadian way of life. I threw my clean, bikini clad body into the cooling water, only to emerge covered in muck from head to toe. This river was dirtier than the Teltow shipping canal had ever been and I wasn't impressed about the local facilities for cooling off. Scraping the dirt off my body, I came face to face with another morally outraged official. It seemed that bikinis were against the law in Montreal and I was again on the verge of being arrested. Sister repeated her speech about newly arrived ignoramuses and her silver-tongued explanation avoided a trip to the police station and incarceration.

The picnic was cancelled, I was declared a proper nuisance and further trips were cancelled indefinitely as I absolutely refused to get myself a one-piece bathing suit. I figured that with that kind of water I wasn't missing much anyway.

I spent the first two weeks in Montreal cleaning all day and visiting Sister and her friend in the evening - where everyone spoke German. This wasn't getting me anywhere in the language department and now it got worse.

Apparently, unbeknownst to me, my stint upstairs was only temporary. My real job was looking after the Greek pair's parents in the country. Sister was ecstatic. "It will be simply wonderful," she said, "the Laurentians are beautiful with lakes and rivers and you'll be in the fresh air and the two old people won't be any bother at all." I was also told that I would soon have to learn how to drive a car because during the winter I was to drive the old people to Miami, Florida and spend the winter there. Wonderful! I didn't think it necessary to tell anyone that I didn't like cars, couldn't reach the pedals in even the smallest version, and had never met a car which permitted me to see anything over the steering wheel. In addition, I had been a disaster on my bicycle with which I had had numerous accidents due to a lack of attention to what's happening around me. Bowling over humans on a bicycle is pretty painful - doing it in a car would have disastrous consequences. Winter was a long way off and anything could happen - and did.

The night before we left, my hosts and a newly arrived family relation visiting from New York invited me for a stroll to the nearest Dairy Queen. I hadn't been anywhere except the lousy beach and the bus stop since my arrival and the invitation was too good to be true. What I encountered was more than I ever expected. Ice cream in plastic containers, covered in chocolate, candies, cherries and bananas, a veritable paradise for ice cream lovers with unimaginable treasurers in bright lights, garish colours and a multitude of flavours. I settled for a milk shake - banana please. Nothing like it on earth. Cool, filling, delicious and entirely satisfying.

I don't know whether it was the milk shake or these people's earnest attempts at making me understand, but the words coming out of their mouths started to make sense. It appeared that the young visitor wasn't at all agreeable to my leaving for the country and was trying to talk her friends out of the prospect. I appreciated the effort but also realized that it was too late to change anyone's mind. I have forgotten her name but I can still see her face, laughing over the Banana Split. She was the first person I actually talked to in English and who seemed to understand what I was talking about. She never knew what it meant but she gave me back my confidence and my spunk. She made me remember who I was - a highly-trained Berliner secretary out for an adventure and not just the maid upstairs who cleaned silver. When we packed the car in the morning, she hugged me tight and wished me luck. I've been pretty lucky ever since.

Sister was right. The Laurentians were beautiful. Lakes, rivers, hills and the smell of pine trees. We passed very small villages where three cars on the road constituted rush hour and five people talking on a corner was a mob. It was all very far away from city life and entirely alien to a city dweller used to the hustle and bustle of a modern metropolis. I hadn't yet arrived at my destination and I was already homesick for the silver in Montreal.

The two old people who greeted us at their country cottage on a lake were delighted to see their relatives but not too impressed with their new companion. We had a problem. They couldn't speak English very well and neither could I. The language they all communicated in was totally Greek to me, literally. We had supper together, where I functioned as the local deaf-mute, and then my English-speaking employers got back into their car and disappeared over the horizon.

The old lady ignored my presence, but her husband took pity on me, showed me my room and brought me a cup of hot milk while I was unpacking. It was really a very beautiful place but it wasn't very suitable to having adventures.

For the next three days I scrubbed floors, washed all the walls in the kitchen, peeled potatoes, helped with cooking lunch and dinner and made breakfast. The old lady screamed every time I misunderstood her intentions, which was practically all the time, and the old gentleman tried to make my life easier by teaching me words, pointing and gesticulating and making me repeat them. I was learning fast - only problem was, I was learning Greek and I didn't think that would help me much in getting a job in an office in the near future.

Every night I sat at the lake and cried my heart out. To feel sorry for one's self is a wonderful luxury and not to be underestimated but there comes a time when there is too much of a good thing. On day six I stopped crying and called Sister.

Basically, I gave her two choices. Either she was going to get me out of there or I was walking back to Montreal and going to the Immigration offices to see what they could do with me. She didn't really have much of a choice because, had I approached the Immigration authorities, I would very likely have been removed from her custody and been taken over by the Canadian department- in which case her name would have been mud with Papa. She came next day, with her boyfriend driving, and I bade my employers a fond farewell - in Greek.

During the two hours it took to get back to civilization, I learned that I was a total failure, a terrible inconvenience, a nuisance and a debtor. Turned out that the money Sister had paid for my trip was a loan, not a gift, and I was expected to work my debt off as soon as possible. Running away from positions wasn't helping the situation any. So the money I had earned for three weeks of work went against my loan and, seeing as I was stone broke as a result, Sister, out of the goodness of her heart, had already procured me another job. I was going to be dropped off at a mansion in the Town of Mount Royal area of Montreal and become a Nanny to two adorable children.

We arrived at 3:00 pm at an ivy-covered old house on a corner lot and I had an interview with my new prospective employers. They must have liked my looks because they never heard my voice, as Sister covered the questions in her usual formidable manner and I never had a chance to reply - not that I knew what they were asking anyway.

I started being a Nanny in the morning. Boyd was 4 and Sarah was 3. My job was looking after them, nothing else. There was an English housekeeper named Olive who lived out and arrived every morning around 8:00 am to take over the running of the house. I served breakfast at 7:00 am to the master of the house who was a charming young man who said please and thank you and smiled. A definite improvement over the Greek Witch of the East.

The children and Olive proceeded to teach me English, which on occasion resulted in calamities. The kids asked to play hide-and-seek. They hid - but I didn't seek. I didn't know what seek was. They got

114

mad and it took Olive to straighten things out. Every night I sat at their beds and read them stories. My pronunciation left a lot to be desired but they seemed to get a kick out of correcting me. The four of us spent all our waking hours together and at night I sat and watched TV and tried to figure out what everyone was talking about. Mitch Miller was a great help.

The show was called "Sing Along With Mitch" and there was a men's choir who sang their little hearts out for an entire hour. Whatever they sang was written on the bottom of the TV screen and a little ball jumped from word to word as they intoned it. Dictionary in one hand, I sang along with Mitch and the Gang, learning without effort every American and English folksong they presented. It was fun, entertaining and the German accent on 'Dat's a long vay to Tibberery' sent Olive into hysterics.

On the culinary front, Olive made the meanest Shepherd's Pie I've ever tasted. On the gossip front, Olive was a bottomless pit of saucy tidbits about her own employers and everyone else in the neighbourhood which led me to the second major decision in my life, next to never owning silver, namely never to employ help. There are no secrets in a house that employs servants. Olive showed me things in drawers I never wished to see and elaborated on secrets I had no wish to know. Housekeepers from across the street and down the lane came visiting when the lady of the house took off for her 3-times-a-week visit to the hairdresser. Coffee cups filled to the brim, they settled down to exchange the latest news about their respective salary providers. It was an eye opener about how high society functions and I think it effectively prevented me, albeit unconsciously, from ever becoming a member of that particular rank and file.

Other than that, I thought I was turning into a pretty good Nanny. Unfortunately, my opinion was not shared by the lady of the house. This was one strange mother. All day long, she reclined in a lounge chair in the garden, reading or just sun bathing. If the children came within 10 feet of her, she'd call for me to take them somewhere else. My innocent question of whether she would like to join our game earned me a sharp rebuke and the advice to mind my own business and what in hell did I think she hired me for. Sorry I asked!

Her husband was very handsome and kind and I was beginning to think that the male variety of Canadians were definitely preferable to the female version. My male employer taught me English during his entire breakfast session and he also had a great sense of humour, which came in handy one night during bath time.

The little boy had a habit of playing with his little wiener while I was towelling him dry and I asked him to stop doing that. His reply of, "My Dad plays with his too" was innocent and would have been quickly forgotten had I not turned around to find myself face-to-face with the adult version of the wiener player. The both of us turned purple and then burst out laughing. What else could you do? Sometimes I wonder what happened to Boyd and whether or not he's still playing with his.

I had been with them for one month when the not very 'motherly' Mother called me into the dining room and informed me that I was fired. No reason given. I had never been fired; it was an experience in humiliation, especially as I believed to have done a good job. Calling Sister and informing her of my misfortune wasn't inclined to make me feel any better.

I had now been in Canada for one month and three weeks. I had hardly seen anything of my new surroundings and I was getting a little grumpy. Adventures were not supposed to consist of cleaning, scrubbing and baby sitting. My one free day a week was usually spent at Sister's new apartment, doing exotic things such as washing, cleaning and setting up house. Sister had been asked to leave her basement suite after I vacated my position with her Greek landlords and had also lost her job at the office, apparently because of my many phone calls. My life was riddled with guilt, I was totally in debt, I had almost been arrested twice and I hadn't had a day of fun.

The silver lining on the horizon was a new job for me that my caring relative had found in the paper five minutes after my phone call. Off we went for the interview, which I passed with flying colours, speaking for myself this time.

My new job did not start until Monday and, this being Saturday, I implored Sister to take me out of the house and into society, threatening suicide and whatever else came into my head. It worked. We took the bus downtown and ended up in a place called the "Palais D'Or" which vaguely resembled my favourite nightclub, the Klosterkeller of Berlin fame. The Pailais D'Or was ostensibly a German Club but was frequented by every nationality that had invaded Canada during the 1950's. Yugoslavs, Hungarians, Germans, Austrians, Swiss, Dutch, French and English and a smattering of Canadians shared tables and danced to a big orchestra playing swing and rock'n'roll. I thought I'd died and gone to heaven.

It is an unfortunate fact of life that making friends is a lot easier when you have a pleasing face and a shapely body. I had both, so there was no scarcity of men asking me to dance and wanting dates in the process. It was a wonderful evening that promised life after cleaning and I revelled in it. Sister found an old friend and decided to go home early after having been assured by one of my new acquaintances that he would take me home safe and sound at a reasonable hour. 1 o'clock in the morning is pretty reasonable for a Berlin night-clubber. We sat in his truck outside Sister's place and my new friend asked if I wanted to have him as a boyfriend. I already had one, however far removed, and I graciously declined. But I did ask him to help me find a girlfriend, which I was in dire need of. He promised to see what he could do and we parted company.

Entering Sister's abode, I found the atmosphere icy to say the least. Sister was definitely taking this 'responsibility' bit too far. I had not had a curfew to speak of since I turned 18 and being told that it was unsuitable to sit in cars in the middle of the night with a young man was a little over the top. Enough was enough. I told her to shut the hell up, leave me alone and went to bed. I was the breadwinner in the house; I had rights. I went to bed, praying that my new friend would keep his word.

Monday morning I was dropped off at my new position. Nanny to two young girls, aged 11 and 13. My bedroom was in the basement, a black hole without windows and an old couch for a bed for which I was handed sheets with great big holes in them. I never even unpacked. I looked after the girls, learned more English and scrubbed. By this time, I was even getting pretty good at it, albeit never getting to the point of either enjoying or liking the procedure.

Two weeks into my tenure, spending my free time at Sister's, I received a phone call. "It's a female," Sister explained in a derogatory manner as she handed me the phone. "I'm not a female," screamed a voice into my ear. "I gave her my name which is Erika. You tell that woman to mind her manners." Now there is a Berliner for you, straight forward and right to the point. I fell in love instantly with a girl I'd never laid eyes on but had every intentions of getting to know better. We made a date for my next day off. "We'll meet at Dunne's. You can't miss it," she said. "Best smoked meat sandwich in town." She was right about that. I've never had a better one.

Five days later I sat in a booth and found myself looking at the warmest smile in a cheerful face that ever lit up a room. More than 40 years later, she's still the best friend I've ever had and that's saying something.

It was pure heaven to sit in a restaurant with a friend and just chat and find out how other people lived in this city that to me was an endless row of dirty pots, dirty sheets and grubby windows. Erika was a Maid and had been for almost a year. But, unlike me, she ruled the house. Her employers were full of praise even though the only thing she ever mastered to cook properly were steaks. It was all they lived on, steaks and salads. Interesting diet. She had two days off a week and had no intention of leaving a profession that left her alone in the house to do as she pleased for most of the day. She made good money, wasn't overtaxed and still properly appreciated. What a difference. It sounded good for her but it wasn't good enough for me. I had my eyes on getting back into the groove of things as a functioning secretary. Somehow, cleaning after people was just not my vocation.

I was perfectly correct in that assumption as two days later I got the sack again. My employer had looked into the basement and noticed that all of my things were still properly packed away in my suitcases and she thought that was an insult to her hospitality. All I had to do is close the suitcase, call my trusty male acquaintance of Palais D'Or fame and ask him to pick me up. I was getting immune to rejections. As long as my debt was diminishing, I didn't care where I ended up. I felt that, without that debt hanging over my head, I would be free to do as I liked and might even disappear altogether from the sight of Sister's spying eyes and moral admonitions.

Back at the ranch, out came the newspaper, down came the pencil and grab went the telephone. I was off to my next interview within the hour. A small house, a neat room for myself, a husband, a wife and a son to look after. No sweat. I'm an expert.

I moved in next morning. First thing, put on the uniform. I used to have to wear a uniform when I looked after Boyd and Sarah and I looked like a sack of potatoes in it because there never had been a maid, before or after me, who needed to be fitted for a small frame of 4 feet 11 inches and weighing 95 pounds. My new uniform was white for daytime and had to be held up with a belt. Every evening, I had to change into a black dress with a white apron and a peculiar contraption was put on my head which I had last seen in an English movie dealing with butlers, maids and murder.

I was taught to only serve from one side, take away from the other and never to stack two plates on top of each other. To a sensible human being this doesn't make sense at all but they were paying me good money, so what did I care. Cleaning the pots, adorned with copper bottoms, took at least two hours but the food my lady served was worth the effort.

In the morning I got breakfast ready for the man of the house. I had to walk through the dining room, down the hall to the kitchen to get his grapefruit, coffee and toast. Coming out of the eating area one faced the bathroom before turning to the kitchen. On my second morning, I was surprised to find the door to the bathroom wide open, the shower door ajar and a spectacularly naked male figure vigorously scrubbing his particulars.

I am a total idiot when it comes to the subtleties of life and to this day, some jokes go right past me. All I perceived in my innocent 20-year old mind was that the poor man wasn't aware of the spectacle he presented, having forgotten to close the door - so I did it for him, eyes properly averted. It can happen to anyone, right?

However, on my second trip, wouldn't you know, the door had miraculously been re-opened and the saga continued. I closed it, he jumped out of the tub and opened it. It went on for days without either one of us ever mentioning the fact. I had never heard of sexual harassment and no one would have believed me anyway.

The female portion of my employers, on the other hand, was charming, polite and absolutely gorgeous, albeit only after 2 pm. She liked sleeping in. So at noon she called for a pot of hot, black coffee and spent the next hour sipping that concoction. When she finally emerged from the bedroom, it was a bleary-eyed, dishevelled, lipstick-smeared woman who entered the bathroom, only to emerge one hour later as a Beauty, every hair in place and every lash painted to the exact amount of mascara it could hold. It was amazing and totally against every rule about make-up removal I had ever learned. You were supposed to take it off at night before you go to sleep or it would ruin your skin. I should have told her. She probably paid a heavy price for her negligence and she was very nice to me.

I asked her for books and was given the liberty of exploring her young son's library. I chose books that had pictures in them and in the process learned about Ruth and Naomi and the Jewish religion in general. All the picture books happened to be religious. Heroes, battles, prophets and ladies in distress. Fascinating stuff that.

Being a servant means being invisible. I had a hard time with that. Being a servant means you're not allowed to laugh when someone cracks a joke. You're not supposed to sing out loud when you're scrubbing pots, thereby bothering the lord and lady of the house taking their coffee in the next room. When you're a servant, you're a nobody. You're a ghost, a non-existent object, you move without sound and you leave no shadow. I don't work that way.

I was down to humming when my lady was kind enough to let me in on my problem. "You're not right for this profession," she said one day. "You know enough English to try for something else." Good advice, but where do I go? "Dominion Textile sometimes employs newcomers whose English is not quite up to scratch for simple jobs," my lady advised me. And with a pat on the back and an unscheduled day off, she sent me on my way to a new life. God bless her!

Chapter 19

ANYTHING GOES!

Dominion Textile turned out to be the biggest textile company in Quebec. Their head office was on Sherbrooke Street in downtown Montreal, which was easy enough to find. The staff at the Personnel Office gave me an application form and left me to my own devices. I tried but I didn't get any further than the second line. What am I? F or M? Female or male? I didn't know what either meant. Back I went to the desk where I was cheerfully advised that, indeed, I was of the female variety and could safely tick the F.

From there I went straight downhill but, with the assistance of an ever-increasing audience who seemed to find the filling out of an application form hilarious, I managed to complete every question to my fan club's satisfaction.

With their help, we proceeded cheerfully to the next step. An aptitude test. In every column there were three words on one side of the page and one word on the other. The three words said 'knife, shingle, tree' and the one word said 'house'. I had to figure out which one of the three words related in any way to the one word. However, when one doesn't know what a shingle is, one cannot connect that word to a house. My audience was not allowed to help me with that one and things began to look pretty bleak until the manager came up with an excellent idea. He took away my word test and handed me a sheet of paper covered in numbers. A row of numbers on the right and the same numbers on the left, albeit sometimes one or two of the numbers on the left were different from the ones on the right. I cheerfully ticked off the mistakes in record time and proudly presented that kind man with proof of my excellent eye coordination. Everybody cheered up and I was asked if I thought I was capable of filling a position where I had to "check". I thought they said "Cheque" and presumed they wanted me to write cheques.

Why on earth I would think that they would ask an ignorant immigrant to write out cheques for the biggest textile company in town is totally beyond me and entirely due to the fact that I was 20 years old, full of myself and sure that, once I was back in an office environment, there wasn't anything I couldn't do. Conceit runs in my family and I got most of it.

Having done everything in my power to their satisfaction, I now expected to be employed on the spot. Apparently it didn't work that way. I was told to leave my phone number and I would be called when something came available. I couldn't do that.

Desperation took hold. I was at the end of my rope. I couldn't face going back to scrubbing and cleaning and being a nobody. I shook my head and told them "NO," I needed a job and I needed it now. I wasn't going to budge until they gave it to me and they got the message. Four feet eleven inches of misery dared them to remove me from the premises. Short of bodily force, there wasn't anything they could do to move me. I was told to start on Monday.

Having only a few days to sort out my new situation, I called my truck-owning friend from the Palais D'Or. He knew of a German family who were renting out rooms on Sherbrooke Street and that evening, my lady let me go early to inquire into lodgings.

The room looked alright, the bed was firm and two other lodgers welcomed me into the fold. It cost $10 a week and I was allowed to use the kitchen. I didn't bother telling them that I didn't know how to cook and wouldn't be using the facility overly much. My new landlord was a taxi driver at night and a construction worker in the daytime and my landlady, highly pregnant and in definite need of some iron in her blood, weakly assured me of her friendship and promised advice, having spent some time at my new employer's facilities herself.

I finished up the rest of the week in high spirits, advised my parents by mail of my new position in life and the perks that went with it, collected my last salary on Saturday and left servitude behind in a cloud of smoke exiting from the exhaust pipe of my helper's ancient truck.

Sister was not pleased. Expecting to be lauded, I was subjected to a barrage of negativity that painted my entry into the office work force in the bleakest colours and promised dire consequences for my decision to leave the shelter of sisterly love and setting out on my own. I figured on taking my chances anyway.

I paid my first week's rent to my landlord and, with Erika in tow, descended into the bowels of Sister's place of employment at a Restaurant on St. Catherine Street. "SMACK" went the envelope containing my last debt payment and "SLAM" went the door on my way out. Money isn't everything but a debt is a sword hanging over one's head. I stayed away from incurring another one as much as I could help it for the rest of my life. I neither spoke to nor saw Sister again for a long time.

Monday morning I found out what 'checking' meant. My job was to check what other people were typing, a totally unbelievable position which would have sent every one of my co-workers at Telefunken into hysterics. Check your typing? Where I came from, your typing was either perfect or you were not allowed near a typewriter - period. But if that was what they wanted me to do, then so be it.

Not being very good at English, I became the most thorough checker they had ever had. I simply checked every word, letter by letter. When I found a mistake between the hand-written order form and the typed manuscript, I simply ripped the offending page in two and handed it and the original back to the culprit for a repeat performance. It was a very boring job but it beat cleaning silver.

My co-workers turned out to be of a very varied variety. No one had told me that there were a lot of people in Montreal preferring to speak French to English. Girls called Nicole and Madeleine proceeded to educate me on the history of Canada, most of which had not been entirely made clear in my history class. I knew of General Wolfe and the battle on the Plains of Abraham but I had no idea that the French had managed to hang on to their language, their identity and their culture to such a degree that they seemed to be basically still fighting the same battle.

I learned about Voyageurs and French Canadian heroines and tortured monks. Growing up with the stories of Sitting Bull and the Sioux, I knew a lot about the Plains Indians of America but not much about the Iroquois, Hurons and Seneca on the East Coast. The Battles fought in subduing these tribes were exciting news to a romantic mind and the French Canadians of history were presented as fun-loving, adventurous travelers who opened up the continent.

The English seemed kind of drab in comparison. However, my first priority was to perfect my imperfect English; conversations with the

French had to be curtailed until later. Every day I learned a little more and every week I got a little more comfortable in my new surroundings. Then I learned that there are people and then there are people and it doesn't matter what country you're in, there are always some one can do without.

In 1959, the subject of Word War II and the German population in particular was still a sore point to some people who did not seem to understand that the generation born during and after this tremendous occurrence could not possibly be held to blame for what happened before they ever got onto the scene. There were people who greeted me with "Heil Hitler" and a proper arm salute. There were people who in all earnest asked me how many Jews my Father had killed and there were people who would not speak to me at all. As I had pretty much got over my guilt feeling on the subject, I gave them the victory sign and smiled. There is not much one can do with that sort of people, so it's best to ignore them.

Until I met one I couldn't ignore. He asked me my name and told me I looked familiar. He said he had been a soldier in Berlin and had slept with numerous Frauleins and would I tell him my Mother's name as I might be one of his. My hand was in the air before he had finished and the slap on his cheek resounded around the office and resulted in a total work stoppage on all fronts. This was exciting.

Five minutes later I was back in the Personnel Office where my sojourn at Dominion Textile had started. It felt familiar. My protagonist, sporting a five-finger impression on his flabby cheek, tried to explain his transgression on the cultural level as a joke gone bad. I elaborated on filial responsibility and loyalty to family in particular and demanded an apology.

No one was more surprised than I when I got the apology, not only from this ignorant idiot, but also from my immediate superior and from the Personnel Manager in particular. I had fully expected to be fired on the spot. Like I said, there are people and then there are people. There was also another German.

Her name was Anna but that was the only thing she had in common with my mother. A few days into my sojourn into this strange new world, someone was trying to explain something to me and we got stuck. We tried sign language, painting pictures and gesticulated frantically but it wasn't working. We went to Anna for help. "Sorry," said my compatriot from Munich, "I leaned English the hard way. So can you." Thank you and may you rot in hell.

A month into my employment, I was promoted. My new job was again checking what other girls were typing, only this time they didn't type on a typewriter but on something called a teletype machine. As they typed out their orders, a yellow ribbon with holes oozed out of the machine. When fed into another machine, this tape could send the entire order to a receiver, miles away in another town and spit out a complete page, identical to the one typed in our office. Miraculous! My new position came with the added responsibility of having to find the tape relating to a misprint within a mountain of yellow ribbons. Upon finding a mistake, I had to dive into that mess, usually disappearing entirely from sight only to emerge scratched and dishevelled but victoriously clamping the offensive tape. It was fun.

My old job was taken over by a girl newly arrived from Holland who spoke English very well, German and French a little and Dutch to perfection. Now I had someone to go to when communication came to a standstill. Between her Dutch and my German, the English problems disappeared. What started out as an assistance turned into a friendship that has lasted to the present day.

The new location brought me closer to the typewriting order typists, two girls who were hammering away on the most sophisticated machines I'd ever seen. At Telefunken, the only electric typewriter belonged to a lady afflicted with some sort of nerve pain which prohibited her from hammering away at the ordinary manual variety. In Canada, there was no manual typewriter in sight. I didn't miss them.

What I did miss were the keys. The English version of the keyboard left a lot to be desired. There was no o, a or u with two dots on top. The Z had relocated to the far corner on the left, the Y was hiding and my typing speed of 120 words per minute went the way of the Dodo bird. I needed to practice - and fast.

As soon as the girls went to lunch, I borrowed their machines. Letters were pouring forth to Germany at an unprecedented level and with ever-increasing speed as my fingers familiarized themselves with the new board. I soon ran out of people to write to and asked if I could type some of the order forms while everyone was out to lunch. They didn't have a problem with that at all and pretty soon my lunch hour was spent typing my little heart out and very quickly doing it faster than any one of them. I ended up going like a bat out of hell through my mountain of tapes to find enough time to get back to typing. I thought I was helping myself getting back into the groove, the girls thought I was slightly crazy but one of them started taking two hours for lunch and disappear frequently for visits to other departments, asking me to take over for a while. It was a good arrangement but it wasn't entirely agreeable to the powers that be, who where observing an employee who seemed to be slacking off.

As if I didn't have enough guilt trips put on me already, I now got saddled with another one. They fired the slacker and put me on the typewriter. In my defence, I kept telling myself that my intentions had been entirely honourable but in 40 years I haven't been able to shake off the feeling of guilt of having taken someone else's position away from them. I never heard from the slacker again. I hope she got married and lived happily ever after. She was the girl who, upon hearing that at the tender age of 20, I was neither married nor engaged nor did I date anyone seriously, proclaimed to all and sundry that she would commit suicide if she wasn't married by 21. She was 18, very pretty and I hope she didn't die by her own hand. Personally, I had no idea what she was talking about. Marriage was not on my agenda.

On the professional front, things were looking up. It had taken me two months to get back to the typewriter, advance to the astonishing salary of $40 a week and add another girl to my ever-widening circle of friends. On the personal level, things were a little bit more complicated. I still couldn't cook and on $40.00 a week, restaurant food was out of the question.

Breakfast was a bowl of cereal, lunch was a hearty sandwich, but dinner was a definite problem. To the rescue came Mr. Campbell and his soups. Every night, seven days a week, 31 days a months. Mushroom, Vegetable, Hearty Beef, Chicken Noodle - there is only so much a stomach can take. Mine went on strike. To this day, a mere whiff of a Campbell's soup sends me into convulsions. I needed help and the Palais D'Or was the place where I found it.

In the Montreal of 1959, drinks were not served on Sundays until accompanied by a meal. In the Palais D'Or, the problem was solved by serving a piece of German bread accompanied by a European wiener with a drink order. Everyone ordered drinks but left their wieners to rot. Except me. I ate my own portion and everyone else's in the process. When I couldn't eat any more, I wrapped up the leftovers and my dinner menu was set for at least three days. For the rest of the week, I agreed to dates. Every date was confronted with the challenge of buying me something to eat before going to the movie house, my excuse being that I had to work late and had had no chance of satisfying the cravings of my body. Hoping that, after having satisfied my stomach, they could then concentrate on some of the cravings of their own, dinner was forthcoming promptly. Sated and happy, I enjoyed the movie, thanked them profusely, kissed them good night and disappeared rather quickly into the bowels of my apartment building on Sherbrooke Street.

It wasn't an ideal arrangement but as far as I was concerned, it was survival of the fittest. It couldn't last, of course, but by the time everyone caught on to my scheme, I had met girlfriend No. 3 and was well on the way to become, if not a gourmet chef, a good, solid, everyday cook.

Having shared my life with two other roomers and the couple inhabiting the apartment, it was time for a change. My Landlords were kind but becoming involved in their personal life was a pretty horrible experience. Having to help out with birthing problems was not my idea of fun and I wasn't going to wait around for an encore.

The man of the house was hardly ever there, not even when his lady started contractions and proceeded to howl, indicating a lung capacity of enormous proportions, never to be guessed at in such an anaemic looking individual. I called a cab and accompanied her to a dismal hospital where nurses relieved me of my charge. I spent the rest of the evening walking the halls, trying to avoid being overrun by screaming women who waddled in a funny duck-like way, cradling their huge bellies. It wasn't a pretty sight and any thought I had ever had of having a baby went right out the window.

I spent hours on the telephone, trying to locate the culprit of this situation who was merrily driving around town in his taxi cab but the baby arrived before he could be located and I was therefore delegated a family member and called in to admire the newborn. I wasn't quite sure what to make of it. I had never seen a newborn and the object cradled in the proud mother's arms did not in the least resemble the rosy-cheeked, pudgy-faced baby on the Gerber baby food advertisements. Nothing ever turns out the way you are led to believe. For years I believed that newborn babies were probably the ugliest little critters I had ever come across. Until I had my own.

Chapter 20
IN SICKNESS AND IN HEALTH
- Oh Yeah?

Christel could do everything. Sew, cook, bake and clean to the point where you could eat off the floor. We met through some mutual acquaintances, all of whom were from Berlin and all of whom were very different from the people I had left behind. They were older than I was and much wiser in the ways of the world. Taking me home one night, one of them advised me that it was entirely old-fashioned not to invite him into my bedchamber as it didn't really matter in the end whether I knew him one day or one year. It mattered to me. Being old-fashioned has its advantages. I showed him the door politely. In his brave new world, I would have kneed him where it hurts.

My new girlfriend lived in a different part of town but under the same circumstances. A room of your own at $10.00 a week, share the bathroom and kitchen and not much privacy. We talked and a week later we found an apartment on Goyer Street in the Cote des Neiges district of Montreal. This was a proper apartment that we would share with an English lady named Olive who occupied bedroom No. 1. We decided to make one room into the bedroom, the other into a living room and thereby created a total home atmosphere to be shared by everyone. Our new roommate happily agreed to the arrangement.

Olive was quite a few years older than the two of us and provided a calming influence on our hectic lifestyle. We shared the cooking, the cleaning and the shopping and saved ourselves quite a bit of hard-earned and much needed money.

Winter had arrived with a vengeance and winter in Montreal is not something to be taken lightly. I needed leotards, thicker pants and boots. It is not possible to go out without having the ears covered and no one in their right mind sets forth to brave the elements without gloves. Everything I had saved went for these necessities of life and Christmas seemed doomed. I knew that Mama would understand if I didn't send anything but I wouldn't have been able to live with myself if I didn't. Erika came to the rescue. She lent me $20.00 and we went shopping.

Something for Brother, something for Papa, something for Mama - it wasn't much and there was still room in the parcel. In desperation I bought an item that looked like a book but, when opened, showed rows upon rows of Lifesaver candies. Everybody loves candies. Right? Wrong! My family never let me forget it. Every year they made me promise not to send Lifesaver candies. They were spitting them out all over the place all through Christmas. The German experts on candies did not think that Canada was a place were people knew the slightest about candy making. Canada was written off as barbaric. You just can't win them all.

It took me a month, $5.00 a week, to repay my loan. But Mama was happy, Papa had a good laugh and Brother had a conversation piece. What more can you ask for?

Living arrangements organized to everyone's satisfaction and working conditions being excellent, we were now able to concentrate our leftover energy on entertainment. There was the Palais D'Or, the big band dance hall where all the newcomers from Europe got together and practiced multi-culturism before the word was invented. Every Sunday night, halfway through the evening, the band would strike up and play folk dances from all over Europe. There were the Yugoslavs, arms around each other's shoulders, travelling at great speed around the dance floor. The Greeks in long lines, hands linked high in the air, knees bending and legs crossing, faster and faster until they basically collapsed. There were the Hungarians, whirling their dance partners in circles to the beat of violins. And then there were the Germans. Or rather, they were not.

None of the Germans I knew in Montreal had any inkling of the dances I had learned with my tall girlfriend of folk dance fame so long ago. How I missed her. We could have shown them a thing or two. But Annelies had absconded to Australia and, as my feet pounded the floor to the sound of the good old German folk dance beat, I hoped she didn't run into the same problem over there.

Friday nights were reserved for the "Badewanne" (Bath Tub), a small nightclub upstairs on St. Catherine Street, just up from Dunn's famous Smoked Meat Sandwich shop. Here we could dance until the early hours of the morning and then head down the stairs and stuff ourselves with Dunn's speciality.

There was the Hofbrauhaus with the definite Bavarian flavour and the Queen Elizabeth Hotel Bar for the more sophisticated dates. And there was Bar-B-Q Chicken.

Montreal style Bar-B-Q Chicken is not to be confused with any ordinary chicken meal. It was juicy, it was delicious when dipped into the accompanying gravy, and it was cheap. The Paris Bar-B-Q at the corner of Goyer and Cote des Neiges was frequented on a regular basis and never lost its attraction. Adventures were fast in coming and we did not turn our backs on them.

One evening at the Palais D'Or, someone mentioned a desire to see Niagara Falls. It was January, but that didn't deter Christel and myself from jumping at the chance. We took off on a Friday evening, drove all night and arrived at Niagara Falls sometime in the morning. The town and the falls were deserted but that didn't put a stop to our desire to get up close and personal. They gave us rubber boots, coats and hats and sent us on our way. It was great sliding on our backsides down a staircase that was totally covered in ice. It was another thing trying to climb back up on a surface as slippery as the "Schlitterbahn" of childhood fame. While crawling on all fours, we spun tales of being marooned all winter on a platform overlooking a spectacular show of frozen ice castles. The falls still roared, albeit with a diminished force, and as the spray was thrown up into the air, it froze, providing us with an array of extraordinary sculptures that glittered in the sun. It took a long while and great effort by our, fortunately, stronger male companions to extricate ourselves from the slippery slopes. It also took at least three cups of hot chocolate to unlimber our frozen extremities. Rubber boots are not conducive to walking on ice for any length of time.

Niagara Falls was great and Toronto was not far away. Why not?

Compared to Montreal, Toronto was totally and utterly dull. There was a rivalry in those days between the two cities and, upon first sight, I heartily agreed with my fellow Montrealers that we lived in the better place. Everything seemed to close around 11:00 pm and being tucked up in bed at midnight on a Saturday night was not my idea of having fun.

Back in Montreal, life was good and I thought it was time to tell my love in Calgary that I had given up on the idea of joining him in the country. The deal had been that if one of us decided that the relationship was over, we would send the little Buddha, which still hung around my neck, to say 'fare thee well'. I had too much fun. I couldn't even remember my lover's face. I wrapped the symbol of my love into tissue paper and sent him on his way.

Winter seemed eternal in Montreal, with snow banks on the sidewalks so high I could not see over them and a temperature so cold I sometimes thought I'd freeze to death waiting for the Bus to arrive. Spring finally put in an appearance around Easter time and everyone got itchy feet. Someone mentioned a trip to New York and Christel and I jumped at the opportunity. When I finally took off in a car with five other passengers, my roommate waived from the window, being confined to bed with a nasty cold.

It was an odd assortment of travelers to say the least. The driver was French Canadian, his navigator was English, two passengers were from Belgium and only myself and the instigator of this adventure happened to be from my own country. Neither the two Belgians nor the French Canadian spoke much English, so the conversations were limited. What was even more limiting was the ability of both the driver and his friend to read a map. I remember visiting a Fort Henry somewhere along the way, the rest was a blur of backtracking and side winding and finally getting to New York four hours behind schedule and in the wrong part of town.

Utterly lost, we parked the car with the intention of asking the friendly natives for directions to Times Square. It didn't take us long to realize that all was not well in the neighbourhood. We were the only white people on the entire street and the looks from the darker-skinned variety of the human race could not possibly be considered friendly. However, ignorance is bliss and we proceeded accordingly.

I dashed into the nearest restaurant and petitioned the waitress behind the counter. I told her we were from Canada, very much lost and needed help urgently. She dropped whatever she was doing, escorted me back to the car and proclaimed to all and sundry in a very loud voice that what we had here were some lost Canadians from the country up north who needed to get back to civilization, namely Times Square. The mood of our audience, which grew more numerous by the minute, changed from one of hostility to bemusement. I could see on their faces what they were thinking. Stupid Canadians. Stupid Tourists. I didn't care. Just get the stupid kids off the block and on the road, please.

They did, amidst laughter and catcalls and, finally, friendly waves. Until I got back home and related our story, I never knew that going into Harlem was not on the official tourist list of recommendations.

Near Times Square, the driver and his navigator told us to assemble in the same place three days hence, revved up the engine and left the rest of us to our own devices. The German knew a hotel near the Square but, upon checking in, we found that most rooms were taken and all that was left was a suite. What's a suite? A suite is like an apartment with two bedrooms and one bathroom. That's nice. Was I to sleep in this suite with three young, nubile males without coming to any harm? There is a solution to every problem and mine was, although ingenious, also utterly naive.

We stood in front of an incredulous audience of hotel personnel, who watched in amazement while I made the three promise me - with a sombre handshake - that they would behave themselves like proper Gentlemen for the time allotted to us to share this "suite" thing. Then we booked ourselves in. To my generation, a handshake was a solemn promise and it never occurred to me, or them, to break that oath. They considered themselves gentlemen and I thought I was a lady. It's not fashionable anymore. Too bad.

In the elevator, the operator pulled out some postcards from his pocket and asked whether or not we wanted to buy some. All of us looked, recoiled and bolted. They were very dirty postcards of people doing things we hadn't thought of being possible. We heard the operator laughing all the way to the ground floor. Embarrassing to be so naive but what can you do?

We had three days and we managed to see every sight advertised in New York's brochures including the Easter Parade. I loved the city and its people who were a friendly bunch except when it came to Canadian money. They didn't seem to want it even though our currency was worth more than theirs in 1960. "We don't take Indian money," said the cashier at a movie house on Broadway. Indian money? I hadn't even seen an Indian yet in Canada and I didn't think they were printing the money either. Oh well, everyone has a hang-up.

It was grand but, four days later, we were glad that the driver managed to find our street corner again so we could rest our backsides for a few hours on the return trip. We managed to get out of New York and into the countryside but then the navigator promptly lost his bearings again. In the process, we got acquainted with lots of sleepy little villages and some beautiful scenery which we would otherwise have missed. There is a silver lining everywhere.

Back in Montreal, spring brought tender feelings to lonely hearts and Girlfriend #3 started going steady with a handsome young Austrian who, unfortunately, lacked one important factor in his pursuit of happiness - a car. To countermand this, the enterprising young lad recruited every eligible, car-owning bachelor he knew and presented them to me as blind dates. I didn't mind. We had a lot of fun on the weekends, driving on dusty roads through the country side, swimming in cool lakes, eating in establishments where sign language was the order of the day because the inhabitants of rural Montreal could not, or would not, speak the only language we had found necessary for our survival in Canada, namely English. None of the boys made any lasting impression. Until they brought the young lad from Nuremberg. Blond, blue-eyed, quiet, mild-mannered Theo with the lovely smile. Who could resist?

When we started talking about the rest of our lives, I thought it wise to, maybe, have another look at my Berliner in Calgary. Just to make sure.

Sister had been re-admitted into my immediate family just before Christmas. Papa always preached the value of togetherness in family affairs and had been pretty upset at our falling out. We called a truce and lived unhappily for more years than I care to remember.

At the time I decided to vacate Montreal, Sister's love life with a Swiss boyfriend had hit rock bottom. I talked her into leaving all this behind and together we boarded a propeller plane destined for the distant province of Alberta and the unknown territory of Western Canada.

I had looked forward with great anticipation to my first airplane ride and, true to form, it turned as sour as all my previous 'great expectations'. That plane made stopovers at least three times before it landed in Calgary and, while descending the first time, I found out that I would have been a disaster as a stewardess. My left ear started hurting and wouldn't stop. Between the stewardesses and the advice from every passenger in my vicinity, I tried everything from yawning to swallowing, from holding my nose and blowing to screaming at the top of my lungs. Nothing worked to expel the air out of that orifice and the pain was excruciating. By the time we finally reached Calgary, I was reduced to a snivelling bundle of misery. It wasn't a good beginning to rekindle a long-lost relationship.

Within two days, Sister decided that Calgary was not her bag and took off for Vancouver, British Columbia. I didn't blame her. If Montreal had some laws that appeared totally crazy to a European, Calgary in 1960 was hick-town of the year.

In 1960's Montreal, a man could disappear into a tavern and no woman could go after him to get him out. No ladies allowed. Positively medieval by my standards. A strip club on every corner but no bikinis allowed on the beach, no short pants on the street and no women in a tavern. Crazy. But at least we could be out all night and the town never slept.

In Calgary, the same laws applied with the added benefit of getting kicked out of a dance hall at 11 pm. Night's over, thank you for coming! So what were young people to do? Seems in Calgary, what they did is drive into the countryside, use the car as a means to get intimately acquainted, get pregnant in the process and then oblige the participating culprit to propose marriage. Not exactly my cup of tea.

My ex-boyfriend tried very hard to make me appreciate the other side of the coin. He took me on the grand tour to Banff and Lake Louise and I was suitably impressed. I also found out that Mountains looming all around me dampen my spirit and that looking at flat prairies makes me feel lonesome. I couldn't possibly live there and found that he had no intention of leaving. End of discussion. My spirits lifted when he told me that he had a girlfriend in the wings, waiting for me to board a plane and disappear forever out of her line of vision. I obliged.

Montreal never looked better. I threw conventions to the wind and moved in with my boyfriend, which in the early 1960's was not something one admitted in public or told one's parents. I also started looking for a new job. The Robin Hood Flour Company declined my offer for help and I retaliated by never buying any of their flour. Petrofina thought I would do a fine job - and I did, hating every day for two weeks. I don't remember exactly what I was supposed to be doing but whatever it was, it was boring and no fun. I called my Boss at Dominion Textile and he was happy to have me back but I couldn't, and didn't, expect to dislodge my Dutch girlfriend who had taken over my old job at the typewriter. So I returned to the mountain of yellow tape. I thought it would be alright but, of course, it wasn't. Watching other girls type at a pace which I knew I could top with one hand tied behind my back was not to be borne.

I asked for a job in some other capacity and was sent to the affiliated company of 'Styled Cottons' at the other end of town near Park Avenue. They took one look at my typing speed and offered me the job forthwith. Their typewriter was a combination typewriter and calculator. I typed in the amount of a certain textile, the price and –Bingo-, the calculator typed in the total amount due. When all orders had been entered, the machine added up the amounts to be shipped, the price for all, added tax and gave the total amount. Pure magic. No one had heard of computers yet, so this was one wild typewriter.

There were only about ten of us in the office and I shared the typewriter with a girl who I thought had the most romantic name I'd ever heard - Naomi. I remembered my former employer and her books and my new friend was suitably impressed with my knowledge of the Jewish religion in general and Ruth's mother-in-law Naomi in particular. We got on great.

The office supervisor was English and henceforth proceeded to correct me constantly in my pronunciation, which resulted in my being blessed with more of an English accent than a German one which is very confusing to a lot of people, including myself. My English was getting better by the day but sometimes expressions got in the way and led to disaster.

Every morning my co-workers and I would head down to the Coffee Shop for some toast with jam and a cup of brown water that the natives dared call coffee. It looked, and tasted, like dishwater. Coming from a country where the coffee is so strong one can basically put a spoon in it and make it stand up straight, the Canadian variety left a lot to be desired. The stuff gurgled away in a thing called a Percolator and tasted either burned or like hot water with one coffee bean swiftly dipped in and removed instantly. It most certainly never kept anyone awake but it was something to slurp with your toast.

One day some jam got stuck on my upper lip and my male companion of the day smiled sweetly and said "I'd like to give you a French kiss." I belted him one right across his foul mouth and stormed upstairs in a proper huff while he sat on his high chair at the counter, utterly confused and totally at a loss to know what had made me so upset.

It took four people, sign language, drawings and very embarrassing hand movements before we had the situation under control. In Germany, a French kiss is what a Canadian calls a 69er and it isn't anything you ever talk about in public. A kiss is a kiss is a kiss, but a French kiss is really something else. Well, in Canada, a kiss is something you give your mother. A French kiss is a kiss with the tongue. All the chap had meant to say that he would have like to kiss me and thereby lick off the offending jam on my lip. End of confusion. In Canada you can't wear a Bikini in public, can't wear shorts but you can French kiss just about anybody. Neat!

The Secretary got pregnant and I applied for the job. "Can you do Dictaphone," my Boss asked. I can do anything if it gets me a little more money. It was my one and only time on that machine and it provided a source of amusement around the office that lasted for weeks.

Thanks to Ronnie, the English Supervisor, my language skills had improved dramatically and I managed to type an entire letter without mistakes except for one misunderstanding. Styled Cottons was a textile company. They produced bales upon bales of textiles and sometimes some pattern would be cancelled. The word Mr. Feldgaier used to indicate this was 'omitted'. "This material will be omitted", he said. Having never heard of this particular expression, I proceeded to hear what I wanted to hear, namely, "This material will be home knitted."

Trying to imagine little old ladies, sitting in a big workshop at the Magog textile manufacturing plant, knitting their little hearts out, was too much for everyone. They didn't stop laughing for days. It's just as well that I have a great ego. I laughed along with them and appreciated the fact that I had learned a new word. I laughed even harder when they told me I got the job. The Dictaphone was packed away and I lived happily ever after, typing correspondence from handwritten copies.

Apart from such minor disasters, I had a lot of fun at work and a lot of fun at home.

I'm a born matchmaker and I had friends who were in need of male companionship. My common-law partner had lots of friends and blind dates were arranged with impunity. None of them ever worked out the way they were supposed to. The eager young man, whom I had targeted for Erika, promptly fell for my Dutch colleague who had only come along for the ride on a Friday night. So now we were a foursome, traveling around the countryside on weekends and spending most of that time stopped at the side of the road, taking off tires and walking them to the nearest garage for a fix-up. The boyfriend had a big Buick with very bad tires and a lot of other things that didn't work very well. My young man also had a strange way of looking at things.

One Sunday he told me that the Buick's generator had given up the ghost. I was in the middle of cooking and not paying much attention. I merely shrugged my shoulders and told him to go steal one. I learned that he was another one who took things literally. Two hours later he turned up and inquired as to whether I would mind helping him by holding a light to see by. He was installing a new generator. Halfway through the proceedings it occurred to me that it was Sunday, so where did he get the generator? "I stole it," said the love of my life. "You told me to." Then he proceeded to show me the under-ground garage where there were lots of cars, one of them now missing a generator. Life is very simple for some people.

The Dutch girlfriend and her Beau got engaged and the love of my life didn't lag behind. A ring was put upon my finger in one of the most romantic settings in Canada, the quaint old town of Quebec, and I thought life couldn't get any better. He wrote a letter to my Papa, asking for my hand in marriage, and Papa was suitably impressed. Papa never met my Theo. Lucky Papa. Lucky Theo.

Living in sin was fun and exceptionally daring, being morally not an accepted situation. We were pioneers of what is today a common practice over which no one blinks an eyelid. My Dutch friend was Catholic and not inclined to buck the trend. She and her Beau decided to make it legal and we followed suit. They had a proper wedding in a Church with a Mass being said and a nice reception with friends. A honeymoon followed where they both met their respective families in Austria and Holland. Everyone was happy.

The fiancée and I decided to keep it simple. Erika was my bridesmaid, Theo's pal Karl was his groomsman and some guy called Gerhard came along for the ride and to take pictures. I wore a simple dress with a jacket to match and we said 'I Do" in the dull surroundings of a Protestant minister's office. I could have done without the minister, not having attended church since my confirmation, but City Hall weddings were not acceptable in Montreal, it being a very Catholic town which necessitated a minister. It was neither romantic nor impressive and the situation wasn't helped by a nagging thought of being in the process of making the biggest mistake of my life. If anyone had asked me that moment whether or not I would like to spend the rest of my life with this man, I would have asked them if they were crazy. But no one asked and I was only 22 years old and not brave enough to call it off. It cost me dearly.

My childhood dream of honeymooning in Niagara Falls seemed like a good idea that turned sour within days. The Falls didn't let me down, everyone and everything else did.

The town of Niagara, without the snow cover, was a nightmare of pink hotels, pink bedrooms, heart-shaped beds and garish advertisements in bright neon colours. If anything could turn one off getting married, Niagara was it. In Germany we called it "Kitsch", overblown, crass and totally without taste. 25 years later, I re-visited the place. Even with the best mate in the world next to me, the place still ranked low on my scale.

Traveling around in Ontario, I was forced to come to the conclusion that my husband was not in the least interested in history, didn't have the slightest notion of why I wanted to wander through every fort we encountered and gave up accompanying me altogether after the third historical monument. He went to the nearest beer parlour to drown his sorrow over a honeymoon gone mad. It didn't get any better once we got back home.

When one falls in love, one does a lot of things which don't come naturally, mostly because its fun to be with the love of one's life. I went fishing because he asked me to even though I cannot find any fun sitting for hours in a boat, holding on to a rod, waiting patiently for something to nibble on the bait. Every fish I've ever known takes one look at my bait and disappears into the depth of the lake. I could not put a poor little worm on a hook and, purely by accident, my can of minnows always seemed to take on a life of its own and spill its contents of happy minnows into the lake.

The love of my life gave up taking me along the day he caught a real whopper that I was supposed to catch in a net. I got the fish into the net alright but when my man took the hook out his mouth, the poor little thing started wriggling like crazy. I let go of the net which promptly disappeared below the surface of the lake, taking the prize-winning fish with it. We could do without the fish, but we needed the net.

Man the provider dived in and came up covered in green plants, holding the net and looking like a perfect reincarnation of Neptune. It was too much. I laughed so hard, I tipped the boat over and poor Theo spent the rest of the afternoon reclaiming the contents of his fishing box and everything else that had sunk to the bottom of the lake. I sat on the beach and fumed. My hair was ruined, my make-up was running and I wasn't looking forward to driving home with a man madder than a hornet. Heck, I don't even like eating fish.

Hunting was worse. Hunting was in the fall. It was cold and wet and we had to wear very bright clothing because during hunting season everyone shoots at everything that moves. We saw a cow that had in big black letters written on its side 'I AM A COW.' Apparently it helped.

Hunting was standing very still in the bushes, straining the ears for the sound of a moose approaching. One day we heard some rustling in the underbrush, everyone froze. Faintly from somewhere across came a voice whispering – "Is that a moose?" I wasn't going to wait for him to find out. I yelled as loud as I could "I am not a moose!" Amidst gales of laughter came the answer from the opposite side, "Neither am I." And while we were still doubling over with our prospective hysterics, a moose galloped across the clearing between us and disappeared from sight. I was very happy for that animal but nobody else was. I was not invited on any future hunting trips.

Three months after my wedding, disaster struck. The East German Government decided enough was enough and, basically overnight, built a wall around the western part of the city of Berlin in an effort to keep East Germans from escaping west. They had a point. The joke in the city was, "Would the last one out of East Germany please turn off the lights." What had started as a dribble had turned into a flood and it had to be stopped. The wall was their answer and it was the most terrible thing that ever happened to my city.

Within a few days, families were torn apart, people died jumping out of windows trying to reach their loved ones, and the West Berliners had to listen to the screams of people dying on the ground on the other side of the wall and could do nothing to help them. I was far away, frightened by what the news media showed nightly on television and not convinced that they wouldn't think of taking over the western part of Berlin, thereby cutting me off from everyone I loved more dearly than the man I had married. I decided to go home to look for myself.

Having spent all my savings on a disastrous honeymoon and on furnishing our new apartment, I did not have cash available for a ticket. My man had never heard of the word 'saving' and was not able to provide assistance either and, through that experience, I learned that in this land of milk and honey, it was positively frowned upon to have no debts. I was refused funds at every Bank I approached because my immaculate record of paying cash was considered inadequate security. Funny system this. I had to enlist the aid of a totally indebted, utterly irresponsible friend who owed money at every department store, auto dealer and finance institution to get my loan approved. They couldn't give me money fast enough with his co-signature next to mine.

Within days, having graciously received permission to go on an unpaid vacation from my wonderful Jewish employers, I was on the plane and heading for home.

Chapter 21

HOME IS WHERE THE HEART IS!

Papa ignored the screams of the customs' officers, jumped luggage like a hurdler at the Olympics and had me in his arms before the rest of the family could get to me. They were right behind him. We made a proper spectacle of ourselves but who cared. Papa's little girl had come home, even if only for a little while.

Britz had not changed much, although the streets looked a little busier. There were a lot more cars on the road and new shops had replaced old ones. The neighbourhood greeted my arrival with smiling faces behind lace curtains. It was October, a little late to be hanging out the window, arms on pillows, which is what most of the older generation did all summer.

Home. A good cup of coffee and a salami sandwich. Mama knew me best. The family gathered in the living room, Papa, Mama, Brother and - look who is here - Sister.

Sister arrived in Montreal three weeks before I booked my flight to Berlin. She was also worried about the situation and left for home a week later. By the time I arrived, the goodwill and novelty of her return had already fizzled and what I walked into was the same old problem. Somehow it always seemed she was on the outside, trying to get in.

I spent the next two weeks trying to find old friends and reacquainting myself with old neighbours who seemed genuinely surprised that I still spoke German without an accent. It appeared that most of the young who had immigrated to far-off places like Australia, America, England and Canada sported a terrific English accent upon returning to their native land. I met some of them on future visits home. It was hilarious. They maintained they had lost their German mother tongue but in the process failed to acquire the ability to talk English with the proper grammar. It never ceased to amaze me.

Mama and I watched the workmen at the wall, protected (better say watched over) as they were by the East German Volks-Polizei. The first wall erected was kind of temporary but this one, now in the process of being cemented together, was of a more permanent nature. German workmanship at its finest. Off and on we heard of people trying to escape, being shot and bleeding to death without anyone being able to help. It was hideous.

A lot of the people I had worked with at Telefunken had lived in East Berlin. They got their salary in both currencies, equally divided. Now they were now no longer able to go to work, nor could they make contact with former friends. Families stood waving at relatives until the height of the wall reached proportions that made viewing impossible. Steps were built on the western side to overcome this obstacle but it only prolonged the agony.

It was a horrible contraption and it destroyed not only access to a part of my City, but also the mindset of a whole generation of Berliners. The jokes which had sustained the population during the War were no longer applicable. There was a pall over everything and everyone. There was nowhere to go without running into that Wall. The Underground route could not possibly be shut down completely, so the stations which were situated in the East were simply put under wraps. The train would slow down and, through the windows, one could glimpse the heroes of East Germany, the ever-present Volkspolizei, guarding a darkened platform, guns at the ready and German Shepherd dogs straining at their leashes. A futuristic nightmare straight out of a George Orwell book. The S-Bahn, part of which traveled through the eastern part as well, was only accessible on routes that did not touch the Free German Republic's territory. Papa no longer had a choice as to which route to take to go to work. However, this entire train system still belonged to the East and therefore presented a cash cow for the East. None of the money collected in fares was ever put into maintaining the system and the rails, already in bad shape when I was still in the business of using them, were now getting worse.

Berlin is surrounded by lakes and forests, all of which had now been marked by either fences in front of 'no-man's-land' areas or red buoys bobbing about in the waters. Guard towers sprouted like mushrooms, inhabited by two or three individuals who spent their entire day watching the West German population through binoculars. "Democracy isn't perfect," said John F. Kennedy years later upon visiting the Brandenburg Gate. "But we don't have to build a wall around it to keep people in." How true!

All this went on while the entire Western World watched, protested - and as it had shown in every other major crisis, did nothing. Papa tried to explain the inability of the Western Nations to interfere and what the results would likely be if they did but, looking at the situation from my limited perspective, I prayed they would change their mind.

What with all the sightseeing and visiting, two weeks went by quickly. I re-acquainted myself with my old friends from business school and found them all married ladies and no longer interested in dancing or hanging around. Some were expecting babies and priorities had changed. We were growing up, it was a different world and reality could no longer be ignored. It just wasn't as much fun any more and it didn't seem like home.

Sister left two days before I did and I enjoyed the time I had left with my loving parents. Mama wanted to know everything about my husband and I tried my best to make life with the man of my choice sound like fun. Papa didn't buy it but did not voice an opinion until the time came to say goodbye, when he slyly mentioned the fact that there was always somewhere I could run to if things did not work out.

Then it was that time again and Brother took me back to Tempelhof Central Airport. In what was becoming a tradition, Mama and Papa waved from the window, pretending I was only going to work. Brother and I held hands until my flight was called and he hugged me until I thought he'd break my ribs. I didn't have much in common anymore with this handsome stranger who drove a new car, wore the latest fashions and scolded me every time I broke into Berlin slang, which was, and still is, my favourite medium of communicating in German. It wasn't "in" any longer and in Germany, when something is not **"in"**, it is definitely **"out"**. Brother was following trends with a passion and I took individuality to new heights. We clashed continuously and waged war with furious abandon. But none of that stopped us from loving one another.

At the other end of the world, my husband took possession of my suitcase and escorted his still new bride to her home on Goyer Street. No walls in this city. No police carrying guns, no one dabbing eyes brimming with tears in public. Just a cold wind announcing that winter was just around the corner and people rushing to and fro, seemingly without a care in the world. The Berlin Wall had already stopped being the headline.

Back to work on Monday morning. First a quick jog to Naomi's house, where her mother greeted me with a hot cup of coffee. Jewish hospitality - you can't beat it. Then the usual walk to the bus stop and the remembered conversations on the ride into town. Our bus went to the garment district and was always bursting with Italian seamstresses who had absolutely no inhibitions about conducting their discourse from one end of the bus to the other. It was loud, vibrant, colourful and decidedly Canadian. There were so many different languages floating around on the streets of Montreal, so many different nations living together and getting along. Why couldn't Germans do the same?

At work everyone was happy to have me back and life went back to normal. What wasn't normal were the phone calls I got in the evenings when the love of my life was not there to pick up the phone himself. There were girls calling, asking for him by name and wondering as to who I was. When informed of the marital status, they seemed genuinely surprised and usually hung up. When confronted, my honey proclaimed that it was his friend Karl who had, just for fun, handed out our telephone number to various persons of the female variety. Karl confirmed the joke and the calls eventually stopped. Don't worry - be happy.

After my return, my 'better half' took to working late a lot or disappeared after dinner with his pal Karl to have a quick beer at the local beer parlour. I neither wondered nor questioned his whereabouts. A man is entitled to have a beer after a hard day of work, is he not? Ignorance is bliss but stupidity is inexcusable. If there had been a prize for it, I would have won.

My marital bliss consisted of working all day, cooking at night and cleaning and going shopping on the weekend. My lad was German and did not believe in chipping in with household chores. I had watched my Mother and Father and thought it was the proper way to conduct a marriage. It never occurred to me that my Father, the breadwinner, left home at 5.30 am and returned at 6:00 pm and that my Mother, the stay-at-home housewife, got up at 4:00 am to serve Papa's breakfast but had all day after that to relax and usually took a nap in the afternoon. When my weight dropped to 90 lbs and my monthly period started resembling a haemorrhage, my Doctor advised me to have a serious conversation with my so-called better half. It helped a little but not much. An attitude such as his could not be changed overnight.

Having been away for a little while, I also noticed that almost everyone we knew in our immediate circle of friends was either German or Austrian or Swiss and it seemed as though we had never left home. We partied together, went to the same clubs, which inevitably were of European origin, read German magazines and danced the weekends away with foxtrots and cha cha as though there wasn't a musical revolution going on in the World. It didn't feel right.

The friends I had made at work, originating as they were from all over the globe, were much more interesting and more fun to be with than the people my husband associated with but, trying to get him to meet my new-found friends of the multi-cultural variety brought him only discomfort. He was not comfortable and did not make the slightest effort at conversation which made my co-workers wonder at my choice of a mate. After a few miserable dinners, I gave up.

So this was what life was like as a new immigrant. One clung to the people one knew, one bought one's meats at the German Delicatessen, one read German newspapers and watched German movies at the one and only German Movie Theatre somewhere on Park Avenue. One criticized the Canadian lifestyle, while proclaiming all the while how much better life was in the old country. The home country, in the meantime, was changing rapidly and the memories one carried around in the head did not keep up with reality and people returning from trips seemed a bit shell-shocked before blotting out the experience and reverting back to bitching.

While living the standard newcomer life, my own personality seemed to split from the accepted norm. I dragged my true-blooded German husband to the latest craze.

The "Carry On" movies from England had invaded Canada and they were outrageously funny to watch. Problem was, they spoke the English of London with all its hilarious intonations and my poor hubby had not been exposed to that accent and expressions such as "Cor Blimey" meant nothing to him. At the end, he professed to not having understood a damn thing and refused to see another. Back to the beer parlour.

Seeing as in 1961 no woman was as yet allowed to see the inside of a beer parlour in Montreal, I continued my own adventures among Canadians who did not frequent these facilities and enjoyed my life. Until, on the 22nd of June, 1962, I celebrated my first wedding anniversary by munching a smoked meat sandwich at Dunn's with my friend Erika. We toasted this auspicious occasion with the famously lousy coffee of Canada and something snapped. Maybe it was the coffee. I don't know. But somehow, sitting there with Erika, thinking of my husband who at that precise moment was strolling around in the wilderness of Quebec, trying to find something to shoot at, I realized that things were not ever going to be any better than this. If this was my first anniversary, just what did I think I was going to do on my 10th? Smoked meat sandwiches and all, Dunn's did not seem the appropriate place for the occasion.

It wasn't much of a problem to come to a decision. Before I left home, Mama gave me a little advice. "You've got one life to live. No one has the right to spoil it for you. Do not believe in words, look at the actions. And the only reason two people should share a life is to make it easier."

Well! There you had it. I didn't exactly have a terrible time but I didn't have a good time either. I had no time. I had married a man whose idea of fun was at the opposite end of my spectrum. Where do you go from there? Absolutely nowhere.

When my hunter returned from the hills, he thanked me for the card I had sent along with his bosom pal Karl and, in reply, I asked him to agree to a divorce. He went into shock. Everything was going so well. Married life was exactly what he had imagined it to be, the only fly in the ointment being that I had not made an effort to learn to sew or knit and had absolutely refused to serve noodles instead of potatoes with my schnitzels. But there was time and I could still learn to be just like the girls at home in Nuremberg who cooked and cleaned and looked after the little ones and waited patiently on Sundays for their husbands to return from the Pubs after the "Fruehschoppen" in the morning, the get-together after lunch and the "Skat" playing after dinner. I pictured the scene in my mind, the happy males, cards in hand, bellies touching the table, swilling their beer being served by the only female attending, endowed with those huge arms carrying 15 beer mugs in one hand as pictured on all Munich Oktoberfest Posters.

I don't know if life in Nuremberg was ever like that and I very much doubt it is so now. I patiently explained that I did not think that the Nurembergers and the Berliners had very much in common and that it was best to part our ways and look for someone more compatible to share the rest of our lives with. If nothing else, the Nurembergers are very stubborn and mine was no exception. We ended up by agreeing to wait six months and, if things didn't improve, we would split.

I doubt he believed me because nothing changed. Six months later

I bought my ticket for an ocean liner leaving on December 1st, quit my job, said a tearful good-bye to my fellow workers and went to the bank to take out my half of the joint bank account funds.

It isn't easy to come to grips with deception. It is a terrible shock to the system to have witnesses to an occasion that could be better handled in private. My withdrawal slip was totally out of line with the amount of money at hand. After 1½ years of saving, we had apparently accumulated $15.00.

Every payday, for the entire time of our marriage, I had handed over part of my salary for deposit into this joint bank account. We were saving for a house and in the world I grew up in, the Man of the House manages the affairs of the money. No one ever told me that some people have absolutely no talent in that region or that some are totally devoid of comprehending the meaning of what is right or wrong or what is mine and yours.

Coming home in tears and confronting my soon-to-be ex-husband, I was told that he only meant to borrow the money and was going to pay it back as soon as possible. The sad thing was that he absolutely believed what he was saying. How does one deal with that?

On the day of my departure, he drank himself into a stupor and good pal Karl took on the role of seeing me off at the Pier. Having participated in my marriage as a sort of third wheel, Karl was familiar with our affairs and totally comfortable with being the shoulder to cry on. Only this time he did not have to worry about wet shoulder pads. I never felt better than when I slammed the door behind me.

Chapter 22

CAT WITH NINE LIVES?

By chance, the ocean liner to take me back to Germany was the same Arcadia that had brought me to Canadian shores three years earlier. I had managed to get myself a cabin a little above D-Deck but, this time, shared the space with a lady from Belgium and a German nurse from Kiel. No one snored and my fellow passengers proved to be very compatible.

Within hours, I became aware of the fact that the passengers on my return trip vastly differed from the ones with which I had shared the voyage coming the other way.

Immigrating to Canada had been families and very young people without much money to spend. Going to Europe were mostly young people with a sense for adventure, on their way to set the old world on fire, plus some returning to the bosom of their families for visits and to show off their newfound wealth and worldly wisdom. I guess I was one of the latter as far as the wisdom was concerned. Wealth had eluded me altogether.

Life aboard ship is a world in itself. The first night is spent exploring the surroundings, finding the right staircases leading to the right venue one wants to get to and usually getting thoroughly lost. Everyone eventually ends up in the Bar and, there, life's miracles happen. On this one, and on every Liner I have been on since, I witnessed the human race sniffing out their most compatible counterparts. Cliques form and usually stick together for the rest of the trip. Sometimes they form by nationality but not very often. Mostly they form by inclination and somehow they all seem to belong. Has anyone ever written a thesis on this? Someone should. It's amazing.

Dinner the first night was not by table setting, which only commenced at breakfast, so the nurse and I sat down at a table of our choice and, within seconds, were joined by three young Canadians of cheerful character. Two lived in Montreal and the third had traveled all the way from Ottawa. All of them intended to paint the old Continent red. On the other, more banal, side, my nurse was returning to Hamburg after a stint curing as many sick babies in Canada as she could and I, the soon-to-be divorcee, was hightailing it back to Mama's bosom.

We got along so well that, right after dinner, we talked the Purser into putting us together for all future meals. That accomplished, we necessarily needed to celebrate. The Bar is the one place everyone finds without trouble. Finding a free table was another thing. We eventually joined up with a group consisting of a lad from San Diego, a girl from Kiel and a Mick from Dublin. Last, but not least, another passenger pulled up a chair, joined the group and found that he couldn't join the conversation. The very handsome Alain Delong look-alike hailed from Geneva, didn't speak a word of English and made up for the lack of conversation by smiling a lot. We didn't want him and more or less ignored him. It wasn't until we hailed the waiter that we started appreciating our new pal.

Our repeated, polite requests for drinks were totally ignored. Granted, that man was very busy and he probably realized that the motley crew assembled in this particular quarter were not of the great tipping variety nor did they look as though they had the money to be rated 'champagne class.'

"GARCON!!!" It snapped like a whip and it stopped the man with the drinks tray dead in his tracks. "Oui Monsieur?" The monsieur said something and then pointed fingers at each of us. We got the message. As the finger made the rounds, we stated what we wanted and our suddenly attentive garcon wrote the orders rapidly on his pad. Within minutes we were served, monsieur paid the tab, we toasted his generosity and everyone learned their first french words. Merci Beaucoup!

There is something about people who have had money all their lives. People who are used to having other people do things for them. People who know how to order others around. There is an assuredness, a not-to-be-denied quality that I can only dream of. There are also some people who accomplish this feat without being rich. Sister has the facility and so has Brother. In Germany, people pretending to belong to this class are called "Hochstapler" (Impostors) and they are fun to watch.

148

I observed my own Sister once in a store on the Kurfuersten Damm. I knew for a fact that all she had in her purse was the subway fare home but she made the owner of this very expensive boutique drag down rolls upon rolls of high quality brocade and silk materials, only to advise him in the end that she would come back with her tailor to make a final decision. The man even held the door for her on the way out. This is definitely something one is born with. I wasn't and neither was the rest of my crew. We needed the lad from Geneva.

So there we had our group and, although we mixed and mingled with others in the coming days and nights, the basic octet played, sang, drank and danced together for the rest of the trip.

At our first breakfast, we found we had been blessed with an additional guest at the table. The most uncommunicative, miserable, positively introverted human being I have ever come across. If he said three words during the entire trip, I missed them. He ate, or more accurately, he shovelled food into his mouth. Anything left over on anyone's plate was confiscated immediately and at the end of each meal there wasn't enough on all our plates to feed an ant. The dishwasher in the kitchen must have been wondering. I think he introduced himself as Herman but he got stuck with the name of "Human Vacuum Cleaner" and that was that. He was no longer young, had spent years upon years in the bush somewhere in Canada chopping down trees and, having accumulated a nest egg, was on his way home to Switzerland to enjoy his life's work. I don't think he could. He didn't have an enjoyable bone in his entire body.

Second night on board was Ballroom Night and I was in for a shock. Having spent 1½ years doing Cha Chas, Waltzes, Polkas, Foxtrots and Rock-n-Roll at the German Clubs, I had totally missed out on the new scene in the music world. It was called "Twist" and when the Band struck up good old Chubby Checker's theme song, I stood rooted on the floor and watched everyone gyrate to a new beat. I didn't have a clue what to do. It was a source of great hilarity to the rest of the gang but thoroughly embarrassing to myself. Another lesson learned, don't lose sight of what goes on around you just because someone else doesn't want to know.

It didn't take long to learn this new craze but I didn't take to it too well. It hurt my stomach after a while. Was I the only one affected like that? I guess every generation has their specialty. Mama's was Charleston which none of us ever mastered like she did. Sister's was Ballroom and Swing. Brother's, and mine, was indisputably 'Rock'N'Roll' or

149

Boogie Woogie, as we called it in Berlin. Twist was OK but I didn't miss it when it left the scene.

After the Big Band in the ballroom closed its doors at midnight, a trio of rock musicians started up in the nightclub. There we could dance until two or three o'clock in the morning, after which the survivors would head back to the ballroom, stretch out comfortably on couches and armchairs and sing songs, tell stories and acquaint one another with languages and customs of other countries. We learned some Gaelic, some French and some strange expressions the English use when they're really mad at someone. We learned to sing Auld Lang Syne, the French Marseillaise and the German component taught everyone how to order beer in Munich. Basically, we invented multiculturalism but it wasn't fashionable yet so we missed out on the patent.

Apart from the first breakfast, I never ate another one. We slept late, ate, drank, danced and had a grand time. It's what you do on ocean liners.

When Ireland came into view, the Irish went crazy. It was late and quite cold but, to celebrate with our friends, we all trouped outside to see the dark speck on the horizon which was pointed out as the Emerald Isle. Everyone was jumping up and down and someone grabbed me around the waist and lifted me in the air. At that precise moment, the ship lurched a little, my handler lost his footing, stumbled and I went head-over-heels over the railing. There I hung, my life in the hands of a highly inebriated young Irishman who held on for dear life to my lower legs. Beneath me a black void and silvery wave caps and nothing to hold on to but the sheer wall of the ship. I don't know how long it took before I felt numerous hands pulling me back over the railing and my feet felt once more the lovely, solid deck beneath them. I promptly collapsed and so did most of the others. We had just discovered a quick way to get sober. My poor Irish friend was crying his heart out, everyone wanted to know if anything was broken, and my nurse friend took charge by picking me off the floor and carrying me back into the ballroom to recuperate on the couch.

Being the centre of attention is a great feeling but the circumstances surrounding this instance left a lot to be desired. We forgot about Ireland and a very subdued crowd dispersed into their allotted cabins to reflect and, if religiously inclined, give praise for a safe delivery. My Belgium roommate gave me a sleeping pill and I made it through the rest of the night without nightmares.

In the morning, a tearful good-bye was said to our Irish pals who had to be transported to their homeland via shuttle boats as our liner was way too big for their little harbour, the name of which I do not remember. After they left, the nightly drunks were sadly reduced in numbers. In England, we lost the lad from Ottawa and after we docked at LeHavre, there were no more lovers kissing in the corners but a lot of girls crying for their handsome Frenchies. At Bremerhaven, the rest of us exchanged addresses, hugged and went our separate ways.

I have never forgotten them. They almost killed me but they also gave me back a self-assurance I had lost and a view of the world that was vastly different from the German-Immigrant version of my ex-husband and his compatriots. They also reminded me of my taste for adventure and foreign countries and peoples. It was very obvious that I wasn't ready for marriage and the life that came with it.

Der Oberbürgermeister der Reichshauptstadt

Berlin, 22. Februar 1939

EHRENPATENSCHAFTEN DER STADT BERLIN.
===

URKUNDE.

Es ist mir eine Freude, den Volksgenossen

Eugen K R A U S E , Vorkalkulator, und seiner

Ehefrau Anna , geborenen Zilling,

wohnhaft: Berlin - Neukölln, Hermannstraße 212,

auf Grund der durch Verfügung vom 16. März 1934 - Ges. VIa 1 -

erlassenen Grundsätze die

"EHRENPATENSCHAFT DER STADT BERLIN

für ihr Kind

Edith Käthe K R A U S E ,

geboren am 27. Dezember 1938 in Berlin- Buckow ,

zu verleihen.

Das Kind ist von nun an

"EHRENPATENKIND DER STADT BERLIN",

die Familie

"EHRENPATENFAMILIE DER STADT BERLIN

Heil Hitler !

Oberbürgermeister
und Stadtpräsident.

Stadtmedizinalrat.

"THE CERTIFICATE"
As it proclaims: I am a Berliner – born, bred and certified by the
incumbent 'Oberbuergermeister' of the City in 1939 to be the
Honorary Godchild of the City of Berlin.

*The perfect German family – tall,
blond and blue-eyed*

*Life among the giants!
Except for the one on my right, we are all the same age.*

*The Evacuees in Saxonia.
Note – At age 5, I'm still
wearing the jumpsuit I
wore at age 3.*

*44 unruly Berliners in Frau Fiedler's class. No. 45 was just one too
many to endure.*

The children of Britz, aka., the wild bunch.

This marriage was not made in heaven.

We got to be experts at changing worn-out tires.
Everyone worked – I supervised!

THE "WALL"
Hideous, demeaning and scarring the landscape and the populace.

My Brother the Artist. A shame Papa never looked at what the Artist could do.

Vancouver, BC, Canada. 1972. When the sun shines, you can't beat it.

Grief can take care of itself but to get the full value of joy you must have someone to share it with. Mark Twain! Mama joined Papa within 3 months.

Chapter 23

YOU CAN'T GO HOME AGAIN!

Papa and Brother were waiting for me at the dock. "Good God," was Papa's first sentence. "What has the bastard done to you?" Done to me? Theo? What did he mean?

What he meant was that I looked like death warmed over. Pale, bags under the eyes, thin as a rail. Papa was ready to board the next plane to Canada and beat up on his soon to be ex-son-in-law but, fortunately, Brother got it right. Honour where honour was due. My current physical condition was totally self-inflicted and Brother knew what a grand hang-over looked like. He looked like that every Monday morning. Papa recovered and we stowed away my luggage in the little Beetle Volkswagen and set off for home.

The object of my relatives driving all the way to Bremerhaven was to make my coming home trip easier. In retrospect, everyone agreed that I should have taken the Bus.

There were now border checkpoints and to get to Berlin we had to pass through two of them. One to enter the "German Democratic Republic" and another one to get out of this so-called democracy which needed walls to keep its people in the country. It was unfortunate that I had missed the changeover and, not being used to such facilities, I pretty well spoiled my perfect homecoming. I was still the Berliner who had left three years before. I had not learned to keep my mouth shut, to be obedient and even smile at people who, because they wore a uniform, felt they had the right to abuse their fellow countrymen - just for the fun of it.

Border guards all over the world hardly ever smile, but the ones guarding this precious republic were the absolute experts on looking grim and forbidding. We stood in the pouring rain, watching them poke flashlights into the trunk, the interior and under the hood. When one particular miserable version of this "Volkspolizei" of the female variety poked the flashlight into the glove compartment, I exploded.

"How many East-Germans do you think we are hiding in there?" I asked. End of friendly relations between east and west. They took the car apart, scattered the contents of my suitcases all over the office and watched, grinning from ear to ear, while I re-packed my luggage and Papa and Brother put the car back together. I thought we had got rid of the SS types but all they had done is move to East Germany and change uniforms. Welcome home!

Halfway to Berlin, my irate relations forgave me my trespass and lectured the innocent on the new world order of Germany in 1962. I didn't think I would like it. Brother actually proclaimed that these people were only doing their job. How much brainwashing had been going on while I was gone? Had the wall sapped my people of their sass? Had they come to terms with a system that should be fought and derided at every opportunity? Something wasn't right with the mental outlook of either Papa or Brother. I hoped it was only them, but it wasn't.

In Mama's arms I forgot, for a while at least, my unfortunate encounter. She laughed and cried and served up my favourite meal. All is well on a full stomach.

I took up residence on the living room couch and stopped being a married woman. I became what I had been all my life - Mama's little girl. Christmas arrived and Papa reverted back to our old routine of decorating the tree in the afternoon. Mama got busy in the kitchen and the familiar smells of the Christmas goose filled the house. In the evening, we waited for Brother to arrive who, because of last-minute changes in shop windows, always made us wait seemingly forever. Once he had arrived, Papa took our presents and put them under the tree, lit the candles, turned on the record player and rang the little bell. It was always magical even if the presents never quite lived up to expectations.

To the end of his day, Brother complained of the endless rows of new pyjamas and undershirts which made up the brunt of his and his sibling's gifts. Neither one of my parents ever acquired the talent to buy something one really wanted and Papa had the annoying habit of leaving the price tags attached to the articles he purchased. He figured to really appreciate a gift, one should know how much it cost. We bitched and complained but we never cured him of this custom. Coming from a family that, until the arrival of Mama, never exchanged any gifts at all or even celebrated Christmas, we forgave him his annoying price tags.

But Sister outdid Papa on this particular night. She had returned from Vancouver to Montreal just before I boarded my escape hatch, the Liner Arcadia. She brought a little parcel for me to take to Mama and, as it sounded like tinkling glass, I paid particular attention to it's safety within the confines of my luggage. I thought they were liquor glasses or some such item.

When we were finished with our presents, I gave Mama the mysterious package and told her to be careful when unwrapping. She was - only no one understood why that was necessary. They were not glasses but glass containers. Four of them, containing pepper, paprika, cloves and nutmeg. Mama maintained to the end of her days that those bottles were even funnier than the Lifesaver candies that I had sent two year's previously.

She was still wiping tears from her eyes when the doorbell rang. Another emigrant had returned from his adopted country of Sweden to the bosom of his family for the Holidays. Lothar Staehler, the south wind who defeated Brother, the north wind, in that memorable Christmas play so very long ago, now paid a visit to his archenemy of old. It turned into one of the best Christmas Eve's I can remember. Reminiscences flowed back and forth, our childhood was re-created and we roared with laughter when the two "Winds" re-created their memorable battle. I drew the line when they asked me to re-light my flame part. It was silly at age 8, I wasn't going to repeat it at almost 24.

After the holidays, I started looking for old friends and found most of them worrying about diaper rashes. My Danish travel companion, was, although expecting a bundle of joy, not yet holding said article and kindly invited me to accompany the family to a New Year's party. Her brother and husband in tow, we spent a very pleasurable evening with some very nice people, all of whom were couples but some of whom were not averse to a little flirting on the side. It seemed that leaving one's husband and seeking a divorce gave one a reputation of a free spirit. Divorces were not yet as common as they are today and so it seemed that, again, I was something of an oddity. I had lived with a man before I married him and then, not having found marriage to my liking, was divorcing him. WOW! We rang in 1963 and had no idea how much life would change within the next decade.

Chapter 24

REALIZING YOUR POTENTIAL!

Looking for work is not my favourite pastime but neither is sitting home, especially when one has not got a room of one's own. I looked for something that would make use of my newfound talent for speaking English and Lothar's mother provided the means of doing so. Mrs. Staehler cleaned the offices for the Americans at the Tempelhof Central Airport and she was sure that they would need my help to run the place. I couldn't argue with that and in the first week of January, I took the U-Bahn to Dahlem, the District the Americans had confiscated for their head office and accommodations right after the war. It was the most expensive real estate in the City, so no one should ever accuse the Americans of not appreciating the finer things in life. It was also the place where they had tried to fatten me up at age 10, in one of the beautiful mansions the Yankees had apparently overlooked, and where they had failed miserably.

It was a very long trip and I was delighted when told that there was a job opening at Tempelhof Airport, a facility basically around the corner from Britz. I filled out the necessary forms and was given a pass to take the Airforce Crew Bus back to Tempelhof for my interview. Wonderful! Everything done in one day! Nobody like the Americans to cut through paperwork.

Riding a comfortable bus, filled with numerous young, virile, full-of-life American soldiers sure beat the subway system. Speaking English felt great and by the time we drove through the gates at the Airport, I was pretty sure I would convince whoever interviewed me that I was what was needed for the job - whatever it was. Then I did the usual - I got lost. I was inside the Base but I couldn't find the Personnel Office anywhere. Time was running out and, in desperation, I marched back to the gate where I promptly got into trouble. I wasn't supposed to be on the inside.

"How did you get in?"

"I rode in on the Bus."

"What Bus?"

"That Bus!"

The driver got called over and defended his actions by insisting he thought I was a "dependent", whatever that was. No one but soldiers and their dependents are allowed on base. I was very apparently neither. He was supposed to let me off at the gate. My English teachers at Styled Cotton had done their work too well. I had no accent, at least not enough of one to make anyone think I was German. I apologized profusely for not having made myself clear to the driver and he and the guard forgave me my trespass and pointed me in the direction of the Personnel Office, wishing me good luck in the process.

I was just in time to join the last girl in a long line of applicants in the waiting room. She was very discouraging. The job I was applying for apparently needed the skills of a translator. Piece of cake, my rival assured me. If you can speak English, you can translate. Famous last words by a woman who thought she knew everything. When she returned from her test, she was even more assured of her chances and reduced me to a quivering bundle of nerves who kind of suspected that speaking a language and then turning it into another one was not quite as easy as she made it sound.

Mr. Gross was a jolly kind of guy who took some of the fear of failure away, but only until he gave me my test. It was a work order. I was supposed to translate a work order and the work order indicated in minute detail how to build a shed, the tools used to make it happen and the measurements that would be needed to make sure it would stand up straight. Wonderful. I can't even hammer a nail straight into a wall. There was no use in trying to do the impossible. I meekly indicated to my tormentor that I couldn't possibly achieve a translation because I did not know many of the names of the tools and measuring instruments used, neither in English nor in German.

He assured me that he wasn't worried about specific words. All he wanted me to do was to translate what I understood and leave gaps where the tools and measuring instruments should be. Well, if he wasn't worried, why should I be. I got down to the business of translating and found I had the knack for it, barring all the important words which I was assured I would find later in the technical dictionaries which he insisted abounded in the office. The typewriter being of the American kind, I had no problem with the keys and hammered away at my usual speed of 120 words a minute. I was a show stopper.

After I handed him my attempt at making sense out of an English text in German, he escorted me back to the waiting room where my friendly rival still smiled away, sure of her victory. I waited for the verdict of which I was sure. Eventually, the roly-poly Mr. Gross returned and walked straight over to the smiling Buddha. "Thank you very much for coming," he crooned. "But we have decided to give Mrs. Roedel a try." Who? Me? Why?

Turned out that I had what it takes and I didn't even know I had it. Translating is not easy. One has to think one way in one language and an entirely different way in another. It didn't matter at all that I had gaps in the text. What I did have was a fluency and a grasp for both languages. I don't believe that that is an entirely learnable skill. I think it is a gift and I am grateful for it. I definitely never worked on it but it got me the job, and I spent the next three years laughing, because there is nothing funnier than to watch the mentalities of Germans and Americans collide. In the process, I found out that I would make a lousy soldier.

Rank is everything. If you're a Sergeant who has been in the service most of his life and who knows how to conduct business from experience, you nevertheless have to take orders from some pipsqueak straight out of officer school who may have a lot of theoretical knowledge but no practical experience. It would kill me.

My rank at Tempelhof Central Airport was 'Work Order Specialist and Translator.' I was in charge of getting things fixed when broken, which applied to all the buildings surrounding the tarmac. The actual fixing was done by the carpenter shop, the plumbing shop, the electrician shop, etc., all of which were manned by German nationals who had passed the rigorous apprenticeship exams in their various professions.

On the other hand, there was the all-round fixer shop manned by the Yanks, who had all the above trades represented with two men each, all of whom had probably attended a 6-months course and, theoretically at least, were thought to be capable of any and all repairs necessary to keep the Base from falling down around our ears.

To keep in touch with all these 'shops,' I was supplied with a switchboard resembling a World War I telephone connecting the front with headquarters. It had wires with little plugs which I had to stick into holes respective of the office I was trying to contact. To make life easy, one of my new colleagues drew little pictures above the holes. The electricians had a light bulb, the plumbers had a toilet seat, the carpenters an axe, transportation a truck and the Yankees had a big question mark. Deservedly so.

They tried, they really did, and they were always the first ones I was instructed to call for repairs. I had to estimate how much time it would take to fix a wall plug, fill in holes in walls, replace a light bulb or fix the linoleum floor. Upon completion of the job, they would call me back and give me the time they had actually needed. I religiously kept track of all this but it never became quite clear to me why. None of my estimates ever remotely came close to the actual time it took to fix anything.

In theory, it worked out like this - the Yanks went off, fixed the problem, returned with their time and everyone lived happily ever after. Right? Wrong! Two minutes after the Yanks left, the injured party would call back and request that I now please send a German labourer. In the three years that I worked my little magic on the switchboard, the times when I didn't have to call in the German experts were far and few between. There was no denying that the 4-year apprenticeship any blue-collar worker in Germany had to endure to get his certificate was superior to the methods employed in the United States and the Airforce in particular.

Working for the Americans necessitated speaking English, which we all did with more or less proficiency. My Boss, Mr. Gross, was better at grammar than anyone I had encountered in Canada but his accent did not live up to the high expectations set by his knowledge of diction. The colleague on my left was still in the learning process and both Mr. Gross and I contributed daily to his advancement. Manfred was small, quick, and boasted a Berliner wit not encountered since listening to the comedians from the Insulaner Troupe on the Rias Radio Station. He had started life in the Airforce as a guard at the Gate and the stories he told about ladies trying to climb fences for secret rendezvous with affluent young soldiers shortly after the war kept us all in his hysterics. His adventures as a last-minute defender of the German Fatherland when he was 15 years of age were probably horrific to one so young but, when related by Manfred with his odd sense of humour, had us rolling in the aisles.

They gave him a gun and told him to shoot the enemy and defend the Fatherland to the last man. The gun was bigger than he was and the first time he encountered a fusillade, he sat down and peed his pants. He never fired a shot and if he had, that gun would probably have sent him flying in the opposite direction of the bullet. Little Manfred and his fellow soldiers decided they had done their bit for Adolf, dropped the guns, held up their hands and were dutifully captured by the enemy. End of war.

The Americans who took them captive had no idea what to do with little children, so they gave them some chewing gum and sent them packing. Manfred fell in love with gum, chocolate and Americans in particular and, as soon as he had acquired a few words of English, applied for a job. His education was furthered by the Yanks with whom he shared guard duty at the gates. Some of that was, albeit usable, not quite up to the standard of a decent conversation. By the time I arrived on the scene, he had managed to improve to the point of getting a job in the office, where his comic talents were greatly appreciated.

The rest of my co-workers were people who had acquired enough English in school before the war to be eligible to be employed by the occupying forces who provided the first employment afterwards. There were some young girls who had married soldiers, gone to the States, England or Canada, and had returned, divorced and disillusioned, for various reasons. By 1963, there were no longer any young girls looking for a soldier husband. Marrying such an individual, of whatever nationality, had totally gone out of fashion and was now frowned upon as lacking in sensibilities. The stories told by returning war brides of life in the States were also not entirely complimentary to a way of life so beautifully described in the movies made in Hollywood.

Our American friends on the Base were like people all over the World. Some were nice, some were terrific, some were lousy and some were downright awful, but they were always fun.

Being a translator entitled me to the privilege of borrowing books from the library. It was supposed to help me retain my English and learn new vocabulary. I didn't care what it was supposed to be for. I was just glad to get back to my Louis L'Amour Westerns, my Arthur Clark's Science Fiction and my American Civil War and Indian Wars histories.

No German was allowed in the Cafeteria but my Yankee crew made allowances for the only person not speaking with the harsh accent of my country. They enjoyed my company and in exchange provided me with the odd cheeseburger with fries, not as yet available in post-war Germany. It was an unfortunate fact, however, that most, if not all, of the young lads stationed at Tempelhof during my sojourn there showed a total lack of interest in getting to know another culture. They worked on the base, went home to their quarters on crew buses, visited their own clubs in the evenings and failed to get even a glimpse of another lifestyle. What a waste of an opportunity.

One who did show an interest in Germany and Berlin in particular was a young man in charge of the Yank crew and, in exchange for hamburgers and fries, he got lessons in German language and culture. I even invited him home one day, which wasn't entirely successful but at least gave the entire neighbourhood a topic of conversation for a long time. Not only was he in uniform, he was also of the dark-skinned variety which, in the days before political correctness became the norm, was still called a Negro.

Arriving by Taxi, we walked the gauntlet of housewives leaning on window sills, elbows comfortably resting on pillows, watching the world go by. I introduced him to my incredulous parents and he made a nice show of slaughtering the German language in his greeting. Mama recovered enough to remember German hospitality and served coffee and cake, all the while yelling at the top of her lungs. Mama had not learned her lesson with the Russian occupiers. She was still convinced that if she yelled loud enough, anyone would understand what she was talking about. The Yank replied with a smile. It's the international language. If in doubt, smile. But my Yank could not sustain his grimace when Papa supplied the only English sentence he knew which was: "This is no place to stay, do your business and go away." I had to explain that one.

Before the war, Papa had a friend who, although of German origin, grew up in England. The poor guy got stuck in Germany at the start of the war and taught Papa the basics of the English language which resulted in his being able to read the above message scribbled on a door while attending to business on the toilet seat. It had always been entertaining but never more so than when explaining it to my co-worker.

After he left, Mama expressed her astonishment on how dark his skin really was. She'd only ever really encountered an American of the coloured variety while they were passing through Kirchsteitz and Mama had not shown quite the enthusiasm her daughter had in exploring the colour oddity. Personally, I never considered our Black Americans as particularly "black". Chocolate brown was more likely. Off and on, we had student applicants coming through the office who originated in Kenya or some other African state. Now that was black.

My chocolate-brown Yank became a great friend, was suitably impressed with Germany and totally spoiled for his next assignment, which was France. He did not encounter the same hospitality and I don't believe he learned a word of that language.

One who wasn't interested in anything German at all and who never let anyone forget that he belonged to an "Occupation Force" occupying a country that had lost the war, was a tall, handsome Lieutenant with an ego that had outgrown his size by a mile. He did not like the country, the mentality of the population and their insistence on following rules. Sometimes, such as when Mr. Gross insisted on his book of regulations, of which he could quote you Paragraph 3, page 43, upon request, he had a point. Most of the time he was nitpicking.

What he especially liked harping on was the murder of 6 million Jews. Somehow we always felt he was addressing the wrong people. Mr. Gross had been drafted into the army right out of school for the entire duration of the war, Manfred was a young boy in the Hitler Youth and I, being of the baby variety during those times, wasn't quite able to voice opposition to mass murder. Most of my fellow employees were in the same boat, so laying the blame on us got a bit on my nerves.

History repeats itself. It is a pity that more people do not take more interest in the past. A lot of mistakes would be avoided. History also comes in handy when accusations are levelled and I am an avid fan of world affairs of the past. I started recounting Indian massacres, such as Wounded Knee and Sandspit, expostulated about generals who told their soldiers to kill Indian children because "nits make lice," continued with the famous Andersonville Prison during the Civil War where humanity to your fellow man was totally abandoned, and worked my way through the Concentration Camps in South Africa invented by the British, where thousands of women and children died of disease and starvation. By the time I got to Napoleon, who to this day is still revered in France despite the fact he oppressed and killed millions all over Europe, I had an audience. I reminded him of the colonization processes perpetrated by all European Nations, which wasn't entirely appreciated by the native populations of Africa, India, China, and whatever other country they set their sights on.

I asked him to name one nation on earth that he thought was

blameless through the ages of committing crimes against humanity. He couldn't. But he found a way to get back at me.

They had a system of rewarding people with outstanding work records and every year Mr. Gross would recommend Manfred and myself for the "Performance Award" and the DM300.00 that went with it. This recommendation had to go through certain channels. Mr. Gross initiated it, the Lieutenant in charge of our department recommended it and the Major approved it.

During my Boss's third attempt to encourage me to type even faster, my paperwork disappeared. Not having heard or seen any reply to his proposal after initiating it three weeks previously, Mr. Gross started making inquiries with negligible results. My recommendation had gone the way of the Dodo Bird - Poof! He searched everywhere but no one in the chain of command admitted to having seen it since it left Mr. Gross's desk. My Boss was, if nothing else, very persistent. He was also very, very German and the regulations did not permit the flow of paperwork to be interrupted by anyone or anything. He turned into a regular Hercule Poirot and he found what he was looking for in the bottom drawer of our Snob Lieutenant's desk, covered by a paraphernalia of used and discarded office equipment, such as broken staplers, chipped rulers and torn folders. All hell broke lose.

In the end, I got my certificate, my DM300.00 and a pat on the rump by the Base Commander. Sexual harassment claims had not as yet been invented and I therefore took the pat for what it was, "sorry about that." I got the message. So did the Lieutenant. He never set foot in our office again for the rest of his unmemorable stay in Germany.

Base Commanders changed frequently; Lieutenants, Sergeants and ordinary grunts came and went. Some were more fun than others.

One Monday morning in May, I came back to work to find the hallway spattered with white paint. Ceiling, floor, walls, everything was decorated with blotches and made for an interesting new decor which, however, was not appreciated by the higher echelons of our society. Upon investigation, it turned out that a group of bored Airmen had decided to present the Base Commander with a little Easter lamb. They are so cute when you hang a bow around their neck.

There were hundreds of sheep on the air base, grazing docilely upon the grass between the runways, lorded over by a genuine sheepherder with a dog to help him keep the flock in check. That Easter, unfortunately, there was no Lamb. What to do? You've got to hand it to the Yanks. They are unbeatable when it comes to innovation. In this case, it didn't work out too well but that's not to say it wasn't a good idea.

They caught themselves the smallest sheep they could find, took it into the hallway and proceeded to colour it white because a normal sheep is such a dull greyish/brown and as such would not have passed muster as a lamb. They hadn't counted on the designated "easter lamb" disagreeing with the treatment. The fight apparently lasted hours and the game was finally conceded to the sheep which was transported back to its normal environment where it went back to munching grass.

The losing team was reprimanded and, equipped with paint and brushes, were made to cover up the stains of their losing bout. That was one of the funny episodes. It wasn't funny when they put a long and expensive transistor radio into a 'Paternoster.'

When I was growing up, every department store had one. It wasn't an elevator but it moved like one. The difference between the two people movers was that the Paternoster had no doors. The cabins rose up to floor level and one just stepped in. Arriving on the floor of one's destination, one stepped out. It never stopped, it went round and round and to my knowledge there was never a problem. It is a people mover, that's all.

On the Paternoster at the Base, there were signs plastered everywhere of what not to do.

DON'T CARRY BIG OBJECTS!

GET OFF ON THE THIRD FLOOR!

STEP IN WHEN FLOOR IS LEVEL WITH PATERNOSTER!

STEP OUT WHEN PATERNOSTER IS LEVEL WITH FLOOR!

Do people read signs? Of course not. So the end of the transistor radio was chopped to pieces because it stuck out too far. That was expensive for the owner of the radio. Another lad cost the Base the reconstruction of an entire cabin. He went so far as to chop the entire cabin to pieces because he forgot to get off at the last floor. I knew what the lad saw when he got there. I'd been there. Huge wheels, lots of noise and darkness. Very scary.

One of the pleasures of childhood was riding up and down in the Paternoster at the Karstadt Department Store, just another game denied to children and therefore to be experienced at all cost. At one point, I got pushed back into the cabin on the last official floor by one of my friends and ended up in the attic with the wheel and the noise. I was as scared as that Yank on the Base, however, our interpretations of the system were very much at odds.

My idea of how the cabin was going to get back down was thinking it would turn on its side, then on its head and go upside down to the floor below. In consequence, I put my foot on the wall, intending to walk around the cabin like a hamster in a wheel. I was still in that position when the cabin passed the floor below and people entering gave me strange looks. All the cabins do is move across the floor and descend again. They rotate in a clockwise fashion.

My rival in imagination had other ideas. He thought the cabin would squash down like an accordion and open up again once it arrived on the opposite side. He managed to demolish the entire cabin with his bare hands in seconds. I don't think there are any "Paternosters" left in Germany. Too dangerous.

Three years of watching people who live by regulations and people who live by ignoring them was one heck of an experience. Then there were the dignitaries passing through.

Queen Elizabeth made her first trip to Germany and the country went wild. Germans love Royalty and loads of magazines attest to this fact. Every week they publish the antics of the "still in position" and the "deposed" broods of Royals from all over Europe, one of the favourites being the ghastly Monaco clan. One wonders why we ever gave up our own brand of Kaisers but, in the end, since most of the still officiating blue-bloods in Europe are related in one form or another to Germans, I suppose it's all the same.

I have never understood this fascination. Take Sweden. During Napoleon's time, the King of Sweden was a childless old man whose mind was wandering. The rest of the Royals in line of succession were a pretty hopeless lot and a strong man was needed at the helm. They got in touch with a Marshall of France, one of Napoleon's best man, Jean Baptiste Bernadotte, and proposed an adoption. He accepted and moved to Stockholm, becoming one of Napoleon's worst nightmares in the process. Jean Baptiste was the son of a lawyer, his wife the daughter of a silk merchant of Marseilles. Their son, Oscar, married the granddaughter of Josephine Beauharnais, the most beautiful courtesan of her time and ex-wife of Napoleon. That's the Royal House of Sweden? WOW!

I was a little left out of the adoration process but my fellow countrymen made up for it. The day Queen Elizabeth and her entourage left the city, the staff at Tempelhof, and whoever we wanted to bring along, were allowed onto the Base. It took her procession a very long time to arrive at Tempelhof because the Berliners were beside themselves and slowed her cavalcade down to a crawl.

Meantime, we sat on the window sill in my office and watched the honour guard drawn up for her leave ceremony. There were the French soldiers, the British, the Americans and the German Police. It was a very hot day and it didn't take long for that fact to take its toll. We started making bets on who would keel over next. Some of the French were first, then some Americans. The British and the Police held fast. No one touched the fallen heroes. They lay where they fell until nature asserted itself and they re-inserted themselves back into line, only to repeat the performance in short order. By the time Her Royal Highness finally arrived, 9 soldiers lay at her feet. Speeches were made, the band played and, in a lull in between, some idiot yelled out of a window "I love you Lizzie." I don't know what "Lizzie" thought of that faux pas. I wasn't amused and, between Manfred and myself who witnessed the incident, we never told anyone that that "idiot" was my Brother.

Another luminary who turned up was Robert Kennedy. I grabbed my camera, dashed onto the tarmac and mixed in with the reporters surrounding this most famous of Americans. I got a beautiful picture of Robert listening to Berlin's Mayor Willy Brandt, extolling the feelings of friendship between Germans and Americans. Willie obviously hadn't had a conversation with the new generation growing up around him who, for reasons unknown, were growing more and more anti-American.

When his Brother, the even more famous Jack Kennedy arrived, the nation outdid itself. Who could resist? Famous, rich, smart and beautiful - the perfect couple. They called it the resurrection of Camelot. I did not think that was a very good name. Camelot did not end up happily ever after.

They were so perfect and so adored that I found it hard to swallow the image. Being totally imperfect myself, I like my heroes to be a little more human. Robert Kennedy, with his brood of children and a wife who didn't have what it takes to be adored, were more to my liking. I always thought he was the smarter of the two and his death was, to my mind, the greater loss.

I got into trouble when Jack made his famous speech at the Schoeneberger Rathaus. As far as the rest of Berlin and most of the world was concerned, Jack proclaimed himself to be a Berliner with the famous ending of his speech wherein he said, "I am a Berliner." Only that wasn't what he meant. What I remember of his speech was more like - "Hundreds of years ago, to say one was a free man, one would say - I am a Roman. Today, to say one is a free man, one says - I am a Berliner." Papa never believed me, nor did Mama nor anyone else I ever talked to in my City. So, to this day, Jack Kennedy said that he was a Berliner, and that is that. Of such things history is made.

When Jack came visiting, he did the obligatory trip to the Brandenburg Gate, wiping crocodile tears from his cheeks and commiserating with the population. It was good enough for the rest of my countrymen but it wasn't good enough for me. I still thought something could have been done and wasn't. When he died in Dallas, Mama made me accompany her to the Schoeneberg Rathaus to sign the book of condolences. We stood in line for hours. It seemed that the entire population of Berlin was in attendance. To this day, they love John F. Kennedy but I have never really understood why. As Mama said, don't listen to words, watch the action. I didn't think he lived up to expectations.

Work at Tempelhof was not work. Work was a lot of fun. So was encountering a new generation of Berliners who didn't resemble the people I had left behind.

Chapter 25

LIFE IN THE SINGLE LANE!

Work kept my mind occupied in the daytime. Evenings and weekends were something else. I had only been gone 3½ years but everything had changed. Another generation had taken the place of my dance-happy friends who were cradling their offspring. The Klosterkeller was deserted and I only found one person I knew and he was there to celebrate his last night on the town. He was getting married in the morning.

There is nothing more mournful than a ballroom with only a scattering of people and a Big Band trying to inveigle the few present to take to the dance floor. I escaped to the Casaleon only to find it had suffered the same fate. There was still the Neue Welt but the second ballroom was closed and in the front one they played waltzes, foxtrot and rumbas and the average age was 40 which was definitely ancient to my 24.

Brother took pity on his frustrated Sister and accompanied me around town on a nightclub tour. Around town meant around the Kurfuersten Damm, which according to Brother was 'the only place to be.'

I never liked the Kurfuersten Damm" area. Not then and not now. Full of tourists, full of wannabies, full of phonies. It is the showpiece of the City, a little snobbish, a little decadent, a little too much pretending to be something it is not - namely the "Potsdamer Platz of the 1920's" which was where everything happened in Berlin and where everyone had to be in those days before the war. Then, Berlin was comparable to Paris, London and New York and the coffee houses and nightclubs were full of the intelligentsia of the time.

I knew all about my City before the War. Mama never stopped

talking about it. Mama watched Josephine Baker dance naked with a bunch of bananas around her waist. Mama was a flapper with a skirt that never reached her knees and sexy curls plastered around her forehead resembling Josephine's. In those days, the KuDamm was a sleepy street with magnificent houses. There was nothing much left of the Potsdamer Platz when the madness was over and, anyway, it ended up in East Berlin. What started the KuDamm on its way was the Black Market around the Zoo Station and the nightclubs springing up on every street corner, accommodating the occupying forces eager to start enjoying life on a grand scale. First it was for everyone and then it became the in-thing, meaning the prices went up.

Brother could afford them, largely because he made me pay the bill. Despite my generosity, our nightclub tour turned into a complete disaster.

Where Brother's life had taken him in the preceding three years was not somewhere I cared to follow and the people he associated with were out of my league. They didn't seem to work for a living but had money in abundance. Having one of them state that it would be physically impossible for her to sit at a typewriter in an office all day was not something to endear her to a person obliged to work for a living. Watching them in action and listening to their idle conversations, laced with sarcasm and inane remarks, and watching Brother acting as their clown, made me realize that not having had rich parents was not so bad after all. It kept you sane.

Brother had definitely left Britz behind, physically and mentally, had moved to Dahlem and only paid infrequent visits to the old neighbourhood. Family conversations turned into arguments over what was Art and what wasn't and who is to say who was right. He loved Picasso's surrealistic paintings of noses, eyes and other facial features floating around in no-mans land. The rest of his family was convinced that the man simply got out of bed one morning and said to himself, "Let's see what the artistic community will swallow." We figured he was probably more surprised than anyone at the reaction he received for his new style and the money that went with it.

Another problem was presented by poetry. Brother came home with a poem by a new poet with the silly name of Joachim Ringelnatz. That man made poems which lived up to his very strange name. I remember one of them which went something like this:

Die Rehe gehen zur Nacht, hab acht.
Halb Neun, Halb Zehn, die Rehe gehen zur Nacht. Hab Acht.

174

After that recital, Brother was confronted with three people, who stared at him, open-mouthed, in total incomprehension. What the heck was that? There were a bunch of deer that were going to sleep and one should be careful. Then the poet counted from 7.30, 8.30, 9.30, then he mentioned again that the deer were going to sleep and one should be careful. Who should be careful and why? Was there a herd of deer that were going to trample someone? Why is he counting hours?

Brother slammed the door on his ungrateful and totally illiterate family. It was very funny and very sad but to this day I don't think Ringelnatz ever came close to replacing Schiller.

We got the message that he considered his parents and friends to be hicktowners to be avoided at all costs. It was painful to see him walking past little old ladies, who had known him as a charming little boy, their greetings ignored by a very handsome, exquisitely dressed young snob.

He had left me behind too but, off and on, still tried to impress me with his newfound lifestyle in and around the bars on the KuDamm. Sometimes I thought we lived on different planets.

He would take me to bars where he was known and greeted warmly. His very own bottle of Vodka, with his name imprinted on the label, was produced from behind the counter and, after use, put back until the next visit. They still charged him for every drink so I couldn't quite see the advantage. Being introduced as the little sister from Canada, I was looked over by world-weary eyes, found lacking in everything that mattered, namely false eyelashes, the latest fashion and the hairstyle of the season, and ignored for the rest of the visit. That was alright. I didn't much care for the conversations anyway.

Everywhere we went, we played a dice game called 'Chicago', perched upon high barstools and in intimate conversation with the bartender. We never sat at a table. It wasn't done. Climbing up on barstools is not the favourite past time for people under 5 feet tall. Brother was taller and had no problems. So Brother was definitely "in" and I was "out" - way out.

At one stop on our nightmare tour, Brother did the unforgivable. He spotted a lady to his liking, left me sitting at the table and took three turns on the dance floor with a young woman who couldn't wipe the grin off her face every time they came anywhere near my table. How could I tell her that I was only the Sister and not some left-behind girlfriend who put up with an unfaithful, ill-mannered boyfriend. When Brother returned, flushed with success, clutching a phone number, he was met by a sisterly wrath not encountered since he dropped me, head first, into a pond while trying to net some water fleas for his aquarium. I took a taxi home and didn't speak to him again for months, which was easy as he hardly ever showed up in Britz anyway.

There was no help from that quarter and so the only way out was to find an entirely new set of friends who were not yet in the baby business. Easier said than done. The solution came by way of the Berlitz Language School. Speaking two languages is fine, speaking three would be even better. So why not try French and get out of the house on a Saturday morning at the same time.

Berlitz had an office near the Kurfuersten Damm and management gratefully accepted my fee. There were eight of us trying to parlez en Francais and one of them was single and still in the "I love to go dancing" business and, I was told, the dancing business was now being conducted in and around the centre of town. Brother had already made that quite clear to me. I didn't particularly care for my new friend but she was my only chance of getting out and about and fitting myself back into the groove. We made a date for Saturday night.

We met at the Hofbrauhaus, a dance hall situated across the street from the 'Gedaechtniskirche', the ruined church which became the landmark of Berlin and which had been left standing as a ruin to remind the population of what Berlin had looked like in 1945. By now, in 1963, it was the only ruin left. Unfortunately, some idiot in the city planning department had the bright idea to surround the ruined tower with a modern church and bell tower. The ruined church would have made an impact standing on its own. Surrounded by buildings resembling a rubic cube and an egg carton, it lost its impact. But it was definitely 'in' with the new Berlin which was modern and being 'Americanized' wholesale.

The Hofbrauhaus, fortunately, was definitely still very German, albeit of the Bavarian kind, and proved to be extremely popular. It wasn't rock-n-roll or twist but it was one hell of a lot of fun.

It was the last date I ever had with the German Frenchie because, during the evening, I got acquainted with three girls with whom I got along great. We spent the next three years dancing in the fast lane, namely in and around the Zoo station. In-between work and fun, I had to look after my personal situation. I had to get my divorce.

Chapter 26

DIVORCE - GERMAN STYLE !

Papa believed in the old adage "You made your soup, now you have to eat it." I got married without his help, now I had to clean up the mess without his help. He did lean over far enough to get me a lawyer and, typically, proceeded to get me the wrong one. The lad was a company lawyer working at Telefunken. What did he know about divorces? Probably less than I did. The two of us made up a team resembling Don Quichote and Sancho Pansa.

Letters to my left-behind husband went for the most part unanswered. The boy absolutely refused to grant me a divorce, insisting that I return and resume my wifely duties. By that he probably meant continuing to support his gun collection purchases with my salary. I declined the honour.

The first time I had to go to court, Mama accompanied her daughter for moral support. It was an eye opener. There was a dais in the form of a horseshoe, the Judge presiding in the middle and two other black-robed figures occupying the side tables. In the middle of the room was a very tall desk shaped like my old school desk without the chair. My lawyer told me to stand behind the desk, which resulted in my disappearing entirely from the officials' view, as they did from mine. I was used to disappearing behind tall people and structures and automatically stepped aside to get a better view. That's when I encountered the inflexibility of the German Law. They ordered me back behind the desk. Not asked me. Ordered!

If Papa had been there, he could have told them that this was trouble. Papa's little girl never liked taking orders. Papa's girl was indoctrinated in the philosophy that "respect" had to be earned on an individual basis. Respect was not something to be accorded because someone wore a uniform, a doctor's coat or a judge's robe. "When the Queen sits on the toilet, she squeezes just as hard as you do," was Papa's advice to the timid. It had taken root in his youngest offspring and now turned life upside down for four legal eagles who were not used to being disobeyed.

I wouldn't budge. I explained the futility of the position behind the desk and sweetly asked if they didn't think it was more enjoyable looking at me than the stupid wood contraption. Apparently it wasn't. There was a regulation and that regulation stipulated that applicants for justice stood behind the podium and that was that. I told them what they should do with that regulation, which prompted my own lawyer to use my foot as a stomping ground. We now had an attentive audience, which did not sit well with the legal professionals who saw their authority being challenged by a midget with the temerity to disobey their orders. I didn't have a chance. Case dismissed until further notice.

My Lawyer stomped off in a rage and a perplexed Mama took a defiant daughter to lunch. As usual, we ended up laughing till the tears ran down Mama's cheeks. I had lost the battle but the war wasn't over.

The second time around, I made the concession of putting half my body behind the podium and the other half to the side. The judges glared but conceded defeat on their part. We commenced proceedings. I asked them to grant me a divorce from a man whose lifestyle did not remotely resemble my own and with whom I had nothing in common. I told them I had made a mistake and would like to correct it by setting the both of us free to find a more suitable mate. I did not tell them that he very likely cheated on me and that he had spent my money on frivolous purchases. I did not tell them about being left alone almost every weekend while he pursued his passions of hunting down poor little rabbits and grandiose moose, the head of one of whom graced my living room wall in Montreal, glaring at me every day with mournful eyes and unspoken accusation. I did not think that this was anybody's business but my own. I did not know the attitude of male judges in 1960's Germany. Case was dismissed until they were in receipt of a letter from my husband. They wanted to hear his side of the story.

By now, my lawyer had written so many unanswered missives that his secretary claimed to be on a first-name basis with the guy in Montreal. We had reached an impasse until Mama remembered the Sister I had left behind in that city. If anybody could convince, cajole and prod the man into replying, it surely would be Sister who was an expert in such tactics. The reply was enough to make a crocodile weep.

Sister went to see my Theo, found him desolate, despairing and full of remorse, eager to receive me back, all forgiven, into the lonely marriage bed. She told Mama to take a stick to my backside and send me back where I rightfully belonged. What she didn't tell Mama, and what we only found out years later upon my return to Montreal, was that the lonely man was already living with another woman, albeit one whom he promised to kick out as soon as I agreed to resume my obligations.

The third time around at the Law Court was not a success either. Having finally received a reply, all my lawyer friend could produce was a letter from my Ex maintaining the love for his woman was unchanged and his desire to resume the relationship. What do you say to that? My word against his! While the judges pondered the opposing statements, I watched while the one on the right filed away on a fingernail, the one on the left was apparently concentrating on a crossword puzzle and the one in the middle glared at me from his high vantage point as though I were a louse on his shirt he would like to squash. I lost it.

I asked the one on the right whether his Mother had neglected to tell him that it was bad manners to do one's nails in public. I offered to help the one on the left with any problems he might encounter with knowledge outside the legal profession and I suggested to the presiding judge to express a little more interest in my problem as that was actually his profession and was what he got paid for - with taxpayer's money, some of which was mine. I brought them to a state nearing apoplexy and that was very satisfying. Unfortunately, it didn't help my case. Case dismissed until further deliberations. I walked out with my head held high, my lawyer slinking behind me and got a standing ovation from Mama. What more can you ask for.

But during all my trials and tribulations with the German Justice System, I managed to enjoy life at work and at play. Life at home was a different story. By the time I had been living at home for a year, I was overstaying my welcome by a mile.

Chapter 27

COLD-WATER FLATS AND OTHER HAZARDS!

In the summer of 1963, Mama and Papa went on vacation to some forest in Germany. Brother had some business in the vicinity and decided to pick them up on his way home. He arrived at their Gasthaus in his VW Beetle, accompanied by a friend who drove a car with a diesel engine. Papa got carsick a lot, especially in cars with diesel engines. They decided to split up. Mama became a passenger in the diesel car and Papa took off in Brother's Beetle. Anticipating their arrival at approximately 6 pm, I made sandwiches, set up the table, put flowers in a vase and waited. And waited. The last time I remember looking at my watch, it was 11 PM.

I woke, still curled up in Papa's armchair, when I heard the door to the apartment slam shut. It was already light outside and I could clearly see my watch, which now stated 6 AM. Mama and the diesel car driver did not have to say anything. They dropped into chairs and my mind tried to deal with the absence of the two men I loved most in my life. "Are they?" "No," said Mama. And the world came back into focus.

It was an accident. Brother took off and Mama and her driver soon lost sight of him. Brother liked driving fast. Approximately one hour into the drive, traffic slowed down to a crawl and Mama looked out the window at an accident scene that looked horrendous. There seemed to be two people on stretchers being carried into ambulances and their car, a little VW Beetle, turned upside down, looked as though someone had stepped on it and reduced it to the size of a sardine can. A VW Beetle? Two people? Mama screamed.

What came out in the court case was that two young men in a Mercedes had overtaken Brother and, realizing that the oncoming traffic was a little faster than they had anticipated, turned back into the lane, catching Brother's front fender and sending his Beetle flying. Both Brother and Papa went through the sunroof, which in a Beetle is absolutely minute, and landed in a fence. They were alive, but just, and now were looked after in a Hospital in Landsberg an der Lech, wherever that was. Brother was in a coma with a bad head injury and Papa had hurt his neck and had his ear torn off down to the lobe. Mama stayed around until she thought they were well looked after and then came home with Brother's friend.

"We were lucky", was all Mama said. Mama had an unfailing faith in God. She spoke to him every night, told him off when things did not go too well, and was convinced that he took a special interest in her life and her family in particular. I wasn't quite so sure but I also understood that it could have been much worse. She was right - we were lucky.

They kept Papa in the hospital for one month and, upon receiving the good news that he would be released, Mama and I traveled by bus, first to Munich and then on to the town of Landsberg on the River Lech, to pick him up.

In Munich we found out that speaking with a Berliner accent does not invite hospitality or anything resembling gentility. Asking for directions to the country bus, people spoke to us in rapid Bavarian and we were just as lost as though they had expressed themselves in Chinese. The population of almost every Bundesstaat speaks with some sort of slangy dialect but they also learn and speak the official language, namely 'Hochdeutsch,' the high German of school fame. In Bavaria, however, they either couldn't or wouldn't communicate properly. Alright - if they didn't want to cooperate, I had another ace up my sleeve. English! I asked for directions in English and, to Mama's astonishment, everyone was happily trying out their school English and doing quite well. Sometimes you wonder about the German mentality.

In Landsberg, we found Papa resting comfortably in a room otherwise occupied by five very handsome and entertaining young men with casts covering diverse limbs. I had dreaded this visit, remembering my one and only attendance in a hospital at that horrible Maternity Ward in Montreal where my landlady was giving birth. Landsberg's hospital was a pleasant surprise. Sunny, clean, with good-natured attendants, a recovering Papa - and all those wonderful young men. I thought I'd died and gone to heaven.

181

Brother put a damper on things. Pale, with dark shadows under his closed eyes and so very still. He had broken his cranium but was, according to the doctors, coming around quite nicely. Sleep was needed to recover and his body was doing the right thing. The silver lining of it was that I could sit with him, hold his hand, tell him that I loved him more than anything in the whole world and he couldn't talk back. It reminded me of the time when the two of us were inseparable and when I had to sit with him for hours at his bedside, playing cards or reading a story. Brother did not like to be by himself when he was sick and, as soon as school was over, my task was to keep him company. Until he had his tonsils removed at age 15, he went to bed with tonsillitis every spring and autumn. He couldn't talk then either, so sitting there at his hospital bed, making one-sided conversation, was just like old times. It also made me realize that, even though we had nothing in common any longer and fought most of the time, what I had felt for him then would never change. I cradled his head and cuddled up close and everything was as it always had been. At least until he woke up.

Papa was discharged with his ear sewn back on and his neck stiff for the rest of his life. Brother stayed behind for another month and recovered enough to pick up where he had left off, meaning he had to try to regain the business he lost during two months of hospital rest. Brother had taken over the business of his boss, who had died 2 year's previously of cancer. He was therefore self-employed and had to work double time to regain the customers he had lost.

The culprits of the accident got a slap on the wrist. As I had found out, if you have a good lawyer, you don't have to worry in the German justice system. The two young men had fathers who were doctors, with sufficient funds in their bank accounts to afford the best. Not only did they get an acquittal, they never even apologized. They walked out of the courtroom with smiles on their faces and smirked at Papa in passing. It left Papa stunned and disillusioned and took away the last respect he had ever had for the system. He never forgave them and the bitterness never left him

The only good thing that came out of this mess was that Papa finally gave up his job. He was 67 by now and his superiors at Telefunken had enticed him to continue working long after his legal retirement age of 65. Now, the culprits' insurance company was obliged to pay him the salary he would have earned until the end of his contract and that finally persuaded him to try retirement. He took to it like a duck takes to water.

Unfortunately for me, being around more often also made him aware of the disturbances caused by my presence. Papa finally came to the conclusion that life past 60 should not be spent with people of a younger generation. I had come to the same conclusion, however, it wasn't all that easy to remedy the situation.

This wasn't Montreal where one just walked about and picked a spot and rented the flat. Looking for a "Wohnung" here necessitated applying and being told that, unless one had a family consisting of numerous offspring, one wasn't entitled to very much. What they offered were cold-water apartments in dilapidated buildings. I had no choice. Papa and I were coming to a parting of the ways and it was either kill him or move out. We are not a violent family. I took the hovel.

It was a bedroom/living room, kitchen and toilet apartment in the remaining part of a building of which the front had fallen victim to the bombs. I walked through a narrow pathway in-between rubble, climbed up to the second floor and entered my abode which was freezing cold in the winter and never improved much even during the hottest summer day. Being afraid of fire did not help much in the matter of lighting the stove which, in any event, only heated the living/bedroom. Ice-cold water on the face in the morning brought about an instant awakening and dressing became a race between frostbite and pneumonia. I broke every record for getting dressed in under 30 seconds. Every Saturday, I trouped back to Mama for a bath. I had tried the public bathrooms once and it was an experience I did not intend to repeat.

At the Ganghofer Strasse Public Bath, they filled up the bathtub, called my name and gave me 30 minutes. Off came the clothes, in went the body and I was blissfully immersed in hot water, staring up at pipes covering the ceiling and tiled walls that had seen better days. It might have been the same bathtub Mama had used for the entire family in those days when they lived in Neukoelln and before I came on the scene and, simply by being born, got them out of there and into the apartment in Britz with their own bathtub.

Twenty minutes into my soak, someone knocked on the door and yelled, "10 minutes." That didn't leave much time to wash, dry and get dressed but, as expected, exactly 30 minutes into my bath time, the door flew open and the cleaners arrived. German punctuality is something to behold.

Clean, dry and pleasantly warm, I walked into a snowstorm and an icy wind that took my breath away. By the time I got home, I was frozen solid and my bath was a distant memory. This was ridiculous.

I did not think it was fair that I should have to suffer the fate of my ancestors and pointed out to Papa that, but for me, he would also still be staring up at pipes in a dingy little bathroom at the public bath. I guess he remembered those days because I was granted permission to bathe in the family tub. Hallelujah.

In the end, although I loved my family, my work and my new-found friends, I realized that home was not what it had been and never would be again. There was the wall and the wall had changed not only the look of my City but also the mentality of the population occupying these closed-in quarters. Everywhere one looked, there it was. Ugly, monstrous and inhuman, an eye sore and an insult to the very word which the East German government used to describe themselves, namely "The German Democratic Republic." What a joke!

Chapter 28

THE WALL!

First it was a temporary installation of bricks loosely cemented and barbed wire strung along the top. Then German efficiency took over and the second construction looked strong enough to withstand a tank attack. On our side, platforms were erected to be able to peer over the top and wave at relatives on the other side. After a while, this became an exercise in futility unless one was equipped with extremely strong binoculars. The landscape beyond the wall changed from apartment buildings and farmlands to an eerie, desolate and deserted no-man's-land, spiked with land mines and protected from incursion by fenced-in walkways, patrolled by armed-to-the-teeth policemen accompanied by German Shepherd dogs, trained to attack anything that moved.

The rivers and lakes of the City were traversed by red buoys, indicating the border and it was not advisable to drift past these markers. Watchtowers dotted the landscape and binoculars were trained on the unsuspecting visitors at lake-side restaurants, stuffing themselves at the obligatory afternoon "Kaffeklatsch" sessions so dear to the German heart. As there wasn't much in the way of cake or any other luxury item left to be had in the East, I fervently hoped that the Volkspolizei watching us eat were drooling.

Traveling in and out of the City became a nightmare of inspections and intimidating procedures by petty-minded East-German officials who seemed to relish their newfound power to scare the average citizen half to death.

It was also a great source of income for the East Government. Every visa stamp entitling the bearer to pass through the Zone cost money.

Every car, every truck and every person in it had to pay a set price for the privilege of passing through a desolate countryside, as must every train passenger perusing deserted train stations where trains no longer stopped. It was the greatest moneymaking scheme ever invented.

Going on vacation, I wasn't supposed to take the train. The powers in charge of the air base were paying their German employees the difference between the cost of an airplane ticket and a train ride, which was not insubstantial. I take after Papa when it comes to saving money and somehow I didn't think that a little translator was of any importance to the Soviets in the greater scheme of things. I took the money and the train whenever I left the City, but I didn't enjoy it.

Leaving Zoo Station, my first encounter with the border police left me fuming with frustration. Dressed to the hilt in their immaculate, ugly uniforms, they entered the compartment and gruffly demand our passports. The smiles were all on the faces of the passengers and I couldn't understand the mentality. Everyone seemed to pretend that everything was normal, that the impolite and rude demeanour of these so-called 'People Police' employees was a workingman's attitudes towards an unpleasant job. I had the distinct feeling that they enjoyed every minute of it and I wasn't about to give them an inch. I scowled at them and answered questions in the most abrupt fashion I could muster. It gave me the tiny victory of watching their faces registering displeasure and earned me the enmity of my fellow passengers who were afraid my attitude would prolong the agony or, worse, would result in all of us being expelled from the train and transported to a Siberian labour camp. They were probably not that far off but I couldn't help myself. It was too humiliating and to have smiled at these bastards would have killed me. What really galled was that they were Germans. Like us. These weren't Russians dealing with a defeated foe in an occupied zone. These were Germans doing horrible things to Germans in their own country. It wasn't right and it wasn't decent.

On one of my trips, our compartment was blessed with the presence of a young American who didn't think he needed to comply with the procedures. By the time the Volkspolizei had finished with him, he was reduced to a quivering mass of Jell-O and his passport was in the hands of the Border Guard before he had uttered the demand thereof. I sympathized with my Yankee friend. Living all your life in a country where travel is unrestricted, where there are no borders to speak of and the next country is Canada where one simply drives past a border guard, waving a friendly hello, does not prepare one for an encounter of the type Berliners had to live with day-in and day-out. They coped and managed their affairs and on the surface all seemed to have stabilized. Only it wasn't.

The first thing I noticed was the temper of the individuals. Where people would have laughed at unavoidable situations, they now frowned or, in the worst cases, yelled. Tempers flared at the least provocation and smiles seemed to have disappeared. Mentioning my observations to Papa, he told me I was dreaming. Berliners had always been gruff, nothing had changed. Not so!

I remembered the bus driver on the way to Tempelhof Central Airport who always called out: "Next stop, Airport, transfer to London, Paris, New York. But not with our ticket. Sorry!," thereby putting smiles on every one's face. Once, when the bus left a stop and one lady tried to get her money out of her purse with one hand, while waving good-bye to someone on the sidewalk with the other, he told her to relax, get her money, he would do the waving for her. Which he did. To the astonishment of the left-behind relative whose wave, however, never faltered.

I remembered fellow passengers on buses, subways and trains, talking to each other, discussing world events or family histories. I remembered playing cards with my friends on the long way to work at Telefunken and people around us "kibitzing" over our shoulders and making fun of an individual who made the wrong move. I remembered labourers digging ditches yelling at Mama: "Hey, Mother, is that daughter for sale," and Mama shoving me in their direction asking them to please take me off her hands as no one had shown any interest before. I remembered the laughter, the light-heartedness, the wit and the sarcasm and I couldn't find it much anymore. It was a different place in a different time and I was no longer at home in it.

In this new Berlin, I had to deal with a changed attitude. When Mama and I reported my return to the local Police Station, the fellow behind the counter started asking me questions, such as how long had I been in Canada, was I going to stay for good, where did I now live, etc., etc. Mama, being Mama, did not wait for me to open my mouth. By the time she had answered his third question, the uniformed public employee exploded. He did not just tell Mama to let me answer for myself, he yelled at the top of his lungs for her to shut the heck up and let me talk. It was the last thing he said for quite a while.

I somersaulted over the counter, got hold of his tie and started shaking the fellow from side to side, all the while yelling at the top of my own lungs that he had absolutely no right to address my mother in such a fashion and that I immediately demanded to see his superior. It was a sight for sore eyes. Me flat across a very wide counter, Mama holding onto my bottom part and the fellow turning red for lack of oxygen produced by my tight grip on his tie. I got an apology and Mama was told, politely, to keep quiet, which she did until we left the police station. Then I got an earful. Mama did not appreciate my temper and even thought that the officer had been right to tell her off. I didn't get it. It was not the only time I ran into trouble with the new attitudes of my fellow Berliners.

The first time Mama and I went shopping, I saw these absolutely delicious looking bunches of grapes outside the shop in a crate. I grabbed one bunch and proceeded into the store, where I deposited the item of my choice onto the scale. The sales lady was dumb struck.

> *"Where did you get this"?*
>
> *"Outside!"*
>
> *"That's the showcase. You're not allowed to touch that!"*
>
> *"Then were do I get my grapes?"*
>
> *"I give them to you!"*

Which she proceeded to do. What was deposited into the scale was a dilapidated bunch that had definitely seen better days.

> *"I don't want those. I want the ones from outside. Where I come from, the customer chooses what he or she wants, not the other way around!"*
>
> *"What are you? A Guest Worker?"*

Mama had to explain that one. There were so many different nationals now working in the prosperous Germany that the lady may have presumed I was an Italian or Spanish national. Every stranger was called a guest worker, as the object of the game was they would work for a while in Germany and then return to their own country. Having sampled the hospitality, I was wondering why anyone stayed, but they did.

Chapter 29

BERLIN VERSUS THE REST OF GERMANY

Entitled to three weeks vacation, I applied to my trusted Health Insurance Company, the KKH, for a rest and relaxation holiday at one of their contracted guesthouses. I had thoroughly enjoyed my previous outing with them, quite apart from the fact that this was the cheapest way to travel. All I had to pay was 1 Mark a day for three meals a day, plus my travel to wherever I wished to go. I picked the little Village of Oehningen located near the Bodensee and took up residence at the 'Gasthaus Adler.' They provided very modern accommodations, albeit with a shared bathroom. Food was delicious, the scenery beautiful and my fellow travelers a diverse bunch of individuals of all ages. We spent days lazing in the sun, taking trips to Switzerland whose border was in walking distance, and taking delight in smuggling chocolate bars back into Germany at every opportunity. Meeting the locals opened my eyes to a different set of nationals. These were farmers who, every evening, assembled in the Gasthaus for their beer and a game of 'Skat'. They didn't think much of city slickers and Berliners in particular, of which I was the only one. The city slickers in turn turned up their noses at the country bumpkins swilling beers and a good time was had by all. In the end, being forced to share the same locality, we declared a truce and proceeded to slay each other only in card games.

I made friends with two girls from Wolfsburg and one young lady from Kiel and learned a lot about life in the rest of Germany in the process. No one outside of Berlin lived anything remotely like the life the Berliners were living and no one really understood the significance of the wall to the mentality of the population being shut up behind it.

By this time, new expressions had come into use. Everyone in the West was a Wessie and everyone in the East was an Ossie and that was that. Berlin was a long way from little villages like Oehningen and, never having been fond of the Prussians in the first place, the rest of Germany went on with their lives as though nothing had changed. It made me feel a little lonely and a little like an outsider but I couldn't blame them either. Like Papa had said, unless one walks around in the other person's shoes, one cannot understand the situation.

There were no walls in West Germany, no fences, no watchtowers and no guards. All they had in the way of officials was the little chap at the Swiss border who, on our last return trip from Switzerland, asked us politely how much chocolate we were smuggling this time around. He had known all along, everybody did it. We gave him a jaunty salute, bid him adieu and went on our way. There are border guards and then there are border guards. I prefer the Swiss variety.

Halfway through my vacation it started raining and it never stopped until the day I left. So the beach at the beautiful lake was deserted and we proceeded to sightsee our way around the countryside. There was a waterfall at Schaffhausen on the River Rhein. It was called the 'Rheinfall.' The German word 'Reinfall' means to fall for something that is a sham. Someone tricks you, you fall for it - that's a 'Reinfall.' Well, the little Rheinfall of Schaffhausen was advertised as a tremendous waterfall of great beauty. The problem was, I had seen Niagara. The Rheinfall didn't have a chance. It was a Reinfall!

At the end, having recovered our strength via the wonderful food being served in our little Gasthaus, we exchanged addresses, promised to keep in touch and went back to our ordinary lives. They to freedom in the West and I to my imprisoned town in the middle of East Germany.

In the autumn of that year, I joined a bus tour to the Teutoburger Forest to visit the statue of Herman. Now there was a lad Germans could be proud of. He was a warrior of the Cherusker tribe who beat the crap out of an entire Roman legion. In Mr. Kaufmann's history class, I continually fell in love with the Goth heroes fighting the Romans. They didn't always win but, by God, they made it all the way to Italy and almost got Rome. Not bad for little German barbarians. My first love was a young man called Alarich, leader of the East or West Goth. Who remembers. Tall, blond, heroic - and dead of fever by the age of 25. His countryman, being determined not to expose him to the fate of falling into enemy hands even in death, managed to divert the Bosento river, dig a hole into the now dry riverbed, bury Alarich and put the river back in its normal position. Try to find him you filthy Romans. There was a poem about this incident and it never failed to move me.

Then there was Theoderich. He made it all the way to Rome and his tomb stands at Ravenna to this day. Where are these heroes when you need them? Standing in front of Herman's huge statue, I wondered how he would have handled the East German police at the border. He most definitely would not have smiled at them.

Today, the invasion of Italy and other countries is still in process. Only now we don't come with battle axes but tourist visas and a lot of good German currency.

My second summer vacation was planned around the fact that rain is a detriment to enjoying the scenery and it hardly ever rains in Spain in summer. So one of my newfound friends and I boarded a propeller-driven plane for the jaunt to the Costa del Sol.

Torremolinos was a small village turned into a tourist trap of grandiose proportions. We were dropped off at a hotel overlooking the beach. Nice hotel - lousy room. Someone had painted the interior and finished the job about two minutes before we got there. The fumes were enough to make you faint and I wasn't prepared to suffer the consequences of inhaling this for even one night.

Management spoke Spanish and shrugged shoulders at our diatribe in German. OK, let's try the ace up my sleeve. I turned myself into a Canadian and found out that English was definitely turning into an international language. Not only did they now understand our predicament, they also proceeded to move our luggage into an apartment, sporting a bedroom, living room, kitchen, bathroom and balcony and the added bonus of a beautiful view of the ocean. My friend was ecstatic and very relieved at not having to try out her meagre Spanish, the fluency of which she had promised but which now was not forthcoming. School never prepares you for the rapidity in which the natives in any country communicate.

We settled in and enjoyed the pool and our fellow vacationers. There was a young chap from Portugal who had run afoul of the government and was hiding in Spain, waiting for democracy to establish itself in his country. In the meantime, he swam lap after lap and some years later I was very happy to learn that Portugal had changed its attitude and implemented a democratic regime because I could picture the poor lad swimming in that pool, trailing a long beard behind him. Most of the other people were English ladies on vacation from Gibraltar. Loud, quite vulgar and very demanding of the personnel, they did not endear themselves to the Spanish staff. Neither did we.

Being young and on vacation seemed to implicate to the male population of Spain that we were open for business in the raw sex department. I don't think the word 'love' entered their vocabulary where tourists were concerned. Maybe they had a point but it didn't go over too well with me, or my friend.

One could not sit on the beach for two minutes without being surrounded by a gaggle of admirers who did not seem to find anything wrong with touching parts of us that we considered off limits. It was a hassle. Shouting at them produced gales of laughter and pushing gave them an opportunity to grab. We gave up on the beach and the ocean and retired to the pool. It wasn't that much of a loss. The crests of the ocean waves sometimes sported a rather strange, pinkish hue and upon following the flow of the tide one day, we discovered a pipe leading down the cliff from the village, emitting a decidedly unpleasant smell and pouring forth offal left over from the butchering day in the village on top of the hill. The pool was the better bargain.

Our servers at breakfast, lunch and dinner tried their jolly best to get us to date them. They promised untold pleasures, told about places no tourist had ever seen and to which we could only get access in their company and sulked when we said no to all offers. For two days they smashed plates in front of us, made us wait for our food and refused to say hello. I got fed up and decided to fight fire with fire. We put our noses into the air and totally ignored them. It worked. Having decided that we were not what we were supposed to be, namely horny tourists, they became pals, protecting us on the beach, accompanying us into town and guarding our virtues with alacrity in nightclubs which, on our own, we would not have dared to enter.

On Sundays, they turned into paladins of good behaviour, walking their Spanish girlfriends or fiancées through the village streets, followed by an entire congregation of relations on both sides of the family, making sure that holding hands was all they did. Different rules for different folks.

My friend, being of the catholic persuasion and devout at that, dragged me into church one Sunday morning. I thought it was pretty useless as neither one of us understood a word being said. What went on in the streets, on the other hand, was downright spooky and did not need translation. It was a parade of some sort, the custom of which was probably handed down from the Middle Ages. Green leaves were laid down on the streets, men carried a statue of the Virgin Mary in front of a Priest waiving a smoking canister on a string from side to side. There followed a whole contingent of little girls in white dresses and little boys in some sort of uniform, all singing and chanting and very devout. My friend crossed herself and looked to be impressed with the show. I freaked out. I felt as though I was being pulled back through the ages into the time of the Inquisition. It was all so medieval, so ancient and outdated and not right for the 20th Century. For the second time in my life I ran for cover and this time I didn't have a watch for an excuse. There is no explaining the mysteries of the Catholic religion to an avowed Agnostic. It's just scary.

I had better luck visiting the Gypsys who abound in the countryside and, for the proper amount of tourist money, dance in caves and serve liquor in very dirty glasses. I would have liked to see them after all the tourists left but that was not possible. The Alhambra in Granada opened our eyes to a culture that had ruled Spain for 700 years. It just goes to show you that occupation, however long, is not a workable solution to expanding one's own interests. The natives never gave up, threw the Moors out and went back to burning witches in the market places. Progress?

I fell in love with Sangria, Paella, Flamenco, the Spanish language and the ever-present sun. I came back to a cold flat, angry people and the Wall and started saving for the next escape.

At Easter break of my third year at home, I flew to the Island of Mallorca off the coast of Spain. A bungalow village, a pool, a half-hour walk to the beach through the dry Spanish countryside where donkeys were the first mode of transportation and a drink at the bar to die for. Cold chocolate milk with a dash of cognac. At my first try, I managed two, got off my barstool and fell flat on my face. My mind was clear but my legs did not follow orders. It took a few days to acclimatize myself to the potent cognac, but I managed.

We toured the old city of Palma de Mallorca where time seemed to have stood still in the quiet little back streets and the castle towering over the town. We rented cars and visited towns which specialized in pearls and leather goods and we bought items which upon closer inspection at home turned into fakes. My leather wallet lasted three weeks and dissolved in a rainstorm into pieces of cardboard. We took boat rides and watched the natives capture squids and strange fish and we ate food no one bothered inquiring as to what it was. I took pictures of everything, always making sure that there was a lot of colour in them. It was my second attempt at coloured pictures and black and white would not do for such a colourful country as this.

I came very close to killing my Mother upon return. She had bought the film with the instructions to get a coloured one. Mama thought that was too expensive. Mama wanted to save me some money. Mama bought black and white and did not tell me. Mama almost died.

I bought my own film for my next summer vacation in Bavaria. The KKH came through again, believing my request for some peace and quiet in the countryside, and I booked a room in a place called Waltenhofen near Fuessen. The village bordered a lake that had not originally been a lake but another village. It was flooded and when the water level was low, one could see the church tower. Legend had it that sometimes one could hear the bells from the tower, lamenting the town's demise. Unfortunately, the bells didn't ring while I was there. Good food, good company and lots of countryside without restrictions as to where one wanted to go. Mostly what people did in that area was hike. I don't hike. I abhor hiking. I find it a boring, useless exercise where one puts one foot in front of the other for hours on end, only to be faced with the return trip upon arrival at the destination.

The problem with being a Berliner is that every other German taunts one with the statement that Berliners are all mouthy with nothing to show. We fall for it every time.

At dinner one night, people told me about an Alm, 1100 meters up in the mountains, which they would visit on the morrow. I asked them what it looked like, this Alm, and I was told that they would love to take me along and show me but, seeing as I was from Berlin and therefore a wimp, they could not invite me as I would not be able to keep up with them. You never say that to a Berliner and especially not to this one.

I turned up in the morning, dressed in shorts, T-Shirt and open-toed sandals. I was ready to climb Mount Everest if I had to, to regain respect for the citizens of my hometown. 1100 metres later, and having survived a steep climb in beautiful countryside, we stopped at our Alm and were served fresh bread and foamy milk straight from the cow. The butter was homemade and so was the cheese. I've never tasted anything more delicious. The inhabitants of this particular Alm told us stories about living alone all summer in this solitude, about the work that never stopped and the danger of losing cows in crevices and thunderstorms. Not my kind of life but this couple seemed to really enjoy it.

The trip home was a bit more difficult than the climb. By now my feet had swollen, the skin was rubbing against the straps and the pebbles on the road made it difficult to get a grip, making me slip and slide most of the way down.

By the time we arrived at the foot of the mountain, the flesh of both feet was bulging through the straps and I didn't think I would ever get out of these sandals alive. Our tour guide had other ideas. He picked me up and deposited me in the little stream which poured ice-cold snow water straight from the mountains into the valley. It was a shallow, pebbled riverbed and it was so cold it hurt my bones. I screamed and pleaded and cried, but he would not let me come out until he thought it was wise to do so. I owe my vacation to the sadist. By the time we got home, I not only got out of my sandals without problems, I did not even have a blister in the morning for my foolish effort. The pain in my leg muscles was another story but, amid the newfound respect from my fellow hikers, I wasn't going to let anyone in on this. The sandals, however, were history.

For the rest of the sightseeing tours, I took the bus. Bavaria was beautiful, the lakes tranquil and the Castle of Neuschwanstein truly amazing, if slightly tacky. Anytime out of Berlin was a rest for the spirit and I was beginning to understand the exodus of Berliners to the wide and open spaces of West Germany.

Upon return to my City, passing through the ever-present borders, it occurred to me that in a place like Australia, I would never have to worry about firing up a stove or washing my face with pieces of ice chopped out of the washbowl. I would not run into walls or guards or have to deal with an exasperated population letting out its anger on each other.

It was the country I had wanted to go to in the first place, ever since the age of 10 when Brother and I had watched 'The Overlanders' and 'The Children of Mara Mara.' Wouldn't everyone be happy to live in a place called Mara Mara? I knew I would!

Applying for a visa was a piece of cake and having reached the old age of 26, there was nothing Papa could do to stop me from going. I was shopping for a means of transportation when the sky fell in.

If I went to Australia, I would be going as a married woman. The German justice system had seen fit to destroy my aspirations to be a single female. They had cancelled my divorce. I never understood their logic and I still don't. With a single stroke of someone's pen, I was obliged to put Australia on hold and put Canada back on my agenda. It was time to convince the Canadians that they needed me to prosper. It wasn't easy but it wasn't impossible. It helps to be young, pretty and to be able to cry on cue. It's also helpful when the person being subjected to this exercise is of the opposite sex. Women don't fall for it.

Chapter 30

THE RETURN OF THE PRODIGAL WIFE!

I called the Canadian Embassy and was told that, after an absence of three years, I was not entitled to a 'Returning Resident' visa but had to apply for immigration anew. The paperwork involved in that procedure would take at least one year and I didn't have that much time. Patience is not a word in my dictionary and, in this instance, was not to be borne. I made an appointment with the man in charge of dealing with returnees and found him to be sympathetic to my plight.

By the time I had finished blubbering about the horrible living conditions, the ice in the washbowl, the freezing toilet seat in the winter, the bathhouse with a 30-minute limit and the cost of having one's clothing washed at the cleaners, he was pretty much in tears himself. I topped it off with stories of horrendous working conditions involved when having to deal with loud-mouthed, arrogant, over-bearing Americans on a daily basis (Canadians love to be told that they are nicer than Americans) and my tremendous home sickness for the land of the beaver where I had been so happy and which I had only left to please my aging Parents. In the end, I almost convinced myself that all of the above were true, which they most certainly were not. Sometimes you have to lie a little to get what you want. As the whole situation was not of my making, I laid the blame on the German Justice System and my soon to be either ex- or murdered husband. They made me do it.

In any event, the official made me a cup of coffee, handed me the Kleenex box, and proceeded with the paperwork for a 'Returning Resident'. I'm still grateful to him and I'm sorry I lied but - all is fair in love and war. And this was war.

My intrepid lawyer equipped me with a letter stating that my husband would appreciate if the German justice system would grant him a divorce for the simple reason that he already lived with another lady whom he intended to marry. I was promised that if I could make the former object of my affection sign it and have the signature verified by an official at the German Embassy in Montreal, all would be well and I would be single.

At the end of November of 1965, I said good-bye to my fellow workers at the Base, took group pictures of every one I had encountered in my time there, hugged my favourites, cried at leaving behind a lot of friends and promised to write.

On December 1st, I gave Mama and Papa my word to return within two years and watched them wave good-bye through the curtain. I drove off with Brother who, as tradition demanded, saw me off. Parting from Berlin for the second time was not as difficult as the first. Somehow, I hadn't quite fit in. Brother put it in a nutshell when he dropped me off at the train station. "You're not the same girl I took to the Bus in 1959. You've changed". I did not agree but I didn't argue. As far as I was concerned, everyone in Berlin had changed while I had stayed true to form. Who was right? Who knows!

I took the train to Rotterdam, suffered one last time the incivility of our border guards, and boarded the Dutch Liner "Rhyndam" for the return trip to Montreal.

If I had expected another raucous experience, I was very much disappointed. Fortunately, my mind was on other things. I was not looking forward to meeting my ex, nor did I quite know how I was going to make him sign a letter such as the one I was carefully transporting in my luggage.

I've only been on one Dutch liner and have therefore no opinion as to the hospitality extended by the entire fleet. My particular ship, however, should have been named 'boredom city.' What they lacked on entertainment, however, they most certainly made up at meal times. The food was scrumptious and plenty of it.

Our dinner table was blessed with the company of the ship's doctor, a handsome enough individual in a spotless uniform who seemed to be under strict instructions to be nice to the passengers while, at the same time, having a great problem acquiescing to that request. We bored him and he bored us and it did not make for particularly exhilarating conversations.

There was a bar which closed at 11 pm. I don't remember dancing but I remember encountering a new phenomena called "hippies". There were about 20 of them on board and they insisted on running around outside barefoot, dressed in long caftans and both sexes wore their hair long and unkempt down their backs. Being busy in the Augustiner Keller and not listening over much to the radio, I had missed out on the emergence of a new generation. Seeing as they seemed not to like washing very much, smelled very badly of something sweetish which someone explained to me was Marijuana, and didn't have enough sense to put on shoes in the middle of December, I didn't think I had missed too much.

The only entertainment I remember was a disaster for me personally as I lost the only friend I had managed to make on the voyage. There was a 'Fancy Hat Show'.

I am not an artist like Brother. I cannot decorate or drape or embellish like Sister. I am a klutz with a needle and the enjoyment of making a piece of art out of bits and pieces totally escapes me. My friend, on the other hand, set to it with vigour. Her hat was a piece of art before mine had a single piece of decoration attached to it. I was in trouble and, when in trouble, I am smart enough to ask for help. She took over and, in next to no time, I was sporting a creation of paper-made flowers, vaguely resembling the kind of hats Grandma would have worn on her way to church. I look good in hats and I looked particularly good in my hand-made original, which I proudly paraded around the dance floor in the evening. I won a bottle of champagne for the prettiest hat and the creator of this original should have been proud of that, but wasn't. She had expected her own hat to win and the fact that mine was actually hers also did not seem to enter her mind. I even gave her the bottle of bubbly but I couldn't fix what was broken. The ego gets in the way of logical thinking sometimes and there is nothing anyone can do about it.

By the time we spotted land, I had gained five pounds, read almost the entire contents of the ship's library and had encountered boredom for the first time in my life. It was mind-numbing and time wasting and not to be repeated at all costs.

At the pier in Montreal, my Dutch friend, accompanied by her husband and baby son, were waiting to greet me. They and my old Boss at Styled Cottons were the only people I had told of my return to Canada and also given the reason why. They had not kept in touch with my Ex and there was no possibility that they would warn him of my arrival even if they had still associated. He had borrowed and forgotten to return funds once too often to most of our friends and, in the process, lost them all.

My old friends had prospered. They lived in a duplex in the outskirts of Montreal and getting to know them again was a pleasure. My first day was spent calling other old friends and the reception after three long years was heart-warming. The call to my husband was a little less so.

We met downtown at Dunn's where the smoked meat sandwich was as delicious as I remembered it and where, between munching, I explained to the once-upon-a-time love of my life that, if he really wanted to get me back, he would first have to sign a piece of paper granting me a divorce. I had fought too hard and paid too much for it to be all forgotten and forgiven. I promised to return, to try again to make a relationship work, but only after he had given me my freedom of choice.

I don't know if it was my persuasive powers or the wonderful smoked meat sandwich which lulled him into a false sense of security, but he fell for it, 'hook, line and sinker'. Two days later, we sat in an opulent office, facing the German Consulate General and watched him reading the morally reprehensible letter issued by my lawyer's pen in a last ditch effort. I still had doubts it would work, but then, I didn't understand much about lawyers and the law in particular.

Having verified my husband's signature, our official representative of the German nation added his own and a stamp to make it official and then congratulated me on my future marriage. The poor man assumed that I was the new woman in my husband's life, not the one he was leaving behind according to the text of the letter. Laughingly advising him of the circumstances, we left him sitting, open-mouthed, at his desk, very likely despairing of the morality of the new generation.

We deposited the letter into the nearest mailbox and I bid my love good-bye, promising to get together as soon as possible. It was the last he saw of me for months.

I spent the next week moving into a studio apartment on Goyer Street and checking out agencies for jobs. Contacting my old boss at Styled Cottons proved productive only in that he gave me good advice. The company itself was no longer in business and he was semi-retired. He invited me to dinner and in the process showed me a world I had not known existed. It was a very fancy restaurant and, for the first time in my life, I was exposed to what a good chef can accomplish with ordinary meats and vegetables and a few spices.

Good food wasn't all my ex-boss provided me with that night. He complimented me on my work ethic, my typing speed and my ability to spell well in my adopted language and he gave me confidence in my job search. "Go for Dictaphone until you learn shorthand. It pays well", he told me - so I did. Only problem was, I did not remember the Dictaphone. I had only used it that one time in his office. I knew there were pedals and a tape and little buttons one stuck in one's ears. However, a little forgetfulness should never stand in the way of success and it doesn't when one is resourceful. First thing in the morning, I headed for an agency.

Having done my typing test, they had no problem recommending me to the firm of Canadian Factors as a Dictaphone typist of the highest order. My interview went well and I was asked to start on Monday. This was Friday. I spent the entire weekend on the phone asking everyone I knew to tell me everything they had to offer about the quaint little machine called a Dictaphone. Most knew as much or less than I did and on Monday morning I was no wiser as to the machine's intricacies.

Being introduced to new co-workers is always a little like running a gauntlet. Appraising eyes are making judgments, which later have to be adapted to the reality of the real person, and future friends or enemies are at this time non-entities and rapidly passing faces with names that just as quickly disappear out of memory.

The girl I was replacing at the job took me to my desk and, lo and behold, there it was - the illusive Dictaphone. It was a grey box, looking kind of worn, with wires attached to earphones. All I managed to see, and a fact which I grabbed hold of with desperation, was that this machine was definitely not a new model.

"Good God," I exclaimed. "I haven't seen this old thing for a long time. I don't even remember how it worked. Would you mind helping me out here?" The lady totally agreed that management was very remiss in not providing their staff with newer models and proceeded to enlighten me as to the workings of this 'old thing' which had surely arrived on this continent by way of the Mayflower. All is fair in love and war and when trying to secure a good job.

My co-workers were mostly French-Canadians, endowed with their inherent good sense of humour which, unfortunately, they were in the process of losing. Quite rapidly I realized that all was not as it had been. It seemed that every time I left somewhere, the remaining population changed everything around, which made home-coming that much more difficult. In this case, it was the age-old dispute of who had conquered Canada and to whom it should belong.

The Battle on the Plains of Abraham had been lost by the French but they have never, not even to this day, acknowledged that fact or conceded defeat to the British. By now, in the year 1966, it was a battle cry in the streets and at the Universities and the topic of every conversation. Quebec for the French and to hell with the English. That in the meantime half the population was of an entirely different ethnic background than either French or English did not come into the equation. It did not make sense to me as both countries had basically invaded someone else's territory, whose inhabitants, nevertheless, had also arrived from somewhere else at another date in time. So who does the country belong to? They've been arguing forever. Years, and hundreds of French Immersion schools later, the country is no more bilingual than it was when they started making it officially so.

I ignored the battle and concentrated on work and getting reacquainted with Montreal. Nothing much had changed in the area around Goyer and Cote Des Neiges. It was still 'new immigrant country', where at any given time you could hear the languages of numerous nationals up and down the street. Multi-culturism was alive and well on the roof tops before ever it became fashionable on the political agenda. The Paris BBQ on the corner still served the best chicken in the world and Dunn's on St. Catherine Street had not lost their touch with smoked meat.

My apartment had hot water and heat and I could have a bath any time I wanted to. The garbage was thrown into an incinerator down the hall which was very convenient but also contributed to the occasional fire when it somehow malfunctioned, which it did on one occasion in my building while I was in the process of sitting down to dinner, luckily with no dire consequences. What was funny in the aftermath was the fact that the only item I had grabbed out of my apartment was the stuffed monkey I had received on my 6th Birthday. One must get one's priorities right and it seemed the monkey was more important to me than my passport or my money. Such items could be replaced, the monkey could not.

Five weeks into my new life, I received a letter from my lawyer with the good news that the German justices had finally seen daylight and, having understood the need of my husband to dispose of me in favour of someone new, they had granted the divorce. Congratulations and papers will follow. What finally arrived was a thick document, nicely put together, outlining in detail the why and wherefore of my divorce and why one had been granted. I was declared 'not guilty' in the suit and given my freedom to pursue other males. It had taken three years of my life, a lot of hard-earned money and a trip back to Canada under false pretences. I figured, if they would make marriage this expensive and divorce easy, a lot of people would think twice about tying the knot. As far as I was concerned, marriage was no longer on my agenda. Then I met a man who taught me not to judge a book by its cover.

Chapter 31

A CHRISTMAS TREE OR A HANUKKAH BUSH?

Marriage was out but dating was still in. After having spent Christmas 1965 all by myself walking around Town of Mount Royal looking at other people's Christmas trees, I had no objections to being pursued by the tall, dark and handsome fellow at the other side of the office who had a way with words and oozed sincerity out of every pore. Before I knew what had happened, I was watching very artsy films, the kind that never make it to ordinary movie houses, and attending discussion groups afterwards where everyone had a quite definite opinion on what the director had been trying to tell the public.

The new man in my life was definitely out of the ordinary. Born of Romanian Jews, his parents divorced while the Germans were in the process of destroying the livelihood of Jews all over Europe. His father had once owned a very prosperous fur business but ended up digging ditches and saved his life by marrying a Catholic girl from Hungary. The entire extended family ended up in Israel but I don't think they liked it very much as, eventually, they all turned up in Montreal. My lad attended school there, became the local rebel who took a knife to school and had rip-roaring fights with his stepmother. By the time I met him, he had definitely settled down somewhat but his stories left me breathless.

This was very different from growing up in Britz. This was romantic and sad and it brought out the mother-instinct I never knew I had. He wanted to be a writer and that should have clued me in to the fact that, maybe, he also had a vivid imagination and that some of his stories should perhaps be taken with a little grain of salt. Unfortunately,

I was too busy enjoying my new 'intellectual' stage in life while he introduced me to Chaucer and Shakespeare and the glory of English and American literature outside of Science Fiction and Westerns. He opened my mind to new worlds and I am still grateful for that. He also taught me to be wary of manipulative people who, step by tiny step, take over a person's life. Papa had taught me never to trust people who use the word 'love' with impudence. By the time I realized what 'love' meant to my intended, it was almost too late.

But first, we had a lot of fun. In the Spring, we had picnics on top of Mount Royal and spent evenings in coffee shops around the city, discussing the French/English situation with French students who were adamant in their belief that Quebec should not be considered a Province in Canada but be made into a country, where French was the language of the land and no one need be bothered any longer with learning English. How they were going to conduct business with the United States was a topic no one was willing to discuss.

My man was attending Sir George William University at night and Chaucer became my favourite author of the moment. At one point, my lover caught a cold, took to his bed and talked me into attending his course to take notes on the subject of Shakespeare's Hamlet. It was the first time I heard someone dissect a book and, in the process, destroy the entire meaning by imbuing the subject with their own limited imagination and psychological hang-ups. It was mind boggling.

The lady in charge had 'phallic symbol' on her mind and those words were repeated over and over as an explanation for whatever ailed poor Hamlet. If Shakespeare had walked in, he would not have recognized his play. As Shakespeare could not defend himself, I felt it was my duty to speak up for him. No one likes to be told that there is something wrong with their sex life. It didn't go down very well. It was the end of my attendance at Sir George Williams and I was left thinking that, not having enjoyed a higher education wasn't all that much of a drawback.

Going steady for a while usually necessitates the obligatory visit to the parents of the suitor. Fortunately, my man's parents had no desire to meet me due to the fact that I was German and therefore 'persona non grata' in a Jewish household, even if it was only half of one. Things could have continued indefinitely until my young man decided that, father's wishes aside, introductions needed to be made if this affair was ever going to be permanent.

One Sunday afternoon, bearing flowers and a watermelon, we entered the lion's den. Nothing is ever as bad as one's imagination tries to make it. Rica and Manzie took one look at four feet eleven inches of anxiety, threw away their prejudices and opened their arms. Heaven is sitting on a balcony that offers a little breeze in Montreal's hot and humid summer evenings, snacking on an ice-cold, juicy watermelon, watching the world go by. In the ensuing months, Manzie taught me new ways to transform raw materials into delicious food and Rica taught me to never judge a book by its cover.

Here was a man who had had everything and had all taken away from him. As long as I knew him, he never complained about his fate, his misfortune or the people responsible for the whole mess. He told wonderful stories about life in Romania before the War, where he had been commissioned to provide fur coats for very illustrious people. He made us laugh, describing his life digging ditches, an enterprise to which neither his hands nor his entire body had an affinity for. He was glad to be still alive and didn't think that blaming me would alter the circumstances.

When I decided not to marry his son, Rica announced that he had not been good enough for me anyway and that I could do better. I still have his engagement present. When I tried to give it back to him, he asked me whether I was ever engaged to him. I had to deny that and to Rica that meant that we had not got disengaged either. So there. Every time I wear my Austrian gold coin surrounded by a star-like design, on a gold chain, I think of Rica and watermelons and hot Montreal summer evenings.

Paprika Chicken, on the other hand, is solely Manzie's contribution to my recipe book and is still enjoyed by everyone lucky enough to be invited to the feast. She was the best cook I ever knew.

Her other talent was reading coffee cups. We would drink thick, black coffee and, when the cup was empty, turn it upside down. Out of the black muck on the bottom, Manzie would predict our future or the lack of one. By the time I had basically decided that the relationship with my fiancee was turning sour, Manzie's talent nearly cost me my secret. My cup, instead of being covered all over as I had intended while swivelling the coffee grounds around, had one bare streak all the way to the rim of the cup. "You're leaving," announced my Hungarian Cassandra. And nothing I said convinced her otherwise. She was Hungarian and she could tell about people by looking at coffee grounds. She really could.

Going out together and working together is not a good situation.

When my man decided it was time to move in together, I thought it appropriate to look for another job. When I quit, the French Canadian section of my team demanded a French Canadian girl to replace me. Seeing as I had typed only one letter in French in eight months, I thought it a bit lame to insist on a bilingual secretary but times had changed and this was the new Quebec. I found a company where French was not as yet in demand and settled down in the accounting department of Churchill Falls Power Corporation on Sherbrooke Street. There wasn't a French Canadian in sight and, accordingly, discussions at lunch and breakfast counters with co-workers turned to topics other than the separation or secession of Quebec out of Canada. It was a relief. Talking to French Canadians some times left one with the impression that there was no other world outside of Quebec. It was nice to be removed from the subject.

Christmas came and I insisted on a Christmas tree. My man acquiesced to my wish and brought home a lovely, thick fir tree which we decorated just as Papa had taught me. On Christmas day, Rica and Manzie arrived for dinner and looked with wonder at the lit-up Christian contraption in the corner. "But, my son", Rica explained. "That is a Christmas tree. What are you doing with a Christmas tree. You're Jewish!". His son never even blinked. "That is not a Christmas tree, Dad. That is a Hanukkah bush!" Problem solved, dinner could commence and a good time was had by all.

I thought I had arrived in Paradise and forgot that there is a snake in residence. How does one defend oneself against accusations when one has done nothing wrong? It started small, got bigger and nastier and made my life a living hell. He suspected infidelity at every corner and watched my every step. I was asked to drop my old friends as their influence was derogatory. Having a cup of coffee with Erika was tantamount to desertion. My life no longer belonged to me but to him and him alone. Snooping through my belongings one day, he came upon my diary, written when I first arrived in Canada. As he could not read German, he made up his own stories as to why some names had an X beside them. For me, they were people I had especially liked, for the suspicious lad, they were people I had had intimate relations with. He asked me to destroy that book as it bothered him.

It is incredible what some people are capable of making others do. I took the book, took basically the story of part of my life, walked out the door and threw it down the incinerator. When I returned and saw his beatific smile, that forgiving smile that had forgiven me so much already, I knew the time had come to wipe it off his face once and for all.

I threw my engagement ring at him and started to pack. My old pal Karl was only a phone call away and, having hated my fiance with a passion, was only too glad to lend a hand in leaving him.

Two weeks later, Israel was invaded. It has gone down in history as the 6-day war. It was won without the help of my Man but not for lack of trying.

He called me at work to tell me that he was going to the Israeli Embassy to volunteer for the Army. Would I mind coming down and seeing him off? How could I mind? For all I knew, he was going to die over there and I couldn't refuse this invitation. It was an eye opener. We sat in the lobby and watched men and women being speedily processed out of their civilian life and back into a soldier's milieu. All of whom were 'Sabras'. All of them were trained in the forces. All of them were willing to leave their livelihood, their families and their friends behind for the sake of Israel. "See you in Cairo," they all said on the way out. I wondered how many of them would see the next week.

By the time they called my volunteer, I was ready to volunteer myself. Such an exuberance of national pride is definitely catching. Not catching enough for my companion, however, who emerged from the office chagrined and disillusioned.

For myself, I had never imagined that they would hand him a gun and drop him into the middle of the war. Unfortunately, that was precisely what he had had in mind. It appealed to his romantic nature to do so. What they offered him was a free flight to Israel and a nice position on a Kibbutz with training in the army in the future. He declined. There was no glory in shovelling manure or digging ditches. I don't know what his relatives made of this decision. Parties had already been arranged to fete the valiant warrior and would now have to be called off. I didn't care. I left him standing outside the Israeli Embassy. There was now nothing left in Montreal to keep me there.

Wonderful Montreal, where one could find an apartment within minutes, move in within days and be free once again of encumbrances and bad relationships. Wonderful Montreal, where friends were leaving by the train-, car- and bus-loads to parts of the country where English was still the only necessary language for immigrants to learn. Wonderful Montreal, where mailboxes started to explode, store clerks refused to serve customers in anything other than the French language and people started to behave as though they lived in the oppressed, inhuman police state of East Germany. Wonderful Montreal, where they kidnapped and killed a human being during those troubled times. And the people who did this got little prison time and lived happily ever after in France for a number of years. They're back now and active in political life. The man they killed is still dead and his family still grieves.

I stopped listening to their grievances, their imagined slights, their whining and complaining. This was no longer the wonderful Montreal I had encountered in 1959. These were no longer the fun-loving, self-deprecating, friendly French Canadians I had come to love. This was madness and stupidity and, like most everyone else I knew, I pulled up stakes to have a look at the rest of the country. I'm definitely one for extremes. I ran all the way from the Atlantic to the Pacific. No one told me how much it rained in Vancouver.

Chapter 32

WEATHER REPORT - WET, WET AND WETTER

I had not kept in touch with Sister, but I knew that she had left Montreal and moved back to Vancouver some months before my return. When Mama heard that I wanted to give Vancouver a try, she implored me to get in touch with my long-lost relative and patch things up. Whatever Mama wants, Mama gets. I wrote Sister a card, advising her of my imminent arrival to which she replied promptly, offering a room in her house.

Vancouver being on the other end of the continent, Papa insisted on a visit before I disappeared into the nether land of British Columbia. I found myself a charter flight, bid goodbye to friends, co-workers and neighbours, boarded - and watched Papa making a fool of himself again in the Airport. It's called love.

I had only been gone 1½ years and things had progressed. My pal Helga of the Denmark trip fame was now a mother of two and had moved into a new district called Britz Sued. The U-Bahn, which had ended at Grenzallee, was being extended all the way to the little village of Rudow and apartment blocks had sprung up like mushrooms in places where Brother and I flew our kites in those far-away days of our youth.

Dance halls were out and Discos were in. Elvis was a has-been and the British Invasion ruled the airwaves. Skirts went up, way up, and men started growing their hair longer than the girls. Papa thought the world had gone mad and paid a price for not understanding the new regime.

A few days into my visit, Mama and Papa decided to go see a

movie. I watched television and amused myself with the spectacle of 'The Rifleman" speaking German. All television programs bought by Germany were dubbed and I could never convince Mama that the lady advertising Palmolive dish soap was actually American. The woman spoke German fluently and that was that for Mama. The fact that I had seen the same lady in Canada speaking fluently in English only convinced Mama of her versatility. End of discussion.

Halfway through the program, my parents returned home. I thought that the movie had been sold out and didn't think anything of it until Papa went to the bedroom and laid down on his bed. This was not like my Papa and, thinking he might have had another heart attack, as he had once before at a time of stress, I jumped off the couch to follow him. Mama held me back and led me back in the living room. Papa did not want to talk to anyone right now. Papa was in shock. Papa had been hit in the face by a young man and sent flying in the lobby of the movie house.

My parents had been standing in the lobby, waiting for the doors to open. There were very few benches in the atrium, all of them occupied. Next to Papa stood a very old lady and, being a gentleman, Papa asked a young man occupying one of the few seats to please vacate his place for this lady. Being Papa, I could imagine the tone of voice in which he addressed this individual. Knowing Papa, I could guess at the affront to his mind of having to even ask this favour. Unfortunately, the young man in question had not received an upbringing by anyone remotely resembling my Papa. He barely glanced at my irate parent and just said "NO." Whereas Papa grabbed the offender by the front and hauled him out of the seat. Never in his life could he have imagined what happened next. The youngster came at him, fists flying, and landed a proper knock-out on Papa's chin. My Papa was in very good physical shape and, in ordinary circumstances, could very likely have beaten his opponent to a pulp. These were not ordinary circumstances. Papa sat on the floor, stunned, unbelieving and in shock. Mama helped him to his feet and propelled him out the door. They did not speak all the way home.

"No one helped", said Mama. "No one said a word. They all just turned away. This isn't right." No, it wasn't. Welcome to the new world order.

I promised Mama never to mention this to Papa and I never did. I just wish I could have been there when he needed me. I had very long fingernails and they would have left permanent marks on the Punk's face. I would have dealt with that Bastard.

I proved it a few days later when Mama tried to take a nap in the afternoon. There were a few children playing outside the window and Mama, as she had done for generations, asked them politely to please go play somewhere else for a little while. I couldn't believe what came back from the mouths of these adorable little creatures. They called my Mama a Witch and invited her, in an unmistakably Berliner accent, to lick their "arse". My out of date parent, as Papa before her, had no weapon with which to fight this insult. I did.

I was at that window in two seconds and promised them the biggest thrashing they had ever had if they were not gone from the vicinity within two minutes. Three took the warning seriously and decamped forthwith. Two decided to dare defiance by telling me that I was not allowed to touch a hair on their head. I told them that it wasn't their hair I was after and that I would be out - NOW! Then I left the window. Mama watched as they sped up the street to greener pastures. Our new generation of Berliners - how lovely. No respect, no courtesy, no manners. Who was raising these imbeciles?

Two weeks into my stay, and having had the pleasure of viewing Brother's face only twice over the supper table, my sibling thought it was time to go on the obligatory nightclub tour. He promised to pay for the drinks this time around and just seeing Mama's happy face as she watched us departing was worth the effort.

First we attended an 'Afternoon Tea Dance' on the roof of the Hilton Hotel. Most of Brother's new friends were Jewish and not of the working-class kind. I kept thinking that if I were Jewish, Germany would be the last place on Earth I would want to settle. But business is business and there were a lot of 'compensation payments' going on. Anyone who could prove they had left behind a thriving business or livelihood before decamping from Germany was adequately reimbursed for their losses. I remembered the little greengrocer on Hermannstrasse who got picked up in the middle of the night and lost his and his family's life at whatever camp they sent him to. How do you reimburse him?

While listening to the violins, I noticed the newest trend in fashion. Wigs. Everyone was wearing wigs. Brother gallantly overlooked the fact that his Sister was again out of fashion and entertained the masses with his charm and witticism. They loved him. I figured he should charge for the performance, he could get rich.

The talk all during the afternoon was of a little Pub we would frequent later in the evening which sported the endearing name of 'The

Black Button.' All Berlin's Nightclubs had by now acquired English names, they wouldn't have survived otherwise. It wasn't cool to dance at something called "Roswitha" any more. You had to be the Petit Palais, the Eden, the Hungry Horse, or whatever. Which was fine with me. Whatever turns people on.

Afternoon Tea over, we had a bite to eat and then proceeded to the famous 'Button' enterprise. Only it wasn't a button. The neon sign above said in glorious colours and very clearly - "Black Bottom". Once inside, I asked Brother why we changed venue. We hadn't. We had arrived at the Black Button. No we hadn't. I started laughing and couldn't stop. When I recovered, I asked them just how many people they thought had been laughing behind their backs about their lack of knowledge of the English language. I exclaimed the difference between a button and a bottom, which in this case was almost self-explanatory as the entrance to the bar was situated below ground and could only be reached by a stairwell going down at least six steps to the 'bottom'.

I spent the rest of the evening in solitude. They decided I was not quite in the league of entertainment as Brother was. I think they were mistaken. Had they been able to laugh at themselves, they would have had a great time. Mama thought it was hilarious.

Three weeks go by very quickly and before I knew it, I was hugging Papa in his bed, hugging Mama at the door and slamming the car door of Brother's newest acquisition. Whatever else he was, Brother was still Brother and his goodbye of "Don't let the Sky fall onto your head, Mondesglanz," was still appreciated for what it was, a declaration of love from one little Indian, named Sitting Bull, to Mondesglanz, the little Indian sister who shared all his adventures sitting on top of the Kachelofen (tile oven) while being chased by the US Cavalry. He called me by that name for as long as I can remember and it always made me feel good. We had sworn to be blood bothers and nothing could ever change that.

Vancouver started off as a disappointment and didn't improve much after. They didn't even have an airport building. There was a shed at the end of the runway to which we had to walk, being watched by relatives and friends from behind a fence. There, waving frantically and looking very pleased to see me, was my Sister. I cleared customs and met up with my long-lost relative and a friend who had volunteered to drive us the long way to Burnaby where Sister had taken up residence.

It was a beautiful August day and the scenery, as Sister had promised, left nothing to be desired. Surrounded as it is by the Coastal Mountains, Vancouver is lovely to behold. Until it starts raining, which it did as soon as September arrived.

With September and the rain came Erika and Terry, my best friend and one of Sister's old pals from Montreal. As refugees from Quebec, they took up residence in the living room, as my own room was barely big enough for a bed and a dresser. Sister lived in a house on a corner lot, graciously supplied by the Welfare Department of the City. Sister had become a single parent with two children, having married and divorced in short order, adding a baby boy to her family out of a doomed relationship. She had now effectively turned me into an Aunt but nobody called me that. When Sister reminded my new relatives that the proper address was Aunt Edie, they informed her that I was too small to be an Aunt and, anyway, I played like a Kid with them and could therefore not really be considered an adult.

The house was not small but definitely not big enough for all these visitors. Terry went first, renting a one-bedroom apartment in the west end of the city near Stanley Park. Erika took up residence in a small room in a boarding house on Barclay Street and I visited them as often as I could. But, as Sister needed more money, she rented out the attic of her little house to students attending classes at Simon Fraser University. One of them wore contact lenses.

Years before in Montreal, Erika and I had watched a young girl in a restaurant who seemed to be crying her eyes out. Upon inquiry as to her problem, we were told there was nothing wrong except for the fact that her contact lenses were brand-new and her eyes were sore as hell. In those days, they were made out of glass and not very comfortable by the looks of it. I swore I would wait for my own set until they had perfected the method which, by the time I arrived in Vancouver, they apparently had. The young student did not seem to have a problem at all and I was getting sick and tired of getting kicked out of men's washrooms, getting into the wrong cars and smiling at people who, at close range, were no acquaintances at all.

I had been short-sighted since the age of 13. Mama found out when one day, standing on the balcony, she waved at someone across the way. I asked her what she was doing and that's how we found out that I couldn't see across the street. I got glasses that I absolutely refused to wear except in a dark movie theatre or at home for the television. I got a reputation for being a snob because I neglected to greet neighbours and other acquaintances and Mama, after the diagnosis by the optician, was happy to inform the neighbourhood that her little girl was nothing of the kind. I just couldn't see anyone.

By the time I arrived in Montreal, I was reduced to wear the glasses at work as it got harder and harder deciphering the work an arms-length away on my desk. But until I got my contact lenses, I walked through life in a foggy haze and have no idea what all I missed in the process.

Not being very affluent at the time of my arrival in Vancouver, I tried to obtain lenses through an ordinary optician. Another lesson learned the hard way. Don't be cheap when you want quality. It was hard enough to learn to insert the tiny plastic shapes into one's eyes without the lids closing automatically when the finger approached. The lenses I had bought were not fitting properly, which meant that every time I blinked, they moved up and then slowly obeyed the law of gravity and moved downwards. It tickled and itched and I blinked continuously trying to keep them in place. In the process, I looked as though I had a nervous condition. I gave up.

Next stop, the best eye doctor in Vancouver. Dr. Pratt-Johnson lived up to his reputation and I am still grateful for his expertise. What an eye opener, literally. Having spent a lifetime walking around with eyes as big as saucers trying to see clearly, I now started appreciating the little things in life - like seeing the number on the Bus, spotting friends across the street and attending to personal business in the proper wash-room facility. It was wonderful living in the 20th Century.

Endowed with good eyesight and totally out of funds, I was forced to go looking for work, which did not seem to be as easy as it had been in Montreal. There weren't many jobs available. Agencies were pretty much useless and whereas I was used to just walk in, do my typing and IQ tests and walk out with a list of interviews to attend, I was now told by everyone that they would get in touch with me when and if a position became available. Two weeks into this exercise, I saw an advertisement in the paper from the CIBC Bank for a Dictaphone typist. I was on the bus and downtown before the door had properly closed behind me. Speed was of the essence as I wasn't the only one looking for a job.

I did my test, passed with flying colours and filled in the obligatory papers to ensure employment. Sister was pleased because she needed my money of $90.00 a month for room and board. She was a very good cook, it was worth it but it didn't take long to dislike the long trip into town. One bus to the Kootenay Loop in Burnaby, where one had to wait around for the Hastings Express to transport the passengers on to downtown. Public transport is not the first priority in British Columbia. But for someone who doesn't own a car, it's decidedly lacking when it rains buckets.

Work was a room full of typewriters and busy girls with flying fingers. I got introduced to my co-workers who ranged in age from 18 to 40 and to my new Boss, Miss Nelson, an elderly lady who made it clear that under no circumstances was she to be addressed as Mrs. I had no problem with that. The custom in Germany is that if a lady is not married by the time she reaches 30, she is automatically addressed as Mrs., even though she is missing that little golden band on her right hand. If this lady, at the tender age of almost 60, was determined to stay a Miss, who was I to argue. She must have had her reasons.

What I did have a problem with was a friendly foe who insisted on supplying me with stacks of work, while, in my observation, the custom seemed to be that one took however much work one thought one could get through in a day from a pile on the counter. Two days into my work being delivered by hand, I asked her politely whether she thought there was something wrong with my legs. I could write a book on how to make friends and acquire enemies in one easy session. One down, ten to go. Two of my co-workers were smaller than I am and I made the dreadful mistake of taking note of that fact. I should have known better.

To the end of my own days, I will resent people who remark on my diminutive size of 4 feet 11 inches (and ½ if I really stretch), as though I hadn't known the fact all my life. Unless someone is a good friend of mine, in which case he or she can call me a shrimp any time they feel like it, I will snap instantly at anyone making an inane remark to that effect. I don't know why. I no longer resent being small, on the contrary, I take delight in the fact. But the childhood abuse, the catcalls, the snide remarks have left an indelible impression and there is nothing I can do about it. So, as soon as those words were out of my mouth and I saw the expression on the little ladies' faces, I knew I was in for it. They never forgave me, which was sad. I never held it against them, which is true.

I settled into my new routine. It was boring but they paid well. I hated the very long bus ride into town but for the time being there was not much I could do about it. When new in town, one has to check things out first. Erika and I went on the prowl.

First stop, the German Club on Fraser Street. First surprise. In 1967, there were very strange liquor laws in place in Vancouver. I don't know what hoops an establishment had to jump through to get a liquor license, but not every restaurant or club owned one. Here we had a German Club full of thirsty Germans who had to bring their own booze to the dance. Erika and I stood transfixed in the doorway. It looked as though we would have to survive the evening with Coca Cola.

Help arrived in the shape of a gentleman from Austria who inquired whether or not we would like to join him at his table which appeared to be covered in bottles of all manner of alcoholic beverages. How could we refuse?

Erika had a great time. She was homesick for Montreal and this club reminded her of our old haunts which I had not frequented in years. I looked around at these aging immigrants holding on to their nationalities as though life depended on it and despaired. Dirndl dresses look charming on young ladies in Bavaria and Austria. When one gets to be around 50, a Dirndl dress is not only out of style, it also amplifies the lost youthfulness of a once swelling bosom. It isn't a pretty sight. It was 1967 and the people at our table had been in Canada for more than 20 years, yet all of their friends were here and everyone was from 'over there'. There was no way I was going that route ever again. It was my first and last evening at the Alpen Club but it had not been a lost cause altogether. Our host, the Austrian owner of many bottles of liquor, did not just supply us with booze, he also gave us a ride home and, in the process of all that, became a life-long friend.

Vancouver had lots of other clubs and entertainment venues. There was the Cave and Izzies, both Supper Clubs where Mitzie Gaynor and other notables tried out their acts. There was the Down Under Club where sooner or later every Australian in town turned up. There was the Quadra Club with a Quartet which boasted a singer who could have doubled for Frank Sinatra, the inevitable 'Hofbrauhaus' on Robson Strasse and then there was the Johann Strauss nightclub, boasting three rooms, each one of which sported live bands which played a different kind of music. Not a bad assortment of entertainment for a town which everyone in Montreal had called "that rainy hick town back of beyond".

Robson Street was commonly known as "Robson Strasse" as it boasted three German delicatessen, a European cheese shop, Gizella's Swiss Konditorei, the Mozart Café and the European News which sold everything from Beer Steins to Dirndl dresses to newspapers from around the world. German Restaurants abounded with the Heidelberg Restaurant and the Schnitzel Keller among other notables of European origin. I was informed that the German speaking population in the

Province of British Columbia, which probably included the Austrians and the Swiss, was the second biggest nationality occupying the area. In Vancouver, the area around Fraser Street was their preferred locale. Today, the next generation of immigrants inhabit the same area and the signs on shops and the wares sold reflect the Chinese and Indian choice of location. Things change.

I fell in love with the West End, which comprised apartment buildings, single-family housing, office towers and shopping streets in an area bordered by the Pacific Ocean all around. It was the preferred playground of the young and not very rich. It was affordable, in walking distance to anywhere important, including work, and it was beachfront accessible. I could not possibly stay put at Sister's house in Burnaby.

One of my pals from work mentioned looking for a roommate and I jumped. We found a one-bedroom, furnished apartment on Burnaby Street with an ocean view to die for. Summer evenings and weekends were spent on the beach at English Bay while Friday nights were reserved for the beer parlours, a strange institution I had never encountered before.

Every hotel in Vancouver had one. A huge hall with tables and chairs and a bar and not much else. These facilities were, without a doubt, the cheapest way to meet people of all ages and varied nationalities. All they sold was beer, cider and tomato juice. This being Canada and Western Canada at that, strict laws still applied. Getting up from the table and walking about with a glass of beer in one's hand guaranteed immediate expulsion by enormous, and rude, bouncers who took their job very serious. Singing was another 'no no', which brought the bouncers running. The logic of which escaped me, as I couldn't think of anyone less harmful than a person singing his little heart out. However, mine was not to reason why, mine was just to drink my cider and meet a lot of people. Which I did.

Vancouver was the beneficiary of the conflict of interest going on in La Belle Province Quebec and particularly Montreal. The war between the English and the French was of no interest to recent immigrants but the necessity of learning French after just having mastered English was asking a little much of most people. There was an exodus of newcomers and established immigrants which benefited the rest of Canada and Vancouver in particular.

The people we met in the Parlours came from everywhere. The Europeans shared tables with the Australians, the South Africans, the

New Zealanders and the discussions were lively, inquisitive and, per force, informative. Political correctness had not yet been invented so we were free to make fun of each other's idiosyncrasies and wonder at foreign customs and rituals which were alien to one another. Before the end of the evening, someone inadvertently would whisper, "there is a party at .....," and, everywhere being in walking distance, we walked to wherever and need never worry about drunk driving either.

It was a young people's Paradise, never more appreciated than when, in August of 1968, the Russians went at it again. This time the headlines were all about Czechoslovakia and the City of Prague and the Russian tanks smothering the emergence of democracy in that country. They called it the 'Czechoslovakian Spring' and it lasted barely long enough for the people of that country to get a taste of it. We walked the streets of Vancouver where no tank had ever been seen and wondered at the mentality of Russia's politicians. I was living among people who had never experienced a war on their shores and who were blissfully unaware of any other way of life than the one they were leading in Canada and this city in particular. Sometimes it was frustrating but mostly it was a good life. Heaven was living in the West End of Vancouver - until the rains started.

In 1967, the rains came in October and didn't let up until July 1968. Erika gave up in December and hightailed it back to Montreal where she found out that, in this brave new world, even a waitress now had to be fluent in French. Toronto became Erika's haven and I didn't see her again for a long time. I missed her.

Nice summer days in Vancouver are spent at the beach. Rainy spring, autumn and winter weekends are spent in the mountains skiing. Coming from the flat lands of Prussia, and experiencing the freezing cold of Quebec, skiing was not something I had ever contemplated as an option for my spare time. However, if one does not ski in Vancouver, one is left alone most weekends, staring out the window at a grey sky and drizzle.

If you can't beat them, join them. They gave me a week vacation in December and one of my co-workers mentioned the need for a roommate for a skiing holiday in Sunshine Village in Alberta. I went shopping. Wooden skis with metal edges, leather boots, bindings, ski jacket and pants, gloves, hat - this wasn't just a sport, this was an industry and a money pit. All I could hope for was that my body would take kindly to this exercise. I almost didn't make it.

We took the train from Vancouver to Banff, Alberta, which took us through some of the most spectacular scenery on earth, unfortunately we traveled all night and I had to wait for my glimpse of the Rockies on the return trip. In Banff, a bus transported us to our destination, 15 miles out of town and up a very winding dirt road with drop-offs to make the mind spin. I had my eyes closed most of the time. Sunshine Village nestled in a valley, surrounded by majestic mountains, every one of which sported ski runs. The hotel was neat as a pin, our room comfortable and, although not facing the ski hills, still provided a peaceful view of a frozen waterfall and snow-covered trees out the back. All was well - until we faced our first lesson in the morning.

Skiing is not for the faint-of-heart. Assembling at the bunny hill and looking around, I thought that my chances of surviving the chair lifts alone were very slim, never mind descending a mountain covered in bumps, called moguls by the experts. Fortunately, my skiing pal remarked upon the fact that, being a flatlander from a big city I probably wouldn't be able to take too well to this exercise. I remembered the Alm trip in Bavaria and advised her that, having conquered a walk in sandals up 1100 meters and having survived the ordeal, I was ready, eager and willing to conquer a sport eminently more suitable to mountain-bred people but not necessarily exclusively theirs. I am a Berliner. I have a big mouth. It will be my downfall one day. It almost was right there.

We assembled at the Ski School sign and were put into our respective categories. Very Good, Good, Not So Good, Bad and the Downright Awful. The 'Awfuls' went, slipping and sliding, to the bunny hill and proceeded to be instructed in how to stop, using the snowplough routine. In theory, one starts sliding down an incline, then pushes the knees together, making the skis edge on the inside, which slows the descent and gradually stops the skier from doing him / herself or someone else any harm. In theory!

In reality, the knees are straining to the utmost but the skis stay flat and an out-of-control skier smashes into the nearest obstacle or goes on forever and disappears into the woods surrounding the ski hills. Lucky for us, they had a St. Bernard dog on hand which instilled a lot of confidence in all of us.

Two days on the bunny hill and our intrepid teacher thought we were ready to tackle Strawberry Run. My Pal and I shared the chairlift and worried all the way up as to how the heck we were going to get out of that contraption alive. Fear made our legs wobble and, although we managed to leave the lift in one piece, it was only accomplished by sliding on our backsides. In the process, we found out that sitting on your skis is much more comfortable than standing which, nevertheless, did not impress our instructor who let us know that we had definitely let him down.

We weren't asked to go straight down but only to traverse the hill at our leisure and, halfway across, move into the snowplough position and bring the skis around for another run to the other side. Not having mastered the snowplough, I ended up hugging trees and bushes all the way down. It was a painful exercise. On the third day, having decided to announce my retirement from the sport while I was still in one piece, I suddenly managed to turn my skis around in a perfect plod position which brought tears to the eyes of my optimistic instructor who had almost given up hope in my case. Another ski fanatic was born and, although never ever achieving anything resembling expertise, I thoroughly enjoyed winters in the mountains of British Columbia for many years.

Sister's friend Terry became a valued ski companion, being blessed with the ownership of a little TR4 that took us to Whistler, which I didn't like, and Mount Baker in Washington, which I loved. Whistler in 1968 was a no-man's land of three small Hotels, a Gondola and two Chairlifts. They never told us what the weather was like on top and therefore, when buying a ticket at the bottom, watching gentle snow flakes settling on one's nose, one was ill prepared for the conditions prevailing miles above one's head. The result was a Gondola ride to the half-way mark, a switching-over to the chair lift for another 15 minutes and, more often than not, being caught in a blinding blizzard. Frozen and stiff, we would end up in the Roundhouse, holding on to a hot chocolate for dear life, trying to thaw out, waiting for the sky to clear or at least for the visibility to improve. At the end of the day, the ride home was a nightmare of curves which made me car-sick and necessitated numerous stops along the way. A cognac could have settled my stomach but there was no liquor sold on Sundays in this part of the woods or any other place in British Columbia.

Mount Baker on the other hand, had a highway straight as an arrow until the ascent to the top and that was only a short distance of 30 minutes on a wide, curvy but nevertheless, easily traveled road. And no matter what day, at the bottom of the hill, the 'Chandelier Inn" served liquor to the hurt, the tired and the exhausted skiers from all over the US and Canada.

There was also a great difference in personalities on both mountains.

Being a lousy skier meant losing my companions, usually on the first run. I always ended up single, which meant joining up with another lousy skier who also happened to have lost his or her pals. At Whistler, it was hard to get to know the other person. Whistler was snob country and I wasn't wearing the latest apparel. Baker was friendly, how-do-you-do territory and it did not seem to matter who you shared the lift with, there was always fun on the ride.

Skiing made Vancouver winter weather bearable. Spring brought another venture, courtesy of the Canadian Imperial Bank of Commerce, who so generously provided me with a paycheque every two weeks and who now initiated me into another sport, which was neither painful nor particularly difficult to understand. Recruitment started for a Spring Bowling League and five of us volunteered to represent Regional Headquarters. Lucky for us, no one took this game serious. We had a lot of fun but did not even come close to winning any trophy.

Trophies weren't what we were after anyway. The teams with which we were competing came from the Bank's branches all over Vancouver and that gave us exposure to a lot of young tellers of the male variety which, under normal circumstances, we might never have met. One of whom was a young man straight out of England with the most delicious English accent we had ever encountered. Consequently, five lousy bowlers got decidedly worse whenever they were faced with the prospect of competing with the particular team which included the handsome, curly-haired, witty lad from Oxford. Five against one. The race was on and the poor boy never had a chance.

The game is played without rules, without mercy, without fairness. It has been played since time immemorial and no man alive has ever comprehended the situation. Five of us made a covenant. No holds barred, we would go after this Lad with every weapon at our disposal but, in the end, we would abide by his choice, which, of course, depended on the fact that he would fall for one of us, which he might not. In which case we would lick our wounds and live to fight another day. It was fun, especially as the lad did not seem to get the message and made no move in any direction but flirted outrageously with all of us.

Towards the end of the season, we noticed that many teams, including the one that harboured the object of our affection, proceeded to the Dufferin Hotel beer parlour after the games to relax before heading home. It was time to make our move. Watching the lad wasting time at the top of the staircase in conversation, we decided to move past him, one at a time, saying good bye in passing and giving him the chance to make his move, if he was inclined to do so.

Three passed without receiving more than a smile and a good-bye in return. Myself, the number four, ascended the staircase and, pretending indifference, passed by the coveted male without so much as a glance. I was stopped dead in my tracks by the invitation, addressed to my backside, to join him and his team for a drink at the Dufferin. Would I? Need you ask? We had a wonderful time that evening. The lad had a great sense of humour, good looks and a way of speaking which threw everyone into hysterics. For him, the trunk of a car was a boot, the hood was a bonnet and, when he thought we made fun of him, he'd retort: "Pull the other leg, it's got bells on." What that meant I never knew.

Someone asked him if they could see him at home some day and the reply of: 'If I am not there, knock up my Landlady and wait' had everyone howling. This young chap had a lot to learn, one of which was that in Canada you do not 'knock' people up, especially if they are over 70 years old. He was impossible to resist.

Funny, uncomplicated, easy to be with, the life of every party and, in the end, the most boring person I had ever met. We spent the next three years trying to make a go of a relationship which was doomed from the start. I hate routine and he hated change. When we finally split for good, he insisted on keeping the same telephone number. More than 30 years later, he still lives in the West End with the same number. Good grief.

Chapter 33

JOINING THE FOREIGN LEGION

Vancouverites are a strange breed. They are friendly, kind and greet you with a cheerful "Hi" whether you know them or not. They are nice people who constantly let you down.

They are very quick in promising action without ever following up on the words. "We have to have lunch together" is a phrase I came to hate. "You have to come and meet my family" was a another. I got to know a lot of people through work and play but I was never invited to their homes. I wasn't the only one feeling left out by the natives.

They called the club 'Foreign Legion.' It was a loose association of people from all over the world joining together in an effort to belong. My Oxford lad introduced me to people from Australia, New Zealand, England and various other European localities and the mix proved invigorating and entertaining.

There were, of course, a lot of parties at various locations. There was a memorable summer outing somewhere on a farm in the Fraser Valley where most of us slept over in a barn surrounded by chickens who, not having partied all night, insisted on greeting the new day round about 4:30 in the morning. The sound of a rooster is not very conducive to a hang over from the night before and it was just as well that he was a fast runner and the people chasing him were not very steady on their feet. It was a sight to see and to remember.

There were boat rides on an old freighter whose captain got us stuck on a rock at low tide for about two hours. One of the jokers from Australia promised to get us off by making everyone congregate at one end of the boat and, at his signal, induced the crowd to run, tightly bunched, to the other side of the ship. He hadn't banked on the narrow passageway on either side of the steerage cabin. Everyone promptly got stuck there and bodies piled on top of one another with hilarious results and a few scrapes and bruises. The boat didn't move an inch until high tide came in, whereupon we continued our passage along the shoreline of West Vancouver, picking up some live crabs from a crab boat heading back home.

On shore, someone built a fire, heated seawater in huge cauldrons and the crabs met a dreadful end. Feeling sorry for them did not prevent me from partaking of the best crab meal I've ever had.

There were New Year's parties and Anzac Parties and a party celebrating the first man on the Moon. When we weren't partying, we watched Broadway shows at Vancouver's Queen Elizabeth Theatre. Saturday nights were spent dancing at any one of the ballrooms in the best Vancouver Hotels. The action was great but the entire scene had taken on a slightly different tone. There were no live bands.

Disco had arrived with a vengeance and the music went on all night without a break. I didn't like it for the simple reason that it prohibited talking at any great length but, when in Rome, do as the Romans do, so I did. Which wasn't all that easy.

The beat was changing and the rhythm did not compliment my steps, which were still rooted in the rock-n-roll era of Elvis. It was the Twist thing all over again, only this time I managed to accommodate myself to the new beat and enjoyed the free movements it allowed. Now it did not matter any longer whether or not one's dancing partner could dance worth a nickel. He did his thing and I did mine and the possibility of him stomping on my feet was remote. Paradise!

With the girls from work, we joined the latest craze which was taking courses in all kinds of enterprises. We were taught how to be a proper Hostess by the Wife of the British Ambassador, we learned how to crochet, how to cook Italian and how to keep the body in shape at the YMCA.

In between I changed residences so often, Mama asked whether I was moving every time the windows got dirty. She was close.

My pal from work and I parted company because her boyfriend seemed to take up permanent residence in our apartment, half of which belonged to me. I moved into a Studio Suite on the corner of Jervis and Pacific which, although facing the back and therefore not eligible to be called an Ocean View apartment, still made me wake up in the morning to the sound of sea gulls crying and the smell of seaweed in my nose. I would have stayed there indefinitely but my Oxford lad had other ideas.

He was a thrifty lad and he did not think much of the idea of him paying rent for a tiny little room and me paying rent for a Studio when, in reality, we seemed to be spending a lot of time together at either place. After repeatedly praising the conveniences of living common law and the money saved in the process of doing so, I caved in and quickly found myself in a one-bedroom apartment on Pendrell Street. No Ocean view, no sea smell but a man with a decorating sense straight out of hell. He hung a fish net, complete with shells, in the corner of the living room. How cool can you get? It was the first fight, followed by many, that we had in the course of a stormy relationship that never seemed to go anywhere.

To make up, the lad called at work the next day and promised to make dinner for me. I was thrilled until I saw the result of his cooking efforts. What do you do when you are confronted with a plate of food, all of which you detest.

I cannot eat brown baked beans. I abhor boiled cold eggs and do not eat celery unless it is cooked and disappears from sight in a Spaghetti Sauce. There was also cold toast, which tastes awful, and something called Mowbray Pie, which I had never heard of and never want to see again. What do you do when you're in love and you don't want to hurt your loved one's feelings? You do the impossible. You eat the lot, although with great difficulty, then excuse yourself and head for the bathroom. I barely made it. It was the worst meal of my life and I made sure that there was no repeat performance.

To please the palate of an Englishman, I learned how to cook with white pepper to disguise seasoning and got used to using salt sparingly. These were hurdles I was willing to take.

Shortly after moving in together, my English lad was dismissed by the Bank for not wanting to transfer to the city of Victoria on Vancouver Island. Purely by chance, I had picked up an application form for an Airline some weeks previously, made him fill it in and mailed the completed form to Canadian Airline's Headquarters. Having no luck in finding another Bank to take him on, he was enormously relieved to be offered an Air Cargo course, entitling him to stuff airplanes full of wares.

We spent days studying Airport codes and weight problems on airplanes. Imagine someone putting a comma in the wrong place and the airplane takes off with too much baggage in its hold. Whabumm!! Not a good idea. His studies paid off in that he came in second overall at the Exam. The first-place student was sent to Toronto, which was fine with us. The second-place student was assigned to Vancouver International Airport. Everyone else who passed ended up in little towns all over British Columbia.

So the Oxford Lad went to work - at night. Being 'low man on the totem pole', he got the night shift. I saw him first thing in the morning, two hours in the evening and on weekends. It worked out perfect and a good time was had by all.

Whenever he worked on the weekend, my Swiss friend Terry and I continued our merry life on the slopes of Mount Baker and in December of 1969, I booked myself in for one week at Whistler Mountain to improve my skiing technique. It didn't work. I never progressed past the low-intermediate level but as long as one is having fun, who cares. I met a lot of people that way because after the first run I never saw my more accomplished ski partners again until the lifts stopped running.

When I came home, my lad had put up a little Christmas tree, decorated and all, with little gifts tucked away in the branches. An English custom, I was told. There wasn't any room for my own decorations but I figured, if the Jewish boyfriend could live with a Hanukkah bush, I shouldn't bitch about an English tree. Christmas was lovely and my present extraordinary. The lad was extremely talented and, knowing my affinity for anything smacking remotely of English history, he had assembled a model of Lord Nelson's flagship. It was gorgeous and positively the best present I had ever received. Life would have been perfect but then they changed the Lad's schedule to days and things deteriorated rapidly.

We tried, we really did. We met our friends on weekdays at the Rembrandt Hotel on Davie Street and watched a painter recreate "The Nightwatch" on the wall of the Lounge. Beer parlours went out of fashion and slowly disappeared from the scene. We went to movies and played board games or went to parties, every one of which always seemed to end up with an order for Pizza around midnight. We traveled on weekends to places like Victoria and Nanaimo on the Island and once to Whitehorse in the Yukon. Being an Airline Employee meant flying for free and I would have taken advantage of that more often but my lad did not care very much for leaving home. He liked routine. He liked doing the same things, over and over. When I told him that he would likely be the last person sitting in the Lounge of the Rembrandt Hotel, everyone else moving on to bigger and better things, he smiled and replied that there were always other people who would be willing to take our place.

Months and months of routine engagements and grey skies. Months and months of hearing the same jokes at parties and eating food without pepper and salt. Months and months of watching him cradling his mug of beer and refusing to ever try anything else. Months and months of boredom at work and boredom at home. And months and months of that miserable drizzle. I flipped.

It never seemed to stop. They weren't kidding when they called it the rain capital of Canada. The downpours started in October and never stopped until May. In summer, one never said: "I'll see you next week on the beach," because the next time the Sun came out could be four weeks down the road. It drizzled and poured and the sky came so close it felt as though one could touch the clouds and I hated it.

I did not like Vancouver and I couldn't go back to Montreal. Calgary wasn't on my map of favourites, Toronto hadn't left much of an impression either and Berlin was a nightmare. What to do?

"Try Germany," wrote Papa. "You've never really looked," he said on the telephone. "You've got nothing to lose," wrote Mama and, "P.S. We would love to see you," was scribbled underneath. They had a point.

Calling it quits is always hard, especially when you like the person you're with. And I really did like him but not enough to spend my entire life being bored.

Chapter 34
RECONNAISSANCE!

I flew home in the summer of 1970, equipped with a Eurorail Pass for one month and enough cash to explore the Fatherland at leisure. Had the Oxford lad accompanied me, the schedule would have worked as planned with no deviations allowed to upset the routine. By myself, I made a proper hash of it and had a grand time in the process.

Having been interested in anything English for a long time and not really understanding why, I thought it appropriate to interrupt the trip home with a 4-day stop-over in London. We landed at Stanstead and I took a train to Kings Cross station in the middle of London. I had not booked a hotel, didn't know how to go about doing it and, as a consequence, stood forlornly on the sidewalk, watching my fellow passengers disappearing in taxicabs. I finally spotted one young lady and, vaguely remembering having seen her on my airplane, I approached her and asked whether or not she knew of a hotel in the vicinity. She did. As a matter of fact, she proposed to share a taxi there and see whether or not they had accommodation for me as well. Perfect! We took off in the biggest Taxi I had ever seen. This wasn't just a car, this was a room inside a car with seats facing each other with ample room for luggage and passengers. Very unusual.

Arriving at Bayswater, our driver accompanied us to the hotel, carrying some of our luggage. It wasn't much of a hotel, more in the category of a guesthouse, and it smelled of curry which is not one of my favourite dishes. I was advised that it would cost 5 Pounds a night with breakfast included. My companion took it and disappeared up the staircase. My friendly taxi driver advised me quietly that he could do a lot better than that and proposed looking for something cheaper. I took his advice. It was the last time I trusted a London taxi driver. He drove here and there, went into buildings, came out with bad news of no accommodation available or rates being higher than three pounds, and I watched the meter going up, up and away. When it reached four pounds, I told him to drive me back to the curry house. The turbaned Indian at the Reception smiled and gave me my key. I dragged my suitcases out of the cab, without the assistance of my helpful driver, and watched him drive away with a smirk on his face. Another tourist had been had. What fun! How stupid! Lucky for me, the rest of the English population lived up to a better standard.

The English were in the process of changing their currency over to the metric system. At the time of my visit, the money circulating was all mixed up with new and old currency. Their system of counting, with 20 shillings to the pound and 12 pennies to the shilling, had driven me almost insane in school. Now I was faced with all these odd-shaped coins on top of trying to figure out how much goes into what. Nevertheless, I dared to enter a little shop in the vicinity and bought two apples and a carton of milk for my sustenance during the night. "2 and 6," said the little chap at the counter. I gave him 2 pounds and 6 shillings. "Blimey," he exclaimed to the general population behind me. "Not another bleeding tourist." Then he explained the method of expressing a price in English. 2 and 6 meant 2 shillings and 6 pence. That got me wondering as to just how I would know that? What if I bought something expensive? If I bought a gold bracelet, would they say 3 and 4 and mean 3 pounds and 4 shillings? I didn't have time to work all this out so on this and every other occasion, I simply held out my hand with all those coins, professed that I was a stupid tourist, and made them take whatever they needed. No one ever took advantage as far as I could tell. Seeing as most other customers were watching the affair with interest, making humorous remarks in the process, they would have had a hard time cheating anyway.

Next day I took off on my first solo sightseeing trip and fell utterly, irrevocably and with all my heart in love. First with the City of London and then, of all people, with Richard III. That love has endured through the years and all the visits since.

Starting in the morning, I walked from Bayswater to the Tower of London, seeing all the sights on the way. Clutching my street map, I even managed to find the tiny street where once upon a time the great fire of London started in a bakery shop. Whenever I stopped to take my bearings, people would interrupt their frantic pace with a friendly "Are you lost, Luv?" and point me in the right direction. The police in London not only looked handsome in their uniforms, they acted totally unlike any policeman I had ever encountered anywhere else. They smiled and, for the price of a bite out of my popsicle, walked me across a busy intersection and admonished the hapless tourist to pay more attention to the direction the cars were taking. As far as I was concerned, they were all driving on the wrong side of the street. I stood on Tower Bridge and imagined life in the time of the Normans. I admired the White Tower and wondered at a building surviving for so many years and in such good shape. They sure built things differently in those days. I walked around the only room remaining of Whitehall and looked out the window where Charles I lost his head. History assaulted my senses at every corner and I didn't think it could get any better. Then I came face to face with Richard III.

I had not planned to spend much time in Galleries but the people populating history are best looked at in a Gallery. There were faces from every era, smiling, frowning, smirking, vacuous - and sad.

He wore a black hat and a black coat with very few decorations to prove his wealth apart from two rings on one hand. He looked away from the painter with the saddest expression on his face that I had ever encountered. I tried walking away and couldn't. I felt myself wishing I could talk to him, to tell him everything would be alright. I didn't know who he was until one of the guards took notice of my long stay. "Do you know who that is?" he asked. "That is Richard III of England." Richard III? The Hunchback? The killer of innocent young lads in the Tower? No way! Not with a face like that!

I had met a man who was as interested in history as I was and, instead of my planned visit to Buckingham Palace, I spent two hours with a member of the 'Society for the Vindication of Richard III.' I have read almost every book written on the subject since and nothing has ever convinced me more of the fallacy and misrepresentation that has led to history being taught in schools today regarding Richard's life and death. When history is written by the winner, the losing party has not got a chance in hell. Poor Richard, whose motto of "Loyalty Binds Me", did not catch on with his own allies and who, in consequence, became the most defiled man in English history. Not fair.

History was alive and well everywhere in London.

I am a very good walker but after three days traipsing through the city, my legs told me in no uncertain terms to stop. I pulled a muscle in

231

my backside and had to think of another way to spend my remaining time. The brochure advertising the glories of London and surroundings pointed me in the direction of Westminster Pier and the boats plying the Thames River. I limped to the Underground, traveled to Westminster Station and boarded one of the mini-liners for a trip to Hampton Court.

It was lovely being on the water but it would have been a lot lovelier if the weather had cooperated. It was freezing in the cabin and there is only so much coffee one can drink to keep warm. My fellow passengers consisted of families who huddled together for warmth and did not look inclined to invite me into their tight embraces. The only way out was the staircase leading up to the steering house, down which a warm wind gave me the impression that the crew were not lacking a heater of some sort. I climbed.

Happiness is steering a boat down the Thames in the company of fun-loving London cockneys who delight in teaching their own version of the English language to unsuspecting tourists. The freezing passengers below never knew how close they came to disaster a few times.

Docking at Hampton Court, we were advised of the precise time the boat would depart and went on our way. It was magic. History was breezing down my neck and I couldn't get enough of it. There was Anne Boleyn's bed. I stood in front of Anne's bed. Me! I stood in front of a bed in which Anne had been frolicking with Henry. It was almost sacrilege. The whole complex is so beautiful that, for the first time, I could readily see why Henry appropriated it from Cardinal Wolsey. In Henry's place, I would have done the same. It was, and still is, one of my favourite Palaces in all of England.

While the Palace was grand, the Maze was terrifying. I couldn't get out of the darn thing. I have no sense of direction at the best of times and was now confronted with shrubs that swirled and confused and lured me into dead-ends and time was running out. It was my first, and my last, experience in a Maze. I was eight minutes late for the boat and but for the fact that the crew had got to know me, would have been left behind. You've got to have connections in life.

Back in London, the youngest crew member thought to show me London by night, which so far had eluded me. We went across the Thames River to the older part of town and ended up in a Pub where the word "tourist" was a four-letter word. I couldn't understand half of what these people were saying. This was pure London slang and I kept wondering what my English teacher in school would have made of it. They had a lot of fun explaining the intricacies of Cockney expressions to me and, in return, I taught them some beauties of my own. The Berliner slang is as sassy and irreverent as the Londoner's any old time and by the time I took my leave, I left behind some happy Englishmen with new expressions in their vocabulary. They loved the drawn-out 'Mensch', expressing disdain, and the backslapping 'Wie jehts' which any ordinary German pronounces as "Wie gehts." They yelled "Tschuess" when I left and never knew that that word was a Berliner bastardization of the French Adieu. When you travel, you learn a lot of things, not all of them useful.

My helpful Londoner was a bit disappointed at not being invited to share my bed but I was really way too tired for that sort of thing. I hope he forgave me.

After four days in London, I was happy to see my three trusty family members assembled as usual at Tempelhof Central Airport, accompanied this time by some of my ex-coworkers who had taken time off to greet me. Coming home was always a happy occasion. It was the leaving that was a killer.

I spent two weeks re-acquainting myself with the neighbours, helping Mama harvest berries in the garden and turning them into her famous juice which had kept us all healthy all during my childhood. I poured over maps, trying to find a route to include all major towns that could lend themselves to the prospect of my joining their workforce. The northern part of Germany was scratched immediately. Been there! Done that! Hamburg, Bremen, Kiel and Bremerhaven were eliminated through brief association of weekend trips in my youth. I decided to head south.

First stop - Frankfurt am Main. Big, noisy and terribly dusty which is not conducive to people wearing contact lenses. The city was in the process of having a subway system built and everywhere I went, I walked around on wooden boards covering construction going on below ground. I paid my respects to Germany's most famous Poet, Johann Wolfgang von Goethe, and managed to make it to the Roemer buildings, both places being the absolute 'must' on any tourist trip. I scanned the papers for jobs and accommodation and, in the end, decided that I would not be happy in Frankfurt. No one said "HI". Everyone rushed from here to there without paying any heed to the lost soul standing on the corner perusing a map. Everyone was very busy. Everyone was too busy to take any notice of me. Frankfurt lost out.

Next stop - Nuremberg. Much smaller, much older and a lot of history to explore. I booked a sightseeing trip on a bus that promised an English speaking guide for the overseas crowd and entertained myself listening to the poor man's German accent which massacred the Queen's English. When he got stuck, I helped him out and earned myself the gratitude of my fellow tourists who, after the tour ended, followed me around like sheep.

No one knew better what it is like not to be able to speak or read a language. I was only too glad to be of assistance and that almost got me employed. We decided to visit the Rathaus that, in the basement, sported an old Prison in which torture instruments from medieval times were exhibited. There was a problem. The English-speaking guide had gone home with the sniffles and there was no one to guide us through the dungeons. Oh yes, there was. My trusty followers advised the officials that they had a bilingual person in their midst who would be only too glad to translate whatever the German guide was offering. That promised to be fun, and it was.

It was absolutely mind-boggling what the human race in medieval times had produced in the way of machinery intended to hurt their fellow men. It wasn't very sophisticated but, by God, it must have been painful. Translating the meaning of the various instruments took me back to Mr. Gross and the technical words I had never heard of. In this instance, I did not have the benefit of medieval torture dictionaries and was therefore reduced to describing items in a very roundabout way, which wasn't entirely technical but made for merriment which, in these dark chambers, was very beneficial. At the end of the tour, they asked me whether I was interested in doing this for a living. Probably wouldn't have been a bad idea but I wasn't ready to settle down yet.

Over supper, which my fan club provided free of charge for the price of translating the menu, I found myself comparing the easy attitude of my companions from overseas and the aloof attitude of my fellow Germans and wondered about the possibility of ever really fitting in again in this country of mine.

After the usual breakfast of fresh buns, boiled eggs, cheese and sandwich meat, I wandered the streets of Nuremberg, ending up in the Castle crowning the hill with a beautiful view all around.

Joining the tour was very educational as, finally, I was able to figure out a phrase with which Papa had admonished us every time we did something wrong. "Jochimkin, Jochimkin, huete Die. Fange wie Die, so hange wie Die," is what he used to say. It was an admonition to someone called 'Jochimkin' and meant "watch out, if we catch you, we hang you." It was also an advice to Papa's offspring not to step out of line. No one ever knew where that expression came from except that Grandfather Krause had used it to admonish his son who felt obliged to carry on the tradition.

On top of the hill at Nuernberg's castle, the mystery was solved. Apparently there was an outlaw, someone in the order of Robin Hood. He was a Nobleman and he robbed from the rich and gave to the poor. The good Burgers of Nuremberg hated him for the simple reason that he had it in for the rich merchants of the town. His name was Ebbeling von Geilingen and, for short, they called him Jochimkin. I have no idea why.

Well, at one point, the Burghers and the officials of the town put out proclamations to the effect of telling Jochimkin that should they catch him, they would hang him. Jochimkin was full of self-confidence, continued unabatedly and was promptly caught. Everyone was happy. Now all they had to do was find a tree.

Jochimkin apparently resigned himself to his fate but asked for one last favour before kicking the bucket. He wanted one more ride on his famous horse around the courtyard. The trusty Burghers didn't think that was a problem. The castle was high up on a hill, there was a moat around it and the possibility of escape was extremely remote. They granted his wish. Jochimkin saddled up, took a turn around the yard and then suddenly galloped for the wall. Still imprinted on the 4-foot high wall surrounding the courtyard is the imprint of his horse's foot. He flew over the wall, over the moat and landed safely on the lawn facing the castle. "The Nurembergers don't hang anyone unless they have him," he yelled and rode off into freedom.

I laughed so hard, our guide got worried. I couldn't wait to get to a telephone to tell Papa about my discovery. Turned out, Papa had no idea that there really was a Jochimkin. It was a wonderful story and I could imagine it turning into a really great movie but, in the Germany of the late 60's, good movies were a thing of the past.

Next stop - Rothenburg Ob der Tauber. As luck would have it, I ended up in Rothenburg on the weekend when the town was celebrating their deliverance from destruction by the Swedish forces during the religious wars that plagued Germany for 30 years in medieval times. History tells us that, Rothenburg having been taken and scheduled for total destruction, the victorious General decided to have a little fun with the populace. Watching the 'Burgermeister' and his cronies pleading for deliverance, he picked up an enormous tankard and promised to spare the city and everyone in it if they could find someone who could drink a full measure of beer out of this glass. The blacksmith of the town volunteered, drank the entire contents, collapsed immediately and died soon after. For a German, if you have to go, this is not a bad way to do it. Beer was, and still is, the favourite beverage of my fellow countrymen.

There is a famous play about the incident that is now presented on each and every anniversary of this momentous occasion. Having discovered the average tourist's fascination with anything medieval, throughout this particular weekend, the town crawls with people dressed in medieval costumes, pulsates with medieval music and swarms with outsiders. I was lucky to get a room.

My landlord owned the butcher shop around the corner and the restaurant beneath my window. The smells coming out of the kitchen promised excellent German cuisine and they didn't let me down with their idea of a good breakfast. Fortified, I went on the prowl and found that, in addition to the usual tourist crowd, there were scores of uniformed young men in attendance. Hearing an English-speaking guide explaining the intricacies of the town clock to about six of these uniformed individuals, I attached myself to within hearing distance to their group and followed them around. It's inherited. I'm as stingy as Papa ever was and this was saving quite a bit of my meagre funds.

It didn't take the lads, or their guide, very long to notice their shadow. The guide told me in no uncertain German terms to go to hell, which was normal. The lads invited me to join the tour, which was kind. They had been on an exercise nearby in the countryside and the town of Rothenburg had thought it a good idea to invite the entire Regiment of British Infantry to join in the festivities. I was declared their mascot and there was nothing the German official could do about it. It was a lovely trip, ending in the dark on a road outside the gates, watching fireworks being set off all along the still existing wall surrounding the town. The way they did that looked as though the Swedes had never left and were throwing everything they had at the defences. Spooky and very well done.

To round out the evening, we decided to have a good meal before retiring to our respective beds. Remembering the delicious smells coming out of my host's kitchen, I suggested the restaurant beneath my room. None of the lads spoke German and the prospect of having someone explain the menu items was enough to provide me with another free meal. It was getting to be a routine.

In the middle of perusing the menu, my landlady approached the table and asked me if I could please step outside for a minute. I had no idea what she wanted and it took me at least two minutes to comprehend what she was talking about. I had a room upstairs. I had turned up with six young men in uniform. I was advised to find myself other accommodation. This was not that sort of a house. Excuse me? Are you saying what I think you are saying?

I am a pretty happy-go-lucky person but I also have a bad temper. By the time I finished telling her about all the places I would go to in the morning to complain about her attitude towards the occupying forces invited to her town and the publicity her hotel, restaurant and butcher shop would be exposed to regarding her implications towards a guest who had simply recommended a good food outlet and offered translations into the bargain, she was reduced to a snivelling wimp who apologized profusely and offered to reduce the eventual bill by half. I never told my Pals about the unfortunate misunderstanding. It would have spoiled their evening and taken away their high regard for German hospitality upon noticing the reduction in price. In return, they gave me one of their emblems. It has a Crown on top and silver laurel leaves surround a gold inscription on blue background. It says: 'Honi Soit Qui Mal Y Pense,' which I learned later means "Evil is who Evil thinks". My lads from the Royal N.Z. Engineers never knew how fitting that inscription was. I still have the little emblem. I consider it my medal of honour.

Next stop - Heidelberg. On the train, I met two young American ladies and we decided to throw our lot together for cheap accommodation. At the desk in Heidelberg's train station, I watched the incumbent Information Officer dealing with an American couple. She told them that there was no accommodation available in town but she could find them something out of town which entailed taking a taxi. It also cost in the vicinity of $50 American a night. They took the offer and also paid an additional DM 5.00 for a brochure with information as to what was happening in town.

I told my two soon-to-be roommates not to say a word to me or to each other for the next little while and approached the desk. In German, I advised the Lady that we were three travelers on a shoestring, had no money for taxis or brochures and needed the cheapest accommodation available in town. Not a problem. Turned out that, for Germans, there was room at the Inn. There was also no cost whatsoever for the brochure. It was free of charge. My astonished question as to why she had charged the Yankees DM5 produced a laugh and a shoulder shrug. "They're Americans." I didn't think that was much of an explanation. Cheating tourists apparently was a worldwide hobby and did not just apply to London taxi drivers.

Heidelberg was lovely but in desperate need of a paint job. Two days of sightseeing in narrow alleys where the sun never reached the ground did not convince me to stay around. A trip down the River Neckar was lovely but not overly exciting except for the fact that I met a most unusual old man.

I got off the boat at Neckarsteinach and took the obligatory walk to an old 'Burg' on a hill of which there seems to be one in every village in that area. I came down too early and sat down on the pier next to a man who patiently waited for a fish to bite on his rod. We started chatting and I found an individual who had never been anywhere and had no wish to leave his neck of the woods. He'd gone to Heidelberg a few times. Not often. He found it too busy. He was born in Neckarsteinach and he was going to die in Neckarsteinach and he was perfectly alright with that.

He was happy where he was and he looked it. It was incomprehensible to me. I couldn't have met anyone who was more unlike myself had I tried. It made me think. Which one of us was the happier? Me with my unquenchable urge to see new places and meet new people or him, with his limited expectations and his satisfaction with the boundaries of his life. To each his own, I suppose. But one could envy him his simplicity. I never forgot that individual and his, to me at least, foreign way of life.

After three days of gloomy streets, old castles and looking at peeling paint, I bid my companions fare-thee-well and thought to find myself a city with wider streets. Munich provided that in ample proportions. On the night table in my room I found earplugs. Not understanding what they were for, I threw them in the garbage bin and, having traveled a lot and consequently being very tired, I went to bed early. At 2 AM I fished the little plugs out of the wastepaper basket and stuck them into my ears. The traffic was as busy as it had been at 2 PM and I hadn't slept a wink.

Munich was big. Very big. Munich had thousands of people dashing here and there, all of whom entirely too preoccupied to help a hapless tourist find her way around. Especially when that tourist speaks with a Berlin accent. Not until I yelled in English did they deem it necessary to assist the suddenly Canadian national to find the Wiesen with the big tents for the Octoberfest, which was starting a couple of days later. The Wiesen was a huge lawn, the tents were enormous, the famous Berolina Statue was huge and the ladies preparing themselves for serving untold quantities of Beer at the Octoberfest were giants carrying numerous beer steins in each hands as though they weighed nothing. Everything in Munich made me feel like an insignificant little ant. Two days of walking, two nights of not sleeping, and I was ready to cut my visit short and leave Munich to the Bavarians and the beer drinkers. I don't even like the music. I'm a Prussian.

The train taking me to Garmisch Partenkirchen was filled with interesting people. I had started my train journey sitting quietly, reading a book or watching the scenery go by. By the time I left Nuremberg, I had acquired enough nerve to introduce myself to my fellow passengers and thence start a conversation. It was an eye opener to learn how many people were even shyer than I was and how glad most seemed to have someone break through the ice. By the time I finished my trip, I had turned from a normally reticent person facing strangers into what a Psychologist would describe as a rip-roaring extrovert. And that was putting it mildly.

On this particular ride, I got to chatting to an elderly Gentleman from New York who had split up with his wife for this part of their trip, she opting to visit Oberammergau and he wanting to visit Garmisch. He waited for me to find myself suitable accommodation and then let me share his Taxi to my destination. For DM7.00, including breakfast, I got the smallest room in the house.

The bed was just big enough for my head and feet to touch the frame but I sleep curled up anyway, so who cared?

The New Yorker stayed in the best hotel and his invitation to dinner and a trip to the Zugspitze next day could not be refused. There is always more fun to be had when you share the experience. We had a lovely time together and I missed him when he left to meet up with his wife.

Alone, I took the chairlift to the top of the Mountain and admired the scenery below, which was truly breathtaking. It was also very hot. For October, the weather couldn't have been better and, spotting something resembling a lake from my vantage point, I decided to unpack the bikini and head there. It was a public swimming pool resembling a lake in the middle of a forest. It was cool under the trees and the water was lovely. So was the young chap who started a conversation and ended up getting a date for the next day to sightsee in the company of a fellow tourist.

All that had made me very hungry and I headed for the nearest Restaurant. Home-fried potatoes and headcheese. Delicious! Until 10:00 o'clock at night. That was when I started feeling sick. The bathroom was across the hall and I spent the entire night going to and fro, watching the headcheese exiting both ways and destroying my health in the process.

At 10:00 am the next day, my landlady came to the door, advising as to the state of breakfast and inquiring as to whether or not I wanted any. Just the mention of it sent me flying across the hall. The landlady, turning angel of mercy, was back within minutes with black tea and burned toast.

Even that didn't stay put until about 5:00 pm, at which time I came to the conclusion that I might survive this ordeal after all. Then came the flowers.

Apparently, my date from the swimming pool had shown up and, being advised as to the precarious state of my health, had left and returned shortly afterward with the loveliest bouquet of flowers I had ever received. His kind gesture contributed a lot to my getting better and I always regretted not being able to thank him. I had things to do, places to go. I was off to Innsbruck in the morning.

Innsbruck is not in Germany. Innsbruck is in Austria. I should not have sent Papa a postcard from Innsbruck. It did not add to his conviction that I was seriously considering settling in Germany.

Innsbruck was small and beautiful. So small that, on assembling for the obligatory sightseeing tour, my question as to where the bus was, was answered with the short notice of "no bus. This is a walking tour". So it was and we walked. All over Innsbruck and around Innsbruck and up a Mountain where there was a Monument celebrating the Austrian version of Wilhelm Tell and Robin Hood. Another freedom fighter by the name of Kaspar Hauser who paid for his belief with death, betrayed by a confederate. I wasn't in the best of shape for all that trekking. I was still living on black tea and toast. Luckily, most of my fellow tourists were more out of shape than I was, so no one noticed my own lack of stamina.

Austria was truly spectacular. I wondered what Switzerland looked like. I should not have sent Papa a postcard from Zurich.

On the train from Innsbruck, my fellow compartment members advised me that I would very likely not find a room in Zurich as that place was always very busy with tourists. I still wasn't feeling particularly good and what confronted the Information Officer in the Zurich Train Station's Tourist Office was a very pale and shaky little lady with black rings under her eyes whose polite inquiry as to a cheap room was dutifully acknowledged and processed. Armed with instructions, I set off on a 10-minute walk, ending up at a huge gate with a cord hanging to the side which, when pulled, set in motion a bell. When the door creaked open, I was confronted by a Nun. Black outfit and head piece. Unquestionably - a real Nun! I apologized for my error in the house number and proceeded on my way. "Come back here," the black figure yelled.

It was a Convent. They rented out rooms for young tourists. For DM7.00 a night including breakfast. It seemed too good to be true and almost was. Everywhere in Europe, my Passport was checked upon arrival at my destination. Even in a Convent. That's when the Nun spotted my year of birth. 1938. I was too old to stay in the girlie residence. I wasn't a girl. I was a grown woman. Sorry!

I couldn't leave. It was getting dark. I was miserable and I wanted to go to bed. Please! She was a Nun. They were supposed to be nice people. They are! "I cannot lie," the Lady said with a twinkle in her eye. "But I can forget things." Which she proceeded to do. The spot for my year of birth was miraculously omitted from the form and a grateful Agnostic crawled into a big featherbed and found oblivion.

Zurich proved to be a place without a hair out of place. Clean, modern, affluent and sanitized. I have no recollection of Zurich at all but I do have the pictures attesting to the fact that I was there for two days. For something different, I thought I'd try the French part of Switzerland. My train chugged into Montreux and I encountered the first difficulty when dealing with the French Swiss population. They don't speak German. Thank God for English or I would have ended up sleeping on a park bench.

My hotel did not have curtains. Getting to bed was a serious affair of turning off all the lights and fumbling around in the dark undressing. The trip to the bathroom in the middle of the night was an adventure and breakfast in the morning an affair of pointing and nodding. Apart from the tourist office personnel, no one spoke anything but French. I bought a French/German dictionary in the morning and tried out the phrases outlined therein. I managed to eat a proper meal for lunch, got perfectly fluent with "Un café au lait, s'il vous plait!" and survived buying another postcard with stamp for Papa's inventory. It was very interesting but a little lonely. Conversation is very important and the lack of it gets to be tedious.

However, I didn't want the French/German dictionary to go to waste and there was another place I had never seen which was accessible via a simple 4-hour train ride from Montreux. PARIS!

The last time I saw Paris was in a movie with Elizabeth Taylor. I thought of maybe meeting someone romantic on the riverbank of the Seine. I wanted to see the fountain where Gene Kelly danced. I didn't have a clue what I was getting into. But then, if one did, one would never have adventures.

The train station in Paris was humming but the Tourist Office was closed, until when I had no idea as I couldn't read the message on the door. I proceeded to the exit and came face to face with a very busy city. It was scary. When I heard English being spoken by two young ladies on the sidewalk, I pounced. I inquired as to where they were heading and they told me about a book they were following which stated that one could experience 'Paris on $5 a Day.' It also informed them of a hotel where English was spoken and rooms would be available. I offered to share the price of the taxi and we took off. It never occurred to any one of us that even if only 50 tourists bought that book that month, they would all end up at the same hotel. They must have. There was no room available. There was also no one who spoke anything resembling English to help us out in our hour of need. It was quite obvious that management thought little of us and wanted to be rid of the overflow.

It was time for my guardian angel to put in an appearance. His name was Dominique and he had just returned from America where he had practiced his English as a counsellor in a summer camp. We were advised that, in Paris, one walked from street to street, from hotel to hotel until one found one with accommodation available. He pointed to a hotel across the street and one of my new-found friends dashed off, returning within minutes to announce she had a room. For her and her friend. Not for me. I was still faced with finding a park bench for the night.

Not so. Not if the French could help it. The lad offered to walk me around until we found a bed for my weary body and I took him up on it gladly. We left my bag with the girls in their new home and started walking. After almost one hour and numerous futile inquiries, we struck gold. I booked myself in to a very big room with a sink for washing and something called a Bidet but the toilet to be accessed across the hall. Beggars can't be choosers. Now all we had to do is to trek back to the other and find my bag.

That was easy to spot. All alone, in the middle of the lobby, it was a perfect set up for any would-be robber. The girls had gone out and left it there. They were lucky I wasn't around when they returned. As it was, the young gentleman insisted on escorting me back to my home for four days. Which was a good thing. With my sense of direction, I might have ended up anywhere.

He promised to be back in the morning to take me around but I didn't really expect to see him again. He was a student and he was very busy registering at University and finding permanent accommodation for his stay during this semester. I was wrong. He'd said he would look after me and he did. Without him, I doubt Paris would have scored too high on my appreciation level.

That evening, I walked the streets and picked a restaurant that looked a bit more upper-class than the little corner café. I was hoping that there one could converse in English. Wrong again. I found myself staring at the Menu without comprehension and no hope of help from anyone. I ordered what I could decipher - 'Soup de Jour and Escargot'. As it came with a lot of wonderful white bread and butter, I didn't leave the place hungry.

I also found out that I couldn't eat a raw oyster again if my life depended on it. At the table next to mine, four people where enjoying a strange meal. There were shells on a platform, heated from below by a little flame. They broke the shell and ate whatever was inside. It was very interesting to watch and, somehow, my interest became a little too noticeable to the diners. Laughing, one gentleman picked up one shell and deposited it on my plate. He said a lot of things which I presumed to be instructions but which went right past me. I thanked him, in French, and scraped out the raw, slippery mass of something or other which refused to stay put on my fork. I really like being the centre of attention but not the butt of the joke which was what I was turning into. I speared the mess, deposited it into my mouth and swallowed. It not only tasted awful, it refused to stay down. It felt as though the darn thing was climbing up my pipe, again and again, in spite of being flushed back repeatedly with gulps of water and more bread. Ghastly. Different strokes for different folks. I don't know about the French but I like my food cooked.

In the morning, I had been advised by my Saviour to pick up the phone on the night table and put in my request for "Le Petit Dejeuner, s'il vous plait!" That was answered with a long tirade, probably wanting more information, to which I quickly replied that "I no speake de

French". I have a problem with languages. Even if I cannot understand them, I can copy pronunciation to perfection and that gives people the wrong impression. My order had been in impeccable French. The rest was not.

I was still in bed when there was a knock on the door, the door flew open and a smiling Madam presented me with breakfast in bed. This was living. Hot coffee, hot milk, warm croissants and a lovely baguette. Add fresh butter and jam and you're in paradise. Unfortunately, there is no paradise without flaws. Adam and Eve had the apple tree. I had the toilet. Here I was, in the 20th Century, faced with a toilet where one had to stand on two barely raised platforms and aim for a hole in the floor. Sometimes the water swishing around swished a little too hard and I learned to unlock the door, flush and jump. Great exercise. They could have scrapped the Bidet in the room. Did anyone ever use that?

My hotel was close to the Eiffel Tower so that was my first stop. Impressive. We have a smaller version of that in Berlin, it's called the Funkturm but the Berliners call it 'Der Lange Lulatsch'. Compared to the Eiffel Tower, the description of 'tall' for the Berliner version was definitely overdoing it.

I joined the throngs of people working at 'Les Halles', the market that was still situated in Paris but was slated to be moved out of town soon. I was glad it was still there. It was pretty dirty and dusty and loud, but it was definitely Paris. Going by Metro was scary. There were people there who pinched my rear and got too close and I moved from one train compartment to another between stations, trying to get away. They were dark-skinned and black-haired and they enjoyed the discomfort they caused me. They also did not speak French but some other language which I was later told was Algerian. I didn't like them and Algeria was scrapped permanently from the list of countries I would want to visit.

I did not know that there were First and Second Class compartments on the Metro. It cost me a fine for having traveled first class when I only paid for second. Explaining my reasons for jumping about made absolutely no impact on the officiating fellow who shook his head at everything I said. They did not or could not speak a word of English in France. I swore at him in two languages and paid in French coin.

Tired and disgusted, I returned to my hotel to find my bilingual friend waiting at the desk. The French may not be too accommodating to their visitors but this particular one kept his word. He took me to St.Germaine Du Pres for dinner at a little sidewalk café. He translated, explained, expostulated and generally brought me up to date on French life, customs and food choices. The next day and the one after that, he marched me around Paris like a professional tourist guide. We lunched at the Sorbonne which was as close as I had ever come to University since my dishonourable stint at Sir George Williams in Montreal. We had dinner in dark places where the only light came from candles on the tables and where I learned what Algerians enjoy in the way of aliments. They may be rude but they do eat well. We spent hours in a museum for movies, watched the biggest fountain I had ever seen shoot water like a cannon and walked along the walk that borders the Seine. Paris actually looked the way it did in Gene Kelly's 'American in Paris' with the little bookstalls and cafes and paintings exhibited along the streets. For once, the movies hadn't let me down. It wasn't spring and I wasn't in love but I loved Paris.

On the morning of my last day, mon ami joined me for breakfast and I helped him compose a letter to his American friends. "They cannot speak French at all," he complained. "They couldn't even pronounce my name properly. I told them to call me 'Domi' for short but they always pronounced it 'Dummy'." I nearly fell off my chair, I was laughing so hard. It took a while for him to understand that they had made good-natured fun of his name and, in the end, he signed his letter "Yours in friendship, Your French Dummy". We hoped they would have a good laugh over that and we wanted them to think that he had known all along what they were doing. I don't know if it worked as I never saw the little Dominic again. He put me on a train back to my own country and the town of Trier. We corresponded for a little while until they drafted him into the Army. There are people and then there are people. Some you make an effort to forget, some you never do and are glad for having met them. Dominic Attalin is one of my favourite memories.

Trier on the Mosel had enough Roman ruins to rival Rome itself. History on every street corner and tourists in every nook and cranny. But I was tired. Tired of sightseeing, tired of looking at ruins, tired of sleeping in strange beds and tired of getting off trains with no one ever there to greet me. I called home and asked my bewildered parents to please pick me up from the Zoo Station. Just once, I wanted someone there to wave. They didn't promise. It's a long bus ride from Britz to the Zoo. But I knew they'd be there. It's what parents do. They don't let you down. At least mine didn't.

Chapter 35

BACK TO THE FUTURE?

Papa didn't so much as mention my unscheduled stops in countries where I couldn't possibly apply for a job. He knew that a decision had been made and that we would all have to live with it. But he still objected strenuously to my desire to emigrate to Australia. He had a point.

I noticed for the first time that the two of them were getting old. Mama had had a lot of problems with menopause in her 50s and somehow had never again been the cheerful, happy-go-lucky person I had known all through my childhood and youth. Papa still pedaled on his bicycle to the garden every day but I could see that the ground wasn't as well looked after as it had been. Sister hardly ever wrote, Brother paid only infrequent visits and who would be there if something went wrong. Canada was nine hours away on an airplane and that trip was within my sphere of affordability. Australia was 24 hours away and imminently more expensive. There wasn't much I could do. If I could reason that they were always there for me, how could I not offer them the same courtesy. Only I couldn't stay in Berlin. Not any more. Even though Brother informed me that nostalgia had hit the town and I could now use the Berliner slang to my heart's content.

It was 'IN" to 'Berliner', thanks to a Berliner actress turned singer by the name of Hildegard Knef. I am eternally grateful to that lady but it was too late. I was still a Berliner but the rest of the population had put on some very strange airs. In the process, they somehow had lost their wonderful sense of humour. I can't live without laughing at life. There wasn't much to laugh at in Berlin anymore.

What there was were lots of letters from my Oxford lad, asking for my return. I was lonely and confused and didn't know what to do next. He solved my problem. I forgot about the infernal rain, about the boring parties and the food without spices. I remembered the good times with friends, the skiing with Terry and the days on the beaches which, in foggy memory, turned out much better than they had actually been. I decided to give Vancouver another go.

I arrived in time for the rainy season to begin and the weather did not let me down. It poured for months. I got soaked every day walking the streets looking for work until I got fed up and re-applied at the Bank where they welcomed me with open arms.

Christmas came and there were the obligatory little presents in the tree and one of them was a little box that contained a diamond ring. I was engaged again. I didn't like it. I didn't like the ring either. I asked my new fiance if we could possibly find one to my liking and, to my surprise, he agreed. The new one had an even smaller diamond and cost him less but it appealed to me. At work, one of my co-workers pointed out that it was bad luck to exchange an engagement ring and nothing would come of this engagement. I wonder if she ever experienced with coffee cup readings like Manzie. She was right-on with her predictions.

We made it through the winter and into spring. At the end of February, Papa wrote a letter asking for help. Mama had gone strange. He didn't know what to do. She couldn't remember how to cook and they were living on cans of soup. Could I possibly come home for a spell.

Miss Nelson, my wonderful Supervisor, immediately approved three weeks vacation and I was on the next plane out. Being a fiancée entitled me to reduced fare airline travel which, under the circumstances, was really appreciated.

For the first time, there was no one there to greet me at Tempelhof Airport. I took a Taxi home and found myself knocking in vain on the door to our apartment. No one was there. My imagination was doing somersaults. I dashed upstairs to the neighbours and Mr. and Mrs. Goetsch assured me that Mama was still among the living. My parents had taken to eating out a lot.

I called Brother who was as surprised as the neighbours as to what I was doing in Berlin. He hadn't been home for quite a while. He didn't know that Mama wasn't herself. He wondered why Papa hadn't called him. I didn't. He had said 'NO' once to often to Papa's request for help. My Papa had to be on the brink of disaster before he requested assistance and it wasn't Brother he thought of in his time of need.

I was served the obligatory cup of coffee to calm my nerves and then we waited at the window, where, sure enough, we soon spotted my parents coming through the Park. It was a shock. Mama had never been anything but slender which had, over the years, produced enmity in the neighbours who couldn't stop putting on weight. Now, however, she was thin to the point of emaciation and, at only 65 years of age, looked years older than my Father who was nine years her senior. This was too sudden and unexpected. I had to work up the courage to make my way downstairs to greet them.

Papa looked relieved at my sudden appearance and Mama was happy but, nevertheless, kept wondering why I was there. "They think I've gone crazy," said Mama. I assured her that, as she had never behaved as any other normal Mother in the first place, she could not possibly be considered normal at this late stage of the game. It made her laugh, which was the objective. We put her to bed and Papa explained his cry for help.

It had gone on for quite a while. Her mind came and went and no one seemed to know why and what to do about it. The doctors prescribed pills. There were so many pills in the cupboard, I couldn't understand how Papa kept track of them. So many in the morning, so many at midday, so many at night. No one had as yet explained to him just what all these pills were supposed to accomplish.

Mama did not remember how to cook. She got up during the night, intending to go shopping. At supper time, she'd spread the butter onto the wrapping paper which had contained the sandwich meat instead of onto her slice of bread. She no longer understood time and he was afraid to let her out of his sight in case she also forgot where she lived. Papa hadn't slept properly in weeks and he looked it. We sat for a long time, holding hands and talking quietly. He thanked me for coming so quickly and apologized for having had to call me home. When he finally went to bed, he looked a little less scared and a bit more hopeful. That was alright. I was scared enough for the two of us.

In the morning, I ran to the bakery and got fresh buns. It is the custom. After a decent cup of coffee and nice, still warm buns from the baker, the three of us felt much better about the prospect of dealing with Mama's memory loss. Brother turned up and, probably because we were all in shock, there was no friction between any of us. Mama seemed fine and we were able to talk candidly about what was happening. The doctors had assured Papa that it was not Alzheimers but some sort of old-age disability. I wasn't quite so sure but it was hard

248

to convince my parents that doctors could be wrong. That generation's mentality did not comprehend the fact that a doctor is a human being and therefore fallible. They believed explicitly in the wisdom of the medical profession and nothing I said could convince them otherwise. I gave up on that front.

Next on the agenda was an overhaul of the apartment. Mama had always been a meticulous housekeeper but since her illness had somehow stopped seeing dirt. At first she was furious that I would intrude on her duties and it took a while to convince her that she deserved a rest. After a while, I imagined she quite enjoyed sitting back and watching me scrub the kitchen cabinets. It was worse than I had imagined but I appreciated being busy and dead tired at night. It kept me from thinking of what I should do once my three weeks vacation was up.

All my life Mama had looked after us. Capable, sturdy, dependable, full of fun and equipped with a wicked sense of humour, we had simply taken her for granted. Now I missed her because the woman walking around in my Mama's body was not my Mama. It was very eerie at times.

One Sunday, Papa and I decided to visit the garden and promised Mama we would be back at noon. We spent an enjoyable morning, sitting outside the 'Laube' Papa had built so many years ago, watched the first flowers emerging from the good soil which had provided nourishment in the years of hunger, and listened to the birds. And then my secretive Papa, of whose life I really did not know much, started talking.

He talked of his family, about the war years spent slugging around France's mud, how he met Mama and why we had never met any of his relatives. He had stopped associating with all his uncles, aunts and cousins when it became apparent that they didn't think Mama was up to the standards of a Berlin family. Mama was a country bumpkin from the poorest part of Germany. Mama laughed too much, too loud and was considered a loose cannon. Papa made his choice and never regretted the outcome. So now I knew why I never met any Krause relations. I didn't think I'd missed anything. They would not have liked me either. I laugh too loud, too much and am a loose cannon.

At one point, I asked him whether he was satisfied with the way his children had turned out. I should have known better. My Papa did not lie and if I was fishing for a compliment, I was harbouring delusions. No, he wasn't. At the same time, he admitted that he didn't think too many parents were. He had wanted a son to step into his footprints. What he got was an artist and he was incapable to deal with the situation that developed. He had never understood Sister's mentality or why she was continuously at odds with the rest of the family. He figured that both my siblings would have been a lot happier if they had been born into a rich family. For the runt of the litter, he expressed a 'no worries' attitude. I suppose if your parents do not worry about you it means they think you're capable of handling your own life which, in a way, means you've turned out not too bad. "You have a good character," he said. I took that for what it was. The biggest compliment anyone had ever paid me.

I learned more about my ancestors and their problems and joys in two hours than I had ever thought to know. By the end, I was darn glad to have been borne in time for the invention of washing machines, telephones and the opportunity to do with one's life whatever one wanted. It was an eye opener.

In between chatting, we made sure to be back on time so Mama wouldn't worry and, at precisely 12:00 o'clock, we marched through the door, only to be confronted by a furious Mama. "You said you would be back by noon," she screamed. "It's been noon three times." I looked at the clock and realized that she had watched the minute arm going around from 9 to 10, to 11 and then 12. Reality had returned with a vengeance and it was hard to deal with.

It got worse next day when the both of them departed for their weekly visit to the doctor. Enjoying some quiet moments, I was surprised to see Mama coming through the door, on her own, three hours after they left.

"Where is Papa?"

'I don't know. The stupid man told me to get in to the subway, which I did, and then he didn't show up. So I went home."

I had a hard time to get used to her new way of expressing situations and Papa in particular but, at the moment, I was more worried as to what had happened to her better half.

We waited for over an hour. When Papa finally arrived he looked as though he had aged 10 years. What finally emerged was this.

Papa was buying the tickets for the subway trip home and told Mama to wait for him. Mama kept walking, down the stairs, onto the platform, and boarded the first train arriving there. There were two ways to get home from the Hermannplatz subway station. One was to get onto the train to Britz Sued, get off at Grenzallee and walk for 15 minutes to our house. The other was to get on to a train to Leinestrasse, get off there, transfer to a bus to Britz and be faced with only a 5-minute walk. However, Hermannplatz is a big terminal, there are subways going in all directions to various parts of Berlin. Papa had no idea what train she'd got on, whether or not she remembered her address or even her name and where he was supposed to be looking. He alerted the personnel who called through to all stations on route to look for a wandering lost soul by the name of Anna Krause. Then he waited, and waited. No one saw or heard from my Mama, who by that time was happily enjoying a cup of coffee in her own kitchen.

He finally gave up and came home, expecting the worst. What he got was a mouthful from Mama, who swore he told her to get on the train and who insinuated that he was the one who was crazy to think that she wouldn't remember where she lived. It took me a while to calm everybody down and to try to make it sound funny when it really wasn't.

Three weeks passed quickly and I wondered as to what to do. Papa declined my offer to stay indefinitely. Things were looking up. He had had a rest. I had a life to live and a fiance to go back to. I was only nine hours away. He knew I'd come if there was need.

The day before I left, he took me to his Bank and instructed the manager to add my name to a savings bond of DM10,000.00. "It's a sort of repayment for the money you've been losing every time I asked you to come home," he explained. It was the first time he actually acknowledged my contribution to family loyalty and the acknowledgment meant more to me than the money ever could.

Back in Vancouver, I found myself living with three men instead of one. The lad had rented out the living room in my absence and the two roommates had not as yet had time to find other accommodation, nor were they making any effort to that effect that I could see after I returned. We took the easy way out. Our lease was up and, instead of renewing, we found ourselves a new apartment nearer to the beach.

So we kept busy by moving and proceeding to build our own furniture. That is to say, the lad built and I held on to the wooden planks for stability while he sawed away. We built a couch, a chair, a coffee table and book shelves out of two-by-fours, varnished the lot, had cushions made and enjoyed the fruits of our labour.

That summer, the lad's sister turned up, ostensibly to stay with us for one week, find a job as a babysitter for five weeks, and then return to the bosom of her Oxford family. Three weeks of watching the laziest woman I have ever encountered reclining on the couch, bringing home lovers to share that narrow cot, who were encountered unexpectedly in the middle of the night on the way to the bathroom, scaring the heck out of me in the dark, did not endear her to her host. I went on strike. I stopped cooking, cleaning and being nice to an unwanted guest occupying the premises in which I paid half the rent. She got the message but managed to only absent herself on a job for two weeks, after which she quit or was fired, depending on whom to believe. I was glad to see the back of her and hoped the rest of the family would be more amiable.

That summer we started losing friends. One went off to Australia. We saw him off on the 'Canberra' and my heart went with him. Some got married and disappeared from the social scene and some moved away. I was stuck and miserable. Then the sky fell in and I found out what real misery is.

Chapter 36
ONCE UPON A TIME ......

In the fall of 1971, I took up shorthand to facilitate getting out of the steno pool. It was time to think of a proper career. I inquired at the University of British Columbia for a librarian or a journalist course and gave up my dreams in that direction in short order. I would have had to study four years to acquire a Bachelor of Arts degree. Then continue many more years to acquire the necessary diplomas to set me on my course. The amount of money involved was horrendous and, as I was 32 at the starting point, I would be paying back thousands of dollars well into my 50s. There was no option but to go for executive secretary, a profession I thoroughly abhorred. I'd missed the boat but I still had the oars. I just had to keep paddling.

On October 13, the lad drove to Seattle to pick up his parents who were coming for a visit. I stayed behind, practicing shorthand by taking dictation from a record supplied by the business college I attended. Then the phone rang and I was glad for the interruption. I didn't care too much for shorthand.

Sister's voice was very low and I had to strain to make out what she was saying.

"I have bad news," she said.

"Mama," I said. *"Something happened to Mama?"*.

"No. Papa's dead."

"NO."

The mind is a strange phenomena. I hung up the telephone and went back to my shorthand. If I just went on with the ordinary thing I was doing, everything would be fine. Only it wasn't and never would be again.

The phone kept on ringing and there was no way I could ignore it forever. Papa was gone and doing shorthand wasn't going to bring him back. I answered the call.

Sister had received a call from Brother who couldn't bring himself to talk to me. Papa had died of a massive stroke in the afternoon of October 12. Mama needed help. Sister had a family, she couldn't possibly get away. Who was going was a foregone conclusion.

Shortly after that, the lad turned up, happy as a lark at having his family ensconced in a hotel nearby and looking forward to enjoying the reunion. What he found upon his return was a dry-eyed, shell-shocked bundle of misery on the couch that couldn't care less about any news from his home front. All I wanted was a ticket to go home. He didn't let me down.

In the morning, I put in a short appearance at work, told Miss Nelson what happened and handed her my letter of resignation. She wouldn't hear of it. Instead, she offered me 'leave without pay' for as long as I needed it. I gratefully accepted her offer. If there is a heaven, there is a place reserved for people like her.

Some hours after that, I briefly met the lad's parents who escorted me to the Airport. I don't remember much about them. I wasn't in a conversational mood.

On the 14th of October, I was met by one of the survivors of my reception committee. Brother stood forlornly in the Airport at Tempelhof and took me to a restaurant for a quiet conversation before heading home to meet Mama. Then I got the low down of what had happened.

Papa had had a good lunch of his favourite meal - potato pancakes. He had chatted with some neighbours, standing on the balcony perusing his domain, the little garden he so lovingly tended. In the afternoon, Mama served coffee and cake and, in the middle of that, he suddenly stood up, waived his arms around and said "Annie, its over." Then he ran out of the room and, making it all the way into the bedroom, threw himself onto his bed.

Mama had no idea what he was talking about and wasted a few minutes trying to understand. Then she ran after him and found him half on and half off the bed. She tried to push him all the way over and strained her back by doing so, without any success. In the process, she noticed that Papa was soaking wet with sweat, almost as though someone had emptied a bucket over him. She ran for help. The neighbours heard her screams and alerted the ambulance. It wasn't long in coming but Papa had already gone past the point of return. He died in the ambulance on the way to the hospital.

To the end of my days, I keep hoping that in those last minutes of consciousness, Papa knew that I wouldn't let him down and didn't die worrying.

Fortified with the news and holding hands for comfort, we headed home. Mama was ready for me. She heated up the leftover pancakes that Papa had not been able to finish. Brother and I nearly choked on them but could not refuse. All in all, Mama seemed remarkably calm. I had the feeling that she was not capable of properly understanding that Papa was gone for good. At one point, she asked us if we thought it odd were she to marry again. I buried my face in the coffee cup and Brother went for some fresh air out on the balcony.

After Brother left, I set out to make up my sleeping quarters on the couch but Mama thought that was stupid. There was this empty bed now, why on earth did I want to sleep on the couch. I promised to use it after reading for a little while longer and tucked her into her own bed. Then I climbed onto Papa's chair, hugged the back, pushed my nose deep into the cushions which still retained his particular smell, and the dam broke. It is very hard to cry without making a sound. I didn't want to wake up Mama and succeeded in doing so but it nearly killed me. Then I had to go and sleep in Papa's bed.

I don't know how I survived that night but I did. In the morning, we had to look after the funeral arrangements. Papa had taken care of everything. All Brother and I had to do was set the date and sign some papers at the funeral parlour.

We stopped in at the local store with the coffins in the window and found a salesperson who made me laugh despite the sorrow. There was the coffin, which was plain wood, just as Papa had ordered. Well, the lady said, wouldn't it be better to pay a little more and buy the oak one? That particular box was also equipped with a better lining and Papa would be resting so much more comfortably. Excuse me? My Papa would have my head if I spent money on a silly box and as for the silk lining, what was she talking about? We're talking about a dead person here! Brother and I broke up. It was good to laugh for a little while and Papa would have chuckled right along with us.

Then we had to arrange a speaker and the music to go with the ceremony. Papa had never been baptized, although he firmly believed in

God. He never went to church and had never shown any indication for liking church music. The music we offered to play was unacceptable. This was Germany where there are rules and regulations for everything, even death. We were stuck with the organ playing church music. Then came the wreath. On two pink sashes, they wanted to imprint the names of the children of the deceased. Papa had never used the names we were baptized with when addressing his offspring. Sister was his Grosse, Brother was his Pipo and I was his Miefchen. That was what we wanted on the sashes. Not possible. There had to be proper names or nothing at all.

The lady was beginning to think we were from Mars, I started foaming at the mouth and Brother signed the papers and removed us from the premises before some damage occurred.

Next step, the plot. I found Papa's site at one end of the cemetery near Buckow, abutting a garden colony just like ours had been in Marienglueck. As I stood there, I listened to people talking, drinking their coffee on the porch of their little country house, oblivious to the fact that two meters away graves dotted the landscape. When I told Mama, she was delighted. "He'll feel right at home," she said. I was beginning to think everyone was crazy.

The day of the funeral dawned cool but sunny. Brother and I spent 10 minutes with the man who was officiating and who, in that short a time, was supposed to emerge himself in Papa's personality and portray him as the man he used to be. In 32 years, I had not understood my Papa, so how could he. What he came up with was so hilarious that I was afraid the coffin would open up and Papa come out swinging.

He talked of the lovely neighbour whom everyone liked and would miss. Reality was sitting in the audience. Mr. and Mrs. Goetsch, Mrs. Kell and Mrs. Liedke, all neighbours from our particular building. The rest of the population had never got to know a man who couldn't care less about people and barely acknowledged their existence with a snort to their hearty greeting. Papa had been let down a lot in his life by friends and neighbours and when you've been framed by the very people, one of whom now sat in the pew at his funeral, and been forced to vacate Berlin or face a Concentration Camp because of a lack of party fervour, one couldn't blame him for not fostering closer ties.

He talked of the Father who was always so proud of his children and their achievements. He talked of Sister who would have given anything to be here to share her family's sorrow and he talked of Papa's work at Telefunken where they would truly miss him now. By the time the poor man was finished, the three attending family members were in hysterics. "Oh my God," said Mama, wiping tears off her cheeks. "That was hilarious." None of Papa's children had achieved anything remotely resembling his own career. Sister had made absolutely no effort to attend the funeral and wouldn't have contributed much to family harmony anyway and the people at Telefunken hadn't seen Papa in years. He only went there when he needed some material for his own tinkering.

Outside, we assembled at the gravesite and watched the coffin disappear into a black hole. I hated that hole. It was a horrible thought to think that Papa would lie in the dark when he so loved being outdoors. I looked up into the brilliant blue sky - and nearly fell over backwards, joining Papa in his hole. Right above the grave, in a perfectly cloudless sky, there floated a little white cloud. Papa's cloud. I pointed and everyone's eyes followed my hand. Three of us got the message. The rest could not possibly understand.

We used to make fun of Papa who had the habit of lecturing with a finger pointed straight in one's face. He always retorted by stating that, even when he was dead, if we did anything he did not agree with, he would sit on his little white cloud and 'Whabumm,' the finger would come out of the sky and whack us right between the eyes. Papa had never made a promise he couldn't keep. We must not have done anything wrong because he didn't whack us. He just showed up.

The days that followed the funeral were sometimes funny, sometimes hilarious and mostly awful. Mama and I went on a shopping spree which was a new experience for her. We bought new curtains for the living room and the kitchen. We bought nice cushions for the chairs in the kitchen. We dressed Mama in a beautiful pantsuit and a gorgeous long gown for watching TV comfortably. We acquired new blouses, skirts and anything else her little heart desired. Mama had a ball. We went to shows, to movies and to the Operettas on ice which were the latest in entertainment.

I got us tickets for a performance by Germany's most famous Ice Dancing Pair skating to the Operetta 'Die Maske in Blau.' Mama didn't see too much of it because she cried through almost the entire performance, indicating that 'Papa would have liked to see this.' Papa wouldn't have. He hated ice-skating but she didn't remember that.

When the show was over, we tried to find our Bus. I thought he had parked to the left of the entrance. Mama insisted he parked to the right. "You have no sense of direction and I may be crazy but I do know my way around." I didn't trust her and we spent half an hour searching to the left before I admitted defeat. She knew her directions all right and she didn't let me forget it for weeks.

What she didn't like was visiting the cemetery. Papa had bought a double plot. So there was this grave that Brother had arranged very nicely and which was topped with a beautiful green rough stone to which we had, for a little extra money, affixed Papa's signature in bronze letters. We had wanted to install Papa's bench from the big garden to the side of the grave for Mama to rest but the bench did not fit into the decor of the cemetery and regulations did not allow for that. Next to Papa's plot, however, there was this empty space. "I don't want to go down there," said Mama. I didn't blame her and our visits therefore were far and few between.

On one visit we were accompanied by a neighbour whose live-in companion had died recently and who had been cremated. We said 'hi' to Papa and then ambled over to her site. After that, Mama got awful quiet and, when she did condescend to reply, it was with an abrupt rudeness quite out of character. When we got home, I asked the reason for her behaviour. "Well, really," Mama exclaimed. "I know they didn't get along too well but to treat the man in such a shabby way and to squish him into such a little hole is despicable." I cracked up.

Once I had recovered and explained about cremations and ashes and little urns, she saw the light and laughed until tears ran down her cheeks.

It wasn't funny when she called the police and reported me missing for days. She was watching television and I thought I could absent myself for a little while to visit Mr. and Mrs. Goetsch upstairs. I told Mama I would be back within an hour. 35 minutes later, the police turned up at the door and asked Mrs. Goetsch if she had heard from me in the last little while. The protectors of the public were not in the least amused nor did show any empathy for Mama's condition. "Don't waste our time," they thundered. I promised to take Mama with me wherever I went and gave them the finger behind their backs. I have a healthy dislike for men in uniforms, especially German ones.

October and November are the worst months in Berlin. Everything is grey, the trees are bare and the rain puts a damper on already depressed spirits. I walked around the neighbourhood and tried to recall happier times but it wasn't easy. Where were all those people who had come calling for Mama to accompany them on the trip to the forests? Where were the women who had no qualms in sending Mama on dangerous trips through the countryside for their benefit. Where was the woman who had sat for days in our kitchen, crying on Mama's shoulder because her husband had walked out on her? Where was everybody? Was this supposed to be a punishment for Mama's lack of participation in the 'Kaffee Klatsches' where the neighbours congregated, knitted, stitched and gossiped about everyone who wasn't there? I couldn't figure it out. It was very depressing and I thought it was time for Mama to leave the neighbourhood.

We registered at a Care Facility where the older generation lived in their own rooms, with their own furniture and where they were able to do their own cooking but, if they didn't feel like doing so, could eat in the restaurant. It was friendly, people seemed content and I hoped there would be a spot for Mama soon. Mama had other ideas. "There is no way I'm ever going to live there", she pronounced. "I'm going to die in my own home." End of discussion. Easy for Mama to say, but not quite that simple for Brother and me.

Brother invented a remarkable colour system for Mama's pills. There were so many of them, it was hard to keep track of them. In the end, we had the morning pills in a red slot, the afternoon pills in a green one and the evening ones in blue. It worked and took care of one problem. The other one was money. Papa had taken care of everything and given Mama food allowances every month. Now the poor woman was supposed to figure out how to get the pension money out of the bank, look after the rent payments and organize her food money. I cursed Papa's macho attitude of never letting Mama in on the serious aspects of living, like money management, and tried to explain the intricacies of banking and budgeting to my poor addled Mother. We established another envelope system whereby the money collected from the Bank on a monthly basis was divided into weekly installments for food, rent, gas and electricity payments. I did not have too much faith in this but Brother promised to help out whenever the time came when I wouldn't be there.

December arrived and with the cold winds came the Oxford lad. It was a nice gesture that wasn't entirely appreciated. Mama wasn't at her best and I hadn't slept properly for weeks and was, consequently, rather short of temper. Mama was in the habit of wanting to go shopping every time she woke up, which could be anywhere from 1 to 5 o'clock in the morning. I had developed a habit of sleeping very lightly to keep track of her movements, which wasn't conducive to my own health. Getting married or even thinking of what I was going to do with my own life at that precise moment was not something I had time or energy for.

Brother and I took a little time off to show the lad the City but it seemed that every time I stepped outside, I ran into trouble. Talking to my lad in English in a restaurant gave the other customers the impression that I wouldn't be able to understand their conversations and, what they thought were funny remarks about English-speaking nationals, were really rude, insulting, crass insinuations from which Berlin humour was sadly absent. I blew them away in my wonderful, sarcastic Berlin slang, which satisfied me for a little while but only made me more angry in the long run.

Going shopping, taking the bus, standing in line at the cash register, everywhere I went I was accosted by tight-lipped, angry individuals. I was walking too slow, standing in the way of someone, even asked to remove my foot from underneath someone else's who was standing on mine. I wasn't used to that any more. I wanted people to say 'hello' on the street even if they didn't know me. I wanted smiles and patience and good manners. I wanted someone to help Mama when she fell while getting into the Bus. I wanted someone to give her a seat after I had picked her off the floor. I did not want to get upset and scream at people and forcibly have to remove a teenager from his seat in the area reserved for old and the disabled. I wanted to get out of this City in which I no longer belonged.

Between Brother, the Oxford lad and my wonderful Mama, they convinced me that I could not possibly stay forever. Everything I could have done, I had done. Mama was getting better at understanding her situation and promised to move to the Home we had visited when the time came. Brother promised to call every day and visit at least three times a week. Mama told me in no uncertain terms that enough was enough. I had done my duty. It was time to get on with my own life. She liked the Oxford lad and she promised a visit once she had totally recovered. In any event, I was only nine hours away.

Chapter 37
END OF AN ERA!

Around the middle of December, the lad and I flew to London and drove to Oxford to visit his family. I called Mama every evening and she always assured me that everything was just fine. The lad and I toured a part of England, which boasted little villages with very strange names and houses whose door frames seemed made to order for people like myself. Everyone else had to duck. Oxford was wonderful and romantic and the atmosphere alone should have put everything right, but it didn't. I worried myself sick every day as to whether or not I was doing the right thing and by the time we boarded the airplane to return to Vancouver, I loathed myself for having left Mama to her own devices. None of that was conducive to my love life. Halfway home, I took off my ring and declared the engagement over. It seemed alright with him.

Vancouver was kind and covered itself in snow that year. It looked very pretty and helped lift my spirits. The lad made arrangements to find himself a new place and sold me the furniture he had so lovingly made. He could always make new ones, I couldn't. I went back to work and life became a routine of work, eat, sleep and call Mama.

On December 27th, the telephone rang at 2:00 in the morning. The Operator announced that I had a call from Germany and to 'please hold the line'. I held and held and then the line went dead. I broke out in a sweat. It was my birthday and I presumed Mama had called but had not been able to figure out exactly how to do the long-distance thing. Or maybe she was calling for help. Or whatever. I broke down and put in my own call. Mama was fine. No, she had not called me; she was watching television. Oh, and by the way, Happy Birthday. I was relieved and told her that I couldn't talk too long on the phone as my calls were breaking my bank account and we signed off. It was the last time I talked to her.

The lad moved out on January 1st. On January 6th, Brother called to say that Mama was in the hospital. She had collapsed at home and was now taken care off. Not to worry. No, don't come home. There is nothing you can do at the moment. I'll look after her.

He spent the next week visiting Mama every day and watching her deteriorate. They had to tie her arms to the bed because she got out all the time, trying to go home. He put cream on her sore skin where she rubbed it against the constraints and she called him Papa. He went through hell and saved me the agony by insisting that I stay put and far away. He protected me from the brutality of life as he had done when we were children and I will be forever grateful for that. I didn't have to see her die.

On January 10th, two days short of three months since Papa left us, Mama closed her eyes and went to join him on his little cloud. There was no way in the world I would leave Brother to put her into the ground by himself. I made a few phone calls.

The Oxford lad inveigled his supervisor to pretend he still had a fiancée and got me a return ticket home. Miss Nelson approved three weeks vacation for the new year without batting an eyelid and, within 24 hours, I was on the plane home.

"I guess we're orphans now." Brother tried to joke. I didn't think that anyone over 30 was considered an orphan but it sure felt like it.

The apartment was cold and soulless. Brother went in to the living room and returned with the sculpture of a wild boar, put it into my hands and simply said, "It's yours now." Grandfather Krause had galvanized that figure and from the time I could talk, I had proclaimed my love for it and declared it mine. Now it truly was.

Without Mama and Papa, our home was no longer a home. I moved in with Brother and spent the next two weeks cleaning out the life-acquisitions of my parents. That's when I found the certificate attesting to my noble birth and the responsibility of the city it never lived up to. I found my baby curls, my ponytail and Papa's soldier book, verifying his attendance in the First World War and the one medal he ever acquired in the pursuit of staying alive in the trenches. I found my own and Papa's 'Poesy Albums' into which every friend and relative we had ever had during childhood had written poems to remember them by.

Every child in my youth had had a book like that but I had not known that the custom went all the way back to Papa's childhood.

Funny to find out that one's Father had once been a little boy with friends who called themselves 'Leo, der Kahle' (Leo, the Bald) and 'Uncas, der Wildtoeter', (Uncas, the Deerslayer).

I found Mama's photo album of famous movie stars. No different than my own collection. Just different faces and hairstyles. I found out more about my Parents than they had ever intended me to know. Once you're dead, your life is an open book to anyone who dares to peek.

I packed a huge trunk full of everything that had any value. The new curtains that still retained their creases, the pantsuit, the evening gown; all the new clothes Mama had so enjoyed. I took my favourite books, Mama's jewellery and some pots and pans. Brother took the cutlery and the dishes, which were only two years old and a birthday present for Mama from me in the days when I thought she would be using them for a long, long while.

Furniture was distributed to newlyweds but no one showed any interest in my Grandparents beautiful bedroom set. Antiques were not in fashion at the time. It ended up, hacked to pieces, in someone's kitchen stove as firewood. At the end of the day, what is important to one person is entirely devoid of value to anyone else. That's life.

In the middle of this turmoil, we had to make arrangements for Mama's burial. The lady in the funeral parlour remembered us fondly and did not attempt to convince us that Mama needed soft cushions in her last bed. I ordered Mama's signature in bronze, to be affixed beneath Papa's name and Brother promised to look after the rest of the ground. He was a decorator, after all. He would do a fine job.

Mama was baptized in the Protestant religion and therefore entitled to a man of the cloth to send her on her way. He talked a lot about nothing. He talked about some Mountain called Zion, which I was sure Mama had never heard of. He talked about how happy Mama was now that she had achieved the pinnacle, namely Heaven. He was a very young man who had not experienced any grief as yet, had no idea how to express solicitation to the bereaved and he drove us batty. When it came to the point of throwing soil into the grave, Brother and I scooped up a big lump, pushed Mama's wedding band into the middle and jointly deposited it on top of her coffin. It belonged to Mama. They should never have taken it off.

Three weeks later, I had worked myself through every room in the apartment but hadn't had time to visit the cellar. Brother promised to look after that affair and took me back to the Airport. Mama's death had done what nothing else had accomplished for the past 20 years. For this visit at least, Brother had been the Brother I had so dearly missed. We were still Sitting Bull and Mondesglanz, fighting off the Cavalry. We could be miles apart but we would always have each other.

Between the two of us, I was the lucky one. He had to stay behind in a city which daily reminded him of his parents. He had to look after the grave, fill in the hole when Papa's coffin collapsed and was not allowed the luxury of crying because that was not considered a manly occupation by his sometimes too-stern Father. I left all that behind and still had an awful time coming to grips with the fact that, once your parents are gone, you're finally an adult yourself.

Back in Vancouver, the weather had reverted to its normal pattern for that time of year. With the Oxford lad departed, I found myself deserted by the very people who had slept, ate and frolicked at our home. In any break-up, friends have to make a decision as to with whom to associate afterwards. All I got were some discreet inquiries as to the possibility of a sleep-over. When that was not received with any fervour, I was dropped from the list of people to call. I had never been so lonely in my entire life.

Depression is not pretty. It is a downward spiral with no end in sight until one picks oneself up by the topknot and straightens out the mess. I couldn't find my topknot. I was having a grand time feeling sorry for myself. I went to work, ate, slept and cried myself to sleep. It never occurred to me that I was expecting too much of other people and that it was myself who was driving my friends away. There was such a big gap in my life and I didn't know how to fill it.

Until the night I took out the sleeping pills my doctor had given me out of the goodness of his heart and started seriously thinking of swallowing the lot and have it over with. Lucky for me, I have a problem swallowing pills and, while in the process of prying each and every one apart and pouring their powdery insides into a glass of water, it occurred to me that meeting my Father on the heavenly shores would not translate into a pleasant encounter. Papa had no time for losers or quitters. Papa would probably kill me for doing what I was doing.

It was the most ridiculous logic, but it worked. Even in death, Papa's influence dominated and the fact that, once I was dead, he couldn't possibly kill me never entered my befuddled mind. I threw the entire contents of the pillbox into the toilet and flushed them down the drain. It was the first night I actually slept right through until morning.

The next day, my guardian angel whispered sweet nothings into Miss Nelson's ears and, having noticed a worsening in my attitude and worrying about my mental outlook on life, she offered me a week without pay and told me to go somewhere where the sun shone every day. That same evening, on the way home, I stopped at a travel office where I was told that Hawaii had sunshine aplenty and would not disappoint me. I picked the Edgewater Hotel in Honolulu and a flight out of Vancouver the next week.

When I showed the ticket and the brochure to my wonderful supervisor she was delighted and wished me luck and recovery. Showing the brochure to my friends and co-workers at coffee break produced an entirely different effect. "Jeez," one of them said. "Haven't you had enough vacations lately?" Vacations? What vacations? Within less than a year, I had looked after my sick Mother, had buried my Father and my Mother and had taken care disposing of all the family's personal belongings. Is that considered a vacation?

I looked around the table at the people with whom I had spent five years of my life working and having fun. Every face mirrored the statement made by one and something inside of me broke. There are people and then there are people. Some of them you don't want to know.

I picked up my cup and retired to a corner of the room. Until the day, six months later, when I left the company for good, I kept to myself at every break and, apart from business related topics, never again participated in a private conversation. I didn't want to waste breath.

Chapter 38

ALOHA!

Sunshine. Bright, brilliant and burning. A warm wind that caresses the skin and palm trees swaying in the breeze. I didn't waste time with unpacking. All I needed was my bikini and a towel. Hawaii, here I come.

The waters of the Pacific did not in the least resemble the waters on the shores of Denmark. I had never seen water like this. I stood up to my waist in the Pacific and watched a fish nibbling on my kneecap. I could see all the way to the bottom and watch my toes wiggle in the sand. It was totally transparent and changed colours from deep blue to turquoise to green, depending on the depth of the ocean. It was magical. Sitting on my towel, watching everyone around me, I felt, for the first time in months, that bubbly feeling in my chest which was a precursor to an attack of the giggles.

When I was a child, giggles were the bane of my existence. They came at intervals of extreme content and happiness and couldn't be stopped by anyone. Not even Papa. I don't remember how many times I was sent away from the dinner table to control myself, by myself, in the kitchen. Having recovered, and being allowed back into the family fold, I only had to look at Brother's face to start the giggles all over again. We were a happy lot in those days, the both of us.

Feeling the bubbles rise in my chest, I thought that Mother Nature must be asserting herself. I wasn't born a pessimist. I couldn't stay down forever. There was a life to be lived and where better to start the way back than here. On my little towel, on a pleasant beach, surrounded by happy people.

One of them taught me about liquid sunshine. There wasn't a cloud in the sky but, every so often, something like a soft mist would settle on my body and I thought someone was spraying me with water, except there was no one in my immediate vicinity. I couldn't figure this out until a young man approached and explained about 'liquid sunshine', a rain being carried on the wind from far away. You learn something new every day.

I also learned about a profession which feeds on lonely tourists of the female variety. My new acquaintance offered to take me around the Island, to nightclubs and shows and generally provide me with excellent entertainment for my entire stay in Honolulu. Wasn't that nice and hospitable?

I am very slow sometimes. It took me a while to understand what he was offering and it was kind of sad to watch his face turn from high expectancy to low disappointment when I told him that I had exactly $50.00 in my hot little hands to spend for one week. He apologized for not having more time to chat and wished me a pleasant holiday. It must have been a sincere wish - I had the best holiday of my life.

That evening, everyone from my flight assembled at the Reef Hotel for free Mai-Tai drinks and instructions on sightseeing trips all over the Island. I was the only one who didn't like the Mai Tai drinks. Most everyone else took good advantage of the word 'free' and got properly sloshed. I re-acquainted myself with a girl I'd met on the plane and we booked ourselves on a sightseeing trip around the Island and a Catamaran Boat tour at night. Then I left the drinkers behind and retired to my wicker-furniture equipped room to sit on the balcony, locally called the Lanai, and watched people going by.

Next morning I found out that sitting for more than one hour on a beach is not advisable for people living in rainy climates most of their lives. I had burned every exposed part of my body, including my eyelids. Getting in and out of that sightseeing bus was torture and provided a lot of entertainment for the rest of the crew. Our wonderful driver took pity on me and provided me with a moisture lotion which made it possible to enjoy the sights of Hanauma Bay, Pali Lookout, Diamond Head and the Luau at Sealife Park in the evening. The show was terrific but I couldn't understand the Hawaiians enthusiasm for something called 'Poi.' Next to the raw oyster in Paris, this was another awful mush that didn't want to be swallowed. Funny how tastes varied from country to country. To Hawaiians, Poi is delicious. To Hawaiians, Sauerkraut would probably be really awful. To each his own.

Walking is my preferred method of exploring the countryside. My companion from the bus and her roommate joined me in a walking tour of Honolulu and we discovered the Mission Houses and the Palace of Hawaiian Royalty. Were they really happy in that stone edifice? Why on earth did they try to copy the Victorian Royals in dress and accommodation? It didn't make sense and I thought that the statue of King Kamehameha, in his native dress outside the Palace grounds, looked much more natural in the environment. This was a whole new history I knew nothing about. Some of my meagre funds were expended on books forthwith. I like to know where I am and what happened there before I arrived on the scene.

In the evening, we went out for a nice meal and then to a dance hall situated on top of a very tall building where the view was supposed to be spectacular. It was. But first I provided a spectacle of my own.

The entrance to the dance hall was through a narrow hallway, lit up with some sort of blue lights. I was wearing a white dress, white underwear and a white shawl over my shoulders. These particular blue lights made my outer garments disappear to reveal what one normally does not show in public. I only became aware of this fact when my friend behind me let out a shriek to frighten the most seasoned horror show aficionado. I felt myself pushed hard and ended up in the middle of the dance floor. I like to make an entrance but this was ridiculous.

Having attracted attention in this unseemly fashion, it didn't take long for the three of us to acquire an admirer each to accompany us on a tour to various other nightclubs in the vicinity. It was still Disco time and Disco's abounded in Honolulu. What also abounded in town were lots and lots of young American soldiers on R&R. My own date's hair was a little too long for the Forces and I never asked whether or not he was one of them. He was good company, he made me laugh and he had enough money to support our outings, one of which was a flight to Maui. We spent every waking hour together for the remaining days of my stay in Hawaii and that young man from Texas listened to an uninterrupted flow of family stories pouring out of my tortured, lonely little soul. I talked and talked and couldn't stop. I told him the entire family history, its ups and downs and the tragic end of it all. And he listened. I don't know why. It was something I needed to do at the time and he was the right person at the right time in the right place.

On my last night in town, we sat in the dark in one of the numerous lifeguard stations on Waikiki's Beach and watched the full moon reflecting on the water. "See that," he said. "That's my moon. Whenever you see the moon so full and round, you remember me and be happy.

That's a Sid moon."

Until the day I die, whenever the moon is really full, I call out "Hi Sid." Because it's a Sid moon and it reminds me of a young man who listened and, in the process, healed my heart and soul.

Back in Vancouver, the rain slowly slacked off and summer arrived. Sister's friend Terry and I decided on a quick long-weekend trip to Reno, Nevada. As usual, things went haywire. Something was wrong at the airport in Reno and, after circling about for a while, the plane was diverted to Sacramento. From there, we boarded a bus for the trip to our gambling paradise. It was getting dark on the drive through the mountains and it got downright spooky when the tour operator started reminiscing about the sad fate that befell the people known today as the 'Donner Party' who, not being blessed with a modern contraption like our bus, got stuck in the mountains on their way to California and, being extremely hungry, resorted to cannibalism. So hard to imagine in today's world. I've been hungry but never that hungry.

Reno! The Biggest Little City in the World! They gave us a book full of coupons and some money to start our gambling career. Terry did really well on the slot machines and exercised her muscles for a nice little profit. The machines ate my quarters and wouldn't give them back. I decided to try my luck at Blackjack but quickly realized that I did not have the wherewithal to play this game on my own. It involves doing mathematics in your head. I can't do that. Not even if it's only up to 21. I was in trouble but I also had the tools to get out of it. I parked myself on a high stool, dressed in the latest fashion of a bright pink hot pants outfit, crossed my legs and announced to all and sundry that I needed some assistance. Being young and pretty makes life so easy. Within seconds I had acquired four aides to my endeavour and two hours later I was rich. At least by my standards.

With the winnings from Blackjack and One-Armed Bandits, we had acquired enough funds to facilitate renting a car and visiting the obligatory tourist attractions around Lake Tahoe. Virginia City, Carson City and the famous Ponderosa Ranch of Bonanza fame. However, what left an indelible impression on me was the smell of the Ponderosa Pine trees surrounding the lake and the beautiful colour of the water at Emerald Bay. Life was still beautiful, one just had to go out and find it.

Gambling is great when you're winning. Gambling is also an addiction, the peril of which was brought home to me on our trip to the restaurant for breakfast in the morning. I had pointed out some of the people on the one-armed bandits to Terry on the way to bed the night before. I couldn't believe my eyes when, at 8 AM the next morning, we spotted some of the same people still doing their thing. Put the token in the slot, pull. Put the token in the slot, pull. I was reminded of Dante's Inferno. If there was a hell, it might look like this. I took my winnings and ran.

In the end, our luck enabled us to return home in style. Lady Luck had not only paid for the trip and the expenses incurred therewith, there was enough left over for a taxi ride home. This is living.

Finally being able to admit that there was now no reason to ever return on a permanent basis to Germany, I applied for Canadian Citizenship. People thought that after 12 years in the country, I was ready to commit myself to becoming a full-fledged Canadian. Reality was somewhat different.

Being free of restraints and finally able to do what I wanted, I had inquired at the Australian Embassy as to entry to their fair country and been informed that, being a German citizen, I was obliged to apply for a visa from my native country, necessitating a stay in Germany for over a year. Bureaucracy in any country takes time, lots of it. However, being a Canadian citizen entitled me to a visa for work and stay on an indefinite basis by simply filling out an application form. Canada and Australia were Commonwealth countries and the people of each country could move to and fro without great restrictions. Hurrah for the Commonwealth and Canadian Citizenship. I applied forthwith.

Becoming a Canadian necessitated learning the history of the country. Piece of cake. Just ask your fellow Canadians. Right? Wrong! There was not a single person at work who could help with ex-Prime Ministers, dates of Provinces entering the Union, wars, uprisings and the muddles of Canadian politics in general. I disappeared for weeks into the bowels of the Vancouver Library and immersed myself in the history of my soon to be adopted country. It was a very hard slog. There were no great heroes I could fall in love with. The closest I came to admiration was Governor Douglas and the RCMP in the wilds of Canada. There seemed to be two different solitudes. There was the East, which was continually occupied with the differences of French and English speaking Canadians, and there was the West which was continually ignored by everyone in the East. There were the people in the Maritimes who seemed to have an entirely different history from the rest of the country and there were the Native Indians whom no one seemed to know what to do with. Topping it all were some people called Metis who were a mix of Native Indian and French Canadian people who thought they should be entitled to a piece of the country to call their own. It was all very confusing.

Sister thought I was stupid to occupy myself thus as no one had asked her anything of the sort when she applied for her certificate. I ploughed on just in case. I was still German at heart. I was trained to obey orders. The form said to study history. So I did. In the end, I was profoundly grateful for Papa instilling a sense of duty into my heart and soul. I have never met anyone who was grilled as I was by a Judge who must have had a profound sense of patriotism. If you wanted to become a Canadian, he was convinced that the applicants should know everything there was to know about their chosen country.

I turned up for my interview with two witnesses who were Canadian by birth and would vouch for my stellar character. With great difficulty, I had found two people who were not only born in Canada or British Columbia but were actually Vancouverites. This species was very hard to come by. Most everyone in this city was from someplace else. By the time my inquisitor had finished putting me through the mill, my two witnesses were pale and jittery bundles of nerves.

Over a cup of fortifying coffee, they told me of their fear of being interrogated by this paragon of virtue themselves. They nearly peed their pants in the process.

My guardian angel not only looks after me, he's also a joker who plays tricks on me and makes my life a continual parody.

Having passed the test, I was scheduled to receive my Canadian Citizenship Certificate at a proper ceremony, attended by the newcomers, various organizations such as Boy Scouts, Women's Auxiliary and RCMP personnel in their beautiful and distinctive uniforms. I invited Sister to witness the occasion which was supposed to be solemn but, thanks to my joker angel, turned out to be somewhat strange to say the least.

Upon entry to the hall, I was asked what denomination I was. I told them I was baptized a Protestant. They wanted to know what kind of Protestant. Baptist, United Church, Anglican? I had no idea what they were talking about. I was a Protestant. That's all we had in Germany. Lutheran Protestants and Catholics. Aha! Problem solved. I was a Lutheran and therefore entitled to a Bible to comfort me in my days ahead as a full-fledged Canadian. What the Bible had to do with citizenship totally escaped me but they wouldn't take no for an answer. It was a present from the Government of Canada. How could I refuse?

Clutching my Bible, I proceeded to the next person who, beaming happily, affixed a Canadian flag pin to my sweater. Then, standing row upon row, we were asked to swear allegiance to the Queen. I couldn't do that. I'd never been properly introduced to the Queen and swearing allegiance to someone I don't know was not proper to my way of thinking. As a good half of the people being sworn in could not converse in English, the oath itself was kind of meaningless anyway. Then we sang the national anthem and the judge presiding told us how proud we should be now that we had achieved the pinnacle of our career. We had become Canadian Citizens. Not being very nationalistically inclined, that comment went right past me. Had it been a blight on one's character to have been Chinese, Hungarian or, heaven forbid, German? We were changing nationalities because we thought it was the thing to do to be able to participate properly in the country of our choice, not because we thought that being a Canadian made us a better human being. It was a ludicrous speech to say the least.

Then it got worse. There was a woman who was acknowledged as having been a valued member of the Women's Auxiliary, whatever that was, and she was thanked for past services as she was retiring from her position. Next thing we knew, she was up and, brandishing a totem pole in one hand and a book in another, proceeded to lecture the new Canadians on the fact that they were not Canadians at all. The only real Canadians were the Natives, a very much maligned people who, having been mistreated by every immigrant arriving on Canada's shores, were nevertheless surviving and should be treated with respect by us in the future. It was hilarious. The RCMP, the Judge and various other officials tried their best to shut her up, promising to honour her with a speech within the confines of the tea party afterwards, but she wasn't having any of it. It took force to remove her from the premises and the last we saw of her was the totem pole, waving above the crowd of people shoving her out the door.

I've never met anyone who had a better Citizenship party. Nothing like a solemn ceremony going haywire to lift the spirit.

Chapter 39

CHOICES !

In late summer, rumour had it that my wonderful Supervisor, Miss Nelson was going to retire. I was called in and asked to take on the job of Assistant Manager of the steno pool, the assistant manager moving up to manager. I told them I'd think about it. This was not the answer anyone had expected. This was a really nice promotion with a tremendous increase in salary and, pray tell, what was there to think about? As far as I was concerned, one hell of a lot!

I spent an entire night writing lists of pros and cons to a decision that would affect me for the rest of my life.

Pro - nice, comfy life. Good money. Pension payments in old age. No worries!

Con - trapped, lulled into a false sense of security, backed into a corner with no way out.

I figured, if I accepted this position, I would never leave it. One gets used to a steady income and by opting for security, I was selling out on every dream I had ever had. I had only just broken out of my cage which, even though it was a loving cage, had still been a confinement imposed upon my life by my parents. By dying, they had set me free. Was I now going to put myself back in for the price of a monthly paycheque, a secured pension plan and four weeks vacation a year? Did I want to live or exist?

In the morning, I handed in my resignation. At lunch, I picked up a request form for a visa at the Australian Embassy and by the following day applied formally to enter Australia. I was 33 years old and life had been kind enough to make me look years younger. I could get away with pretending I was 24. I could join other enterprising young-sters and not stick out like a sore thumb. I could finally do what I had wanted to do all my life. I could go anywhere, anytime. It was time to go visit a place called Mara Mara.

Brother thought it was a great idea. Sister called me a middle-aged hippie. Everyone else called me crazy. No matter. It was my life and my choice. It was the best choice I ever made.

My ship would leave Vancouver harbour in January. I had time to take Sister's In-Laws up on a promise made. They lived near San Francisco in a place called Roberts Park and had invited me to stay with them any time I felt like it. I had the time and I felt like it. I spent a traditional Thanksgiving day in a log cabin in the middle of a pri-meval forest, walked the streets of San Francisco, was taken on a tour of Sausalito and toured the coastline of Monterey by bus. They, their neighbours and friends were hospitable to the utmost and their efforts in making my stay in California interesting and memorable was highly appreciated. I mentioned one evening that one of my favourite authors was Jack London who had, many years previously, provided me with my favourite phrase.

Impressed by my knowledge of American authors, they took me to Jack's house, or what's left of it. Apparently, Jack was a socialist and not very well liked in the neighbourhood. No one knows exactly what happened but, shortly before the completion of his dream house called 'The Wolfs Lair', someone reduced the building to ashes by ar-son. No one was caught and no one was accused. Jack London left the neighbourhood, never to return. It was sad, looking at the ruins in the middle of a forest. It would have been a beautiful place. How much hate does it take to demolish someone's dream? Jack didn't live very long after this horrible event but his books are alive and well and are still enjoyed by millions.

Being in the neighbourhood, I decided on a trip to Disneyland. For two days I reverted back to childhood and enjoyed myself thoroughly. Brother should have been with me. We didn't call him Peter Pan for nothing. Disneyland is the ultimate child's dream come true. I took in the sights, fell in love with the Pirates of the Caribbean, got really scared when faced with Snow White's Witch of a Stepmother, appreci-ated the superb imitation of an Amazon River ride and went to bed ev-ery night thanking Walt Disney for his imagination and perseverance. It was magic!

Three weeks later, I was back in Vancouver, re-packing my suitcase for, what I thought to be, my last trip to Berlin for a very long time. It would be the first Christmas for Brother not necessitating a rush to his parents' home after work. I didn't think he should spend it on his own. I managed to book myself on a cheap charter flight to take me from Vancouver to Ostende in Belgium and from there to Brussels and Berlin.

It was one of the coldest winters on record. The Wannsee was frozen over and I was very grateful for the warm fur coat which I had bought with the money Papa had put into my name. During the day, I walked the streets in the beautiful neighbourhood of Dahlem where Brother rented a suite, went back to Britz to greet neighbours and visited my school friends of long ago. There was no snow and Berlin in winter is not very cheerful. It's grey. Grey buildings, grey skies, grey sidewalks, grey people. Brother's place was small but cosy and his Christmas decorations of a round globe fabricated out of fir tree branches, decorated with red bows and hanging from the ceiling was very chic. His Christmas tree sported the same decorations and the effect was stunning. It was a decorator's dream, but it wasn't Papa's tree.

We spent a quiet Christmas, reminiscing about the past, laughing about our childhood adventures and trying to bolster each other's spirits. New Year's Eve was celebrated in a bar where we stunned everyone with our still dynamic performance of good old' Rock'N'Roll. On my birthday, he promised me the best Western I had ever seen and which, seeing as the title was in German, I could not recall as having ever heard of it. This movie was, according to Brother, being played in Berlin for months and months and everyone loved it and went to see it over and over again. Must be good, I thought, but could not figure out why it had never arrived in Canada.

Two minutes into the credits, I not only recognized the film, I also remembered that everyone, myself included, had thought this movie to be the very worst western ever. It was called 'Once Upon a Time in the West,' the most god-awful Spaghetti Western ever made and one which turned me permanently off the sound of a mouth organ.

I looked at Brother's rapturous face and couldn't tell him. That day has gone down as the worst birthday I have ever had to live through. I turned 34 to the sound of Charles Bronson piping away on that infernal instrument, Henry Fonda hanging poor Mexicans from trees and Claudia Cardinale pining for the quiet Mexican hero who was supposed to take her away from it all. Happy Birthday everyone!

Three weeks went quickly and, before I knew it, I was back on a plane heading for Brussels. That's when my joker angel decided life had been decidedly too dull lately. There were 13 people on the plane heading to Belgium who didn't know one another. Three hours later and after flying for a very long time in circles above the Brussels's airport, we had become bosom buddies.

The story was that there was too much fog in Brussels and the plane had been re-routed to Luxembourg. "Right," said the fellow across the aisle from me. "Do you know what the name of this airline stands for? SABENA! 'Such a Bloody Experience. Never Again.'." We all had a good laugh and introduced each other for lack of something other to do. In Luxembourg, we were offered a lunch and given train tickets for the trip to Brussels. By the time we got to the station in that illustrious City, we were all a little tipsy from imbuing the free drinks offered along with the ride. It was too late for me to head for Ostende, so my companion from across the aisle in the plane offered to take me along to his hotel. Checking in, they took our passports which, in Belgium, are handed to the police for check-ups on the moral characters of their visitors. Not having a guilty conscience, we submitted to the rules of the country and proceeded to enjoy our stay by enjoying a bit of the nightlife and the beautiful architecture of Brussels's town hall square.

In the morning, I looked in vain for him at breakfast, knocked on his door and finally figured he had departed early. Halfway through my cup of coffee, he walked into the breakfast room, dishevelled, dirty and in a very foul mood. Belgium, he pronounced, is a police state rivalling Nazi Germany. They had come for him at 1:00 o'clock in the morning, made him get dressed in their presence as though he was a criminal and taken him to the police station. Three months previously, he had received a parking ticket in Brussels. Leaving the next day, he had not thought this to be of enormous importance and, within days, forgotten all about it. The police had not. They kept him overnight in jail, made him pay the fine and a fine on top of that for not having paid the fine on time. They also fined him for having to pick him up from the hotel.

They have a saying in Germany – 'Schadenfreude ist die beste Freude.' To laugh at someone else's misfortune is one of the biggest laughs one can have. I tried very hard to keep a straight face but, in the end, we both laughed so hard we almost tipped the chairs over backwards. He went and changed and then was kind enough to accompany me to the train station for my trip to Ostende. I hope they left him alone on future trips. He was great fun to be with and he showed me Brussels at night, which I would never have had the nerve to do by myself.

Upon arrival, I took a bus to the airport, expecting my plane to be sitting on the tarmac. There were a lot of people sitting around on the departure level and rumour had it that the plane had been delayed until the next morning. Some of the people around were the same people who had come with me from Seattle three weeks previously and we re-acquainted ourselves and made plans as to how to spend the night. Two young enterprising Swiss Nationals called their Embassy and demanded assistance, which was promptly forthcoming with the promise of two rooms rented in their names in town. They offered one room to myself and a young lady by name of Barbara at no cost. We accepted graciously, booked ourselves in and promptly disappeared out of their line of vision. We were not quite convinced that 'no cost' really meant what it said to the two lads.

Ostende proved to be very hospitable. We spent basically our last funds on a meal and the best hot chocolate I had ever tasted and, upon telling the waiter of our misfortune, were told that we should forget about paying the bill, save our meagre funds and send the money in the mail upon return to our native shores. Stories like that never make the newspapers.

We paid, being convinced that tomorrow would see us home, and then went to meet the younger generation of Belgians in a Disco on their main street. They couldn't speak English and we had no French. We got along great. Way past midnight, we snuck up to our room, tiptoed past the Swiss lads' lair, and slept the sleep of the just.

After breakfast, shared with a disillusioned couple of young men, we met up with the rest of our fellow passengers, some of whom had slept on benches in the lounge of the airport. Everyone had some idea of what was going on but no one knew the truth until a representative of our charter company turned up with a double-decker bus. Our plane had had a malfunction of some sort and there was another plane being flown in from overseas but said plane would land in Basel, Switzerland, and now all we had to do was to board the bus and be on our way.

Some people did not have time for this. Some people had enough money to say 'to hell with this' and booked themselves on ordinary flights home. One older gentlemen, who according to Barbara owned a candy factory in Seattle and was therefore quite affluent, offered to advance people's fare for repayment upon returning home. Some took him up on that. I figured I had at least 1½ weeks before my ship was leaving the harbour in Vancouver and thought to see this trip through the hard way.

By now my little group of intimates included Barbara and a young fellow named David who had been my seat partner on the flight over. We stormed to the top of the bus and took ownership of the first row. We drove through the day, into the night, and in the process I learned songs sung in summer camps all over the United States from my two intrepid young companions. The whole bus sang: 'I'm a little nut that's brown, lying on the cold wet ground. Someone came and stepped on me. That's why I'm a nut, you see.' Then everyone yelled "I'm a nut" and banged their fist on their heads. We sang 'One Hundred Bottles of Beer on the Wall' until we got sick of it, whereupon the older generation taught the youngsters songs of the Blitz. We kept everyone awake and in good humour and to the sound of 'It's a Long Way to Tipperary', we arrived in good spirits in Basel, a city of which we could see nothing as by now it was past midnight and very dark.

To their merit, the charter people had booked a hotel for us and, within minutes of arrival, we were all tucked away and sound asleep. It had been a long day. After breakfast, we had time to wander the streets of our unintentional stop on the itinerary and expended our last coins on chocolates, the likes of which are not produced as well anywhere else, especially not in North America. Then the Double-Decker took us back to the airport and the much anticipated airplane. We had a good look at it and for a long time. They didn't let us board until late in the evening and Basel presented a beautiful view, as it was quite dark when we finally departed for our last stretch home. Last stretch? Not so fast. A few hours into the flight, we were advised that we had to refuel in Shannon, Ireland. By now we were so used to unexpected stops no one even questioned the validity of the statement. There was a three hour delay in Shannon. Time enough to get out of a cramped seat and tour the facility. It was the most beautiful airport I had seen so far. It was also the most deserted. I had never been to Ireland and the least I was expecting to take away from my visit was a stamp in my Passport. We searched for a long time before we found someone to do us the honour. There was no one to check who we were, what we were doing there and what was in our luggage. Innocent age that.

Back on the plane, we thought to catch a little sleep for the next little while but were rudely interrupted by the pilot's announcement that, according to IATA regulations, they had now flown too many hours and had to make an overnight stop in Boston. Boston? Boston is on the East Coast. Seattle is on the West Coast. Another stopover and a long way from home.

Boston was also asleep. They had to call in some customs officers to check our luggage and that took time. People stood around, asleep on their feet while children fretted and cried and everyone had got to the point of utter frustration with short tempers to boot.

David got through customs before we did and we watched him talking to a young man dressed in overalls, gesticulating all the while back to where Barbara and I still stood in line. Once we got through, he announced proudly that he had accommodation for us for the night. The young man was a technician of sorts at Boston International and had listened to the trouble being encountered with this unexpected planeload of strangers so late at night. He thought he might be of assistance and had picked David, offering him a bed and rest. There was no way David would leave his charges behind. Three of us got into the technician's car and were driven to a huge house somewhere in a Boston neighbourhood. The lad's mother greeted us from behind her bedroom door, told us to make ourselves comfortable and went back to sleep. Barbara and I shared the lad's bed, David got installed on the couch in the living room and before he had even started the car to return to his nightshift job, we were snuggled in and sound asleep.

When we woke, the mother had already departed for work, leaving a note on the kitchen table and three towels to clean up. We showered and washed our hair and finished in time for our host to return and take us for breakfast. We left behind the chocolates we had bought in Basel to pay for the kindness to strangers. There was enough time for a little sightseeing trip through Boston and then we were dropped off at the airport to join up with the rest of the passengers, most of whom had slept little and badly on the benches surrounding the Departure Lounge. I didn't mention my guardian angel to my friends but I am sure that, if I had, they would have totally believed in the existence of said deity.

Five hours later, we saw the lights of Seattle and some of us fell into the arms of friends and relatives. I said good bye to my fellow travellers and my two companions in particular, congratulated the lad's father on a wonderful, responsible 17-year old son, promised to write and boarded the bus on the last leg of an endless trip home.

My last few days in Vancouver flew by in a flurry of packing, sorting papers and saying goodbye to friends. Suddenly I was standing on the railing of the liner Arcadia, throwing streamers into the wind and getting soaked by the ever-present Vancouver winter drizzle. Most people disappeared quickly from the deck, preferring the cosy atmosphere of the bar to the damp, rainy outside. In the end, I was the only one standing at the railing at the back of the ship taking me into the unknown. As we passed beneath the Lions Gate Bridge, I reflected on five years of fun, sadness and downright misery. I hadn't hit it off in this city. I had a wicked sense of humour that did not seem agreeable to the general population. I was a Berliner from the old school. I had run into trouble being true to my nature. I was forthright and utterly unable to tell little white lies just for the sake of being polite. I remembered the promises that were never kept and the friends who were otherwise engaged when I most needed them. I looked at the clouds that seemed near enough to touch and felt the rain soak my hair and run in little rivulets down my face like tears.

I grabbed the railing, turned my head to the grey, drizzling clouds and yelled at the top of my lungs: "I will never, never, never come back to this place".

It was the 17th of February 1973.

No one told me that one should never say never!

EPILOGUE!

In August of 1989, I was back in Berlin, showing my hometown to my 11 year-old son and my husband. We stood on a hill watching the German Shepherd dogs parole the border, watched the 'No Man's Land' peppered with mines, the barbed wire fences and the watchtowers and I had no answer to my son's question of "Why?".

I showed him my home and the grapevine his Grandfather had planted so many years ago to the amusement of his neighbours who didn't think that this would ever fly. "Where does he think he lives? In the Rhineland?", they smirked. Now we looked at a plant that had grown from a spindly seedling to a formidable vine, reaching all the way to the third floor of our building, feeding three tenants with very delicious green grapes.

I showed him the geranium pots adorning the railing of the balcony steps. I told him of the day Papa and I installed the clamps, three on each side, to hold those pots which prompted Mama to exclaim: "Don't we have enough flowers to water around here?" I showed him the abomination scratched into the stucco beneath our living room window. Someone had carved a Swastika deep into the stone and Brother had corrected the symbol by connecting the points and making a window frame out of it. So many memories to share with a grandson who had never had the pleasure of making the acquaintance of his grandparents. Just like me, he could only be told of the generations which preceded him.

Brother took us on a tour around the city that he knew better than the back of his hand. It was lovely in the forests of the Grunewald, at the Pfaueninsel, the Wannsee and on the boat plying the lakes. It was peaceful in the evening, wading in the waters at Glienicke with the moonlight reflecting on the water. It was romantic eating Schwarzwaelder Kirschtorte with whipped cream in the beautiful setting of a lakeside café. Until one looked up and saw the watchtower. Until one was stopped at a street which was blocked off by Police because the night before some people who called themselves 'Chaoten' had totally demolished the neighbourhood. Until one saw the graffiti on every wall, the dirt on the streets and the carelessness with which Berliners were treating their surroundings. Throwing garbage into the street wasn't done in the Berlin I once knew. Now, no one seemed to think twice about it.

Coming from a country where Playboy was considered racy, my Son was appalled by the magazines exhibited at every newsstand. Germans had become sexually liberated and what was displayed on each and every one of them left nothing much to the imagination. The Nation had come a long way from being "Bourgeois" but I couldn't see that it made them any happier.

Going shopping was the usual nightmare of shoving, yelling and generally being unpleasant. Every little corner store had been turned into a 'Supermarket' where tiny carts were pushed around in an area the size of my living room. At one point, I lost my family in the shuffle until reminded of their existence by frantic calls for help. I found them in the vegetable section where a big sign above the door advised the customers to not take their carts into the room because of its diminutive size. Not being able to read German, both husband and son had merrily carried on, only to be faced by two very irate German Hausfraus who shouted at them at the top of their lungs, calling them all kinds of animal names which are the favourite swearwords of my native country. Among other things, they were called pigs, pig dogs, stupid cows, silly goats, etc, etc.

I stormed to the rescue, explaining to the ladies in as polite a fashion as I could muster that these two were Canadian citizens who had no knowledge of the German language, did not know what the heck anyone was talking about and, under the circumstances, would it not have been better to use sign language, i.e., pointing to the sign and making reversal movements. I should have known better. What I got in return was more swearing and a shove of the little cart into my midsection. My husband, being a peaceful citizen, was not prepared to start the 3rd World War over a bunch of bananas. He picked me up and bodily removed me from the premises. My son, being half a Berliner, reversed the cart and, with a mighty push, managed to shove one of the heavy-duty Hausfraus head first into the potato bin. His Grandfather would have been proud of him.

I told Brother of my desire to visit the place in Saxony where we had spent two years of our adventurous youth. He took me to a travel office where I was advised that such a trip was quite impossible as the only way to travel in the 'Deutsche Demokratische Republik' was to book hotels in major towns, then get from one to the other in a given time limit. Getting off the highway was impossible and the little village of Kirchsteitz could not possibly qualify for a stop over. I thanked the agent for his trouble and casually remarked that I would try again when things had changed and the Wall had been demolished. He laughed a mirthless laugh and said: "Young Lady, that won't happen in our lifetime." Three months later he was eating his words.

Back home, in the fall of 1989, we watched in fascination as energetic Berliners chopped away at the abomination that had graced their city for too long. Brother, joining the little woodpeckers on the Wall, sent me four pieces of cement, covered in vivid colours. On the western side, the Wall had been painted by artists, would-be artists and ordinary citizens for so long that, by the time the structure came down, there wasn't a plain, grey cement spot in sight. I took the artifacts to a frame shop and they produced a masterpiece of four little misshapen pieces of colourful cement, placed on black satin in a beautiful frame. A plaque beneath simply states:

BERLIN WALL
1961 - 1989

So the Wall was down and everybody was happy. For about a month. Then the citizens of West Germany discovered that they really had nothing in common with their eastern brethren. Not only that, the whole re-unification was costing a fortune. East Germany had been severely negligent in the upkeep of roads, in their use of chemicals in the ground, in their maintenance of the railway system, etc., etc. All of which had to be fixed.

Re-unification brought families back together and some of them one hardly knew. Brother got a phone call from Aunt Fanny. The last time I had seen her was the year before I immigrated to Canada. Aunt Fanny used to visit us on the pretext that she was traveling to Berlin to see her daughter who had a lucrative job with the East German government. She usually dropped in on her daughter for one night and high-tailed it into the affluent West, to go shopping with Mama and marvel at the food available to the average citizen. Our repeated requests to meet the elusive cousin were, at first, brushed aside with comments as to how busy the said girl was and, later, acknowledged as a bias by said cousin against the West. So we had never had the pleasure of meeting Erika but enjoyed Aunt Fanny's company anyway.

All these years later, we found out that Aunt Fanny had moved to East Berlin 25 years ago to live with her daughter after having had to endure a rather nasty divorce. Her second daughter suffered an aneurism in her 40s and died suddenly, leaving my Aunt nothing much to tie her to the town she had lived in all her life, namely Magdeburg. Whether or not Mama knew all that, I couldn't say. She never mentioned any correspondence.

So all of a sudden we were blessed with an Aunt and a Cousin. That resulted in a visit by myself two years after the City had been restored to its former size and glory. Meeting Aunt Fanny and Erika was harmonious and lucrative. Aunt and I took to each other immediately and made up for lost time by chatting for hours. Cousin Erika was incredibly versed in the history of old Berlin and the walk she took me on was memorable. Brother had a bit of a problem with Erika's outlook on life in general and her leanings towards communism in particular. I figured that, if we had grown up in the East and been brainwashed as children as Erika had been, we might have ended up as ardent communists ourselves. Who knows? Anyone who loved history as much as she did couldn't be all bad. We got along just fine.

Upon bidding goodbye to my new-found relatives, Aunt Fanny pressed DM 50.00 into my hand. "Buy yourself something nice," she said, and wouldn't take no for an answer. Trying to hand it over to Erika was not successful either. Apparently, it was what Aunts do. Never having had one before, I wasn't sure how to handle it. On each and every other visit, we have gone through the same procedure and I have come to understand that it makes her feel good, makes me feel like a little girl and makes the world go round. It's called family.

The both of them lived in a typical East Berlin 'Stalinesque' apartment building that looked to be in dire need of repair and a paint job. But within walking distance, I found the Berlin I had not been able to locate any longer on the western side.

Once the Second World War was over, West Berlin had been rebuilt without any consideration for history. On the western side, everything was new and shiny. On the eastern side, they had protected the old architecture like the Dom, the Zeughaus, the Gendarmerie, etc. It was their way of showing superiority, I suppose but, in the process, they managed to preserve some parts of the City which, had they been in the West, would have gone the way of the Dodo bird. Unfortunately, it is the only good thing I can say about that regime.

Two years after the fall of that darn wall, there was hardly anything to be found to remember it. If nothing else, Germans are very efficient. There were cranes everywhere, new buildings going up and every painter in the city seemed to be employed splashing colour on neglected buildings. So everything looked as though it would work out just fine and things would go back to normal, but they didn't.

Now there were Ossies (East Germans) and Wessies (West Germans) living in Germany and never the twain shall meet. Then again, the future lies in the hands of future generations who do not remember the wall. One day, people will stop proclaiming to live in the east or the west. One day, Germans will just be Germans again. But it won't be in my lifetime.

All through history, people have flocked to Berlin, earning the description of "Rucksack Berliners" (Knapsack Berliners). The names in the Berlin telephone books reflect the diversity of the newcomer's nationalities and origins and is proof of the fact that what made the Berliners strong was their ability to absorb strangers into their midst. Unfortunately, with the arrival of the latest immigrants, this is no longer a factor. My City now boasts the largest Turkish population outside of Ankara and the joke is going around that if one owns a German Shepherd in Russia, one can claim German citizenship and hightail it home. While some of the newcomers have integrated, the majority maintain their culture, their language and their customs. All that translates into Ghettos. Kreuzberg, Neukoelln and many more of my old stomping grounds make me feel a stranger in my own town. I cannot read the signs on shop windows nor do I understand the language spoken on the streets. Immigrants and refugees are piling into Germany at an amazing rate which makes reading a sign of "don't step on the lawn" in any park an exercise in futility. They say the same thing in about five languages.

This is my City now. Ossies, Wessies, Turks, Eastern Europeans, Russians, Arabs, Asians, etc. Each a solitude. Each disliking the others. All living in Berlin.

__But how many of them can actually say "I am a Berliner!__

ISBN 141208566-7

9 781412 085663